# Legas

## Sicilian Studies

### Volume I

**Series Editor: Gaetano Cipolla**

D1280551

# Giuseppe Quatriglio

# A THOUSAND YEARS IN SICILY

## FROM THE ARABS
## TO THE BOURBONS

**Translated By Justin Vitiello**

LEGAS

**Canadian Cataloguing in Publication Data**

Quatriglio, Giuseppe, 1922-
    A Thousand Years in Sicily : from the Arabs to the Bourbons

Includes index
ISBN 0-921252-17-X

1. Sicily  (Italy) --History-    I. Title.

DG86Q8213 1991    945'.8    C91-090628-9

The Italian edition of this book was published by Ediprint Editrice, Siracusa Palermo.  Via Maestranza, 58,  96100 Siracusa, Italy.

### Acknowledgments

This book is being published under the patronage of the Sicilian Regional Assembly (Assemblea Regionale Siciliana).

For information and orders  write to:

### Legas

| | | |
|---|---|---|
| P.O. Box 040328 | P.O. Box 4, Stn A. | 38 Stayner Ave |
| Brooklyn, New York | Ottawa, Ontario | Toronto, Ontario |
| 11204 | KIN 8V1 | M6B 1N6 |

To my daughter Costanza

# Table of Contents

## Chapter XIV: The Intervention of London

## Chapter XV: 1820: The Beginning of the End

## Chapter XVI: The Ultimate Conspiracy

# Preface

This history of Sicilian vicissitudes in the course of a millennium was initially published in serial form in the Sunday Supplement of the Palermitan daily *Giornale di Sicilia*. Widely read in Sicily, the rest of Italy and North America, the articles seemed to friends and colleagues worthy of expansion into book format.

My articles had dealt with Sicily from the landing of the Arabs (827) to the events of 1812. To complete the present volume, I have added the sections bringing my narration up to 1860, the year in which Sicilian history begins to coincide with that of the Italy. Thus, while my treatment of the historical span from 827 to 1812 is a reelaboration of my articles, the parts dealing with the Risorgimento and the Unification as related to Sicily are herein printed for the first time.

In writing this book, I have tried to synthesize for the sake of clarity. I have employed what I considered the most valid of sources: diaries, memoirs, eyewitness accounts and, of course, past and up-to-date historiographical literature. My aim has been to describe how events unfolded and to make their often labyrinthine intricacies comprehensible. Special attention has been paid to chronology so that the reader can easily follow the rhythms of these events. Furthermore, by recounting pertinent anecdotes and other curiosities usually buried in chronicles, I have striven to represent the vital and universal significance of the facts via flashes of images.

I have written this book—whose pages grew on me before I fully realized its dimensions—with mixed feelings of anger and compassion. Ultimately, Sicilian history has struck me as the saga of a proud people with a sense of national identity that has often conflicted over the centuries with its rulers of foreign origin and their representatives on the island. Ever since Sicily has existed, I maintain, its native inhabitants have struggled to defend its nature and, on many occasions, offered creative solutions to the problems imposed by its dominators.

Revolts, conspiracies and uprisings have punctuated Sicily's troubled history. But these explosions, often as liberal-minded as naive, have been based, for the most part, on a resistance to injustice mustered by the popular classes against centralizing despotism and tyranny or, simply, against hunger. Unfortunately, such groundswells have usually lacked political or military organization and have therefore been doomed to failure, if not bloody repression, from their inception.

During the centuries of Spanish domination—when the nobility operated entirely in defense of its own privileges—this endemic spirit of rebellion bent on disaster was a constant of Sicilian history. Yet, under the Bourbons, who devolved from enlightened absolutism to a fiercely repressive regime precluding any forms of liberty, popular awakenings and mass insurrections entailed a genuine intellectual enlightenment, gave shape to the meaning of the Risorgimento and created the conditions making Italian unification possible.

I would stress one more point here: Sicily's political autonomy, now guaranteed by the Italian Constitution, embodies an age-old passion of Sicilians. Their aspiration, clearly expressed by the pro-Unification patriots of the 19th century as well, was, nonetheless, considered until a few decades ago the manifestation of a dubious brand of Sicilianism. Yet today, all over Europe, the issue of regional autonomy and the question of how it articulates with a collective national consciousness are timely subjects of debate and objectives requiring creative thinking. Such ferment is one more example of the contemporaneity of the lesson that Sicilian history, in all its complexity, has to teach us in the present.

G. Q.

# Chapter I: Glimmers from the East and Men from the North

## 1. "Rue de Sicile" in Susa: An Historical Reminiscence

The Arab conquest of Sicily, initiated in 827, was preceded by numerous Saracen invasions of the island while it was still under Byzantine rule. It took the Arabs a great deal of energy expended over a long period of time before they were finally able to mount a totally successful offensive. In 652, at a moment of major Arab expansion when both Cyprus and Rhodes were conquered, Moslems engineered a raid of the island. In his *History of the Moslems in Sicily*, Michele Amari records the sense of consternation weighing upon the islanders with that first incursion. After they occupied a few strategic points along the coast, the invaders, says Amari, "sent marauders to attack towns, sacking them and taking prisoners, yet failing to gain control over the whole territory. But Christians, initially frightened in the face of this unexpected and undreamed of attack, could not muster their forces against the invaders, so strange and new as they were in manners, appearance, language and reckless ways of doing battle."

Seventeen years later, in 669, Arabs struck at Sicily's coasts for the second time. Syracuse was taken and devastated. As the inhabitants of the city, once a rich and powerful State, fled into the mountains of the interior, the raiders proceeded to steal the treasures of the Church.

Subsequently, the efforts of the "Infidels" (as the Moslems were dubbed by Christendom) to conquer Sicily were multiplied precisely in a period when the island's ties to the Roman Church were being strengthened as a direct consequence of the election of Sicilians to the Papal See. Notably, the Palermitan Agathon, becoming the first Sicilian pope (678-681), fought to extend the sway of Rome in both West and East.

Agathon's successor, Leo II (682-683), another Sicilian, waged victorious wars against a number of heresies. Then, in 686-687, Conon, born in Thrace but raised in Sicily, became pope, and, taking the risk of not consulting Byzantium, designated the Deacon of Syracuse as Bishop and Administrator of all the Holy See's Sicilian possessions. Following Conon, another Palermitan, Sergius I (687-701) ascended to the papal throne and defended the integrity of Roman religion against the pretensions of the Eastern Church.

As Sicily secured its ties with Christian Rome, the Moslems, after conquering North Africa, made an all-out assault to dominate the island. Toward the end of the 7th century, they overran, lost and reoccupied Carthage. From that point on, their main objective was to seize Sicily from the Christians. Thus, the Arabs' first step, at the beginning of the 8th century, was to take over the island of Cossura (present day Pantelleria), where many Christians from North Africa had sought refuge. In the following years, the Arab general Musa, after preaching Holy War, led an expedition to a part of western Sicily whose name is not indicated in any historical documents but which Amari surmises was Lilibeo (Marsala).

By 710 the Arabs were totally committed to the conquest of Spain, but this new offensive did not deter them from making raids on Sicily. Similar attacks were launched in 730-731, 734-735, 740 and 752-753. Their ultimate coup, however, was to come 14 years later, in 827. One day in June of that year, from the Tunisian port of Susa, approximately one hundred ships carrying seven-hundred horsemen and 10,000 footsoldiers set sail. Heading the expedition was the seventy-year-old jurist Asad Ibn Al-Furàt who, true to the Koran's teachings, incited his army to fight "according to the ways of Allah in order to exchange this earthly life for the celestial, for he who dies or conquers by and for the way of God will be blessed with infinite mercy."

Still today in Susa, just beyond the old quarter where the soldiers gathered to set out on their invasion of the largest island of the Mediterranean, one comes across Rue de Sicile. It is virtually an alley, but it reminds us of the conquest of a distant past.

## 2. The Occupation of the Island: the 75 Years War

The Arab expedition that disembarked from Susa on June 13, 827, reached Mazara on the 17th of that month. Ancient chronicles report that the Moslem leaders, Berbers and Andalusians recruited for the great adventure that would last two and a half centuries were men who knew very little about the land (occupied by the Byzantines) for which they were headed. Such an account seems unlikely, however, because that stretch of sea from the North African coasts to Sicily had been crossed by hosts of Arab marauders in the preceding centuries. At any rate, tradition has it that the captains of these soldiers of fortune consulted experts in geography to calculate the distance separating their shores from those of Sicily.

The expeditionary forces reached Sicily after a brief stop on the island of Conigli to stock up on provisions and collect more recruits. After an improvised army of Sicilians sent to engage the Saracens was routed and sought refuge on the high plains of Enna, the invaders met with no further resistance. After posting garrisons at strategic points, the Arab army marched toward Syracuse. Its road was long and hard across the mountain passes around Chiaramonte and Palazzolo. Asad's troops, moreover, suffered hunger more than did the besieged because the latter received provisions and reinforcements from the Venetian Republic.

Syracuse, once the richest of Greek colonies in all of Sicily, held out against the invaders for half a century. But after fifty years of bloody battles, the city, subjected to a year-long siege, surrendered in 878.

Asad himself had died during an epidemic one year after his troops had landed at Mazara. But the invaders regrouped to march on Palermo, which fell to them in 831.

These early years of occupation strained the marauders and their victims alike. The Moslem soldiers were forced to live in camps exposed to the elements or in mountain strongholds where they were barricaded. The

**1. The Arabs begin their conquest of Christian lands. From Galibier's *Storia di Algeri*, 1847**

natives, who now found themselves and their lands fair game, had to survive their invaders' forays and various forms of thievery.

When the epidemic subsided, the Moslem ranks went on to conquer the fortified city of Mineo and lay siege to Enna (which they called Kasr Jenna, the name that stuck in its Italian form of Castrogiovanni until the post-World War II period). This assault lasted so long that the Arabs found time to mint coins. Meanwhile, defeated by the Greek general Theodotus, they had to retreat from Agrigento to Mazara. In 830, however, they received reinforcements from Africa.

These new recruits, under the command of Asbagh, were massive: 20-30,000 infantrymen and 300 ships. With these forces, Asbagh trounced Theodotus at Mineo and proceeded with his multi-fronted counterattack. Enna fell in 837, and, between 839 and 841, Platani, Caltabellotta, Corleone, Marineo, Geraci and Grotte surrendered. In effect, all of western Sicily was in Arab hands.

To the east, the Arabs, with Neapolitan help, succeeded in overrunning Messina in 843. Leontini fell in 847 and, one year later, through treachery, the Arabs took Ragusa. Between 863 and 869, Scicli and Noto were subdued; and in 877, the Saracens, after devastating the territories around Rometta, Taormina and Catania, pushed toward Syracuse once more. As I have mentioned, this city fell in 878—but only after a determined siege and unimaginable acts of cruelty. Taormina itself finally surrendered in 902, 75 years after the landing at Mazara.

From that moment on, Sicily belonged totally to the Arabs. Previously, for sixteen centuries, the character of the island as a whole had been Greek. But the violence of invasion annihilated all remaining Hellenic traces, and thus the Arabs were able to sink deep roots.

### 3. At the Roots of Arab Sicily

Adolph Holm's history of ancient Sicily ends with the Arab conquest of the island culminating in 902 with the capitulation of Taormina. As Holm says, "Our story comes to a close the moment Sicily loses its identity as a classical land, when the serene and joyful Hellenic spirit is supplanted by the grave Arab, Norman and Hispanic world view which still constitutes today (1896) the character of the Sicilian people, predominating especially in the western part of the island." According to this German historian, the Arab influence on Sicily was as profound as it was lasting. But such an influence was the result not only of two and a half centuries of Arab presence on the island but also of the Arabization that survived during the Norman Period in the forms and ways of life that made Sicilians forget how much they had suffered under their Moslem lords and that, simultaneously, exalted Islamic cultural traditions, architecture, and civilization.

The Arab Era in Sicily was not without its internal conflicts. Unfortunately though, in spite of Michele Amari's amassing of all available documentation, we know very little about the economic, social or cultural history during this period. Contrary to the view of other historians, Amari makes a positive assessment of the Moslem domination in Sicily, "fecund for having injected new vital lymph into the decrepit shell of Roman/

Byzantine society, reformed the structure of land ownership and agriculture, introduced new arts and forms of culture." Of course, adds Amari, "this progress bore its greatest fruits only with the advent of Norman civilization." In fact, when we speak of the splendors of Arab Sicily, we are really referring to the grand fusion of Arab and Norman elements—a fusion brought about by new conquerors descending from the north after 1061.

While few monuments survive in Sicily that are purely Arab (the most important of which are arguably the thermal baths at Cefalà Diana), we can identify the roots of Moslem cultural influence in linguistic terms. Numerous common Sicilian surnames are of Arab origin: Fragalà, Pittalà, Vadalà, Zappalà, Mandalà, Barillà, Crucillà. Similarly, rooted in Arabic are place names like Buccheri, Buscemi, Mussomeli, Calatafimi, Mezzojuso, Corleone, Raffadali, Sciacca. Moreover, the Sicilian language preserves many Arab words: *balata* (slab of stone or marble), *calia* (roasted chickpeas), *gebbia* (water tank), *giurana* (frog or toad), *giarra* (large clay container), *giummu* (bow, tuft, or flake), *lemmu* (large basin), *matarazzu* (mattress), *naca* (cradle), *nanfara* (nasal voice), *senia* (mill water-wheel), *sciabbica* (fishing net), *zubbibbu* (sweet green grape), *zotta* (whip). Even the Italian words *ragazzo* (boy), *facchino* (porter, drudge), *zerbino* (doormat) and *bagarino* (ticket scalper) are Arabic in origin. Finally, as the ethnologist Giuseppe Pitrè points out, ancient magical rites, popular superstitions, exorcisms, and witchcraft practices are expressions of Sicily's Arab soul.

### 4. The Glorious Conquest as Remembered in Africa

While the Norman Conquest of Sicily failed to eradicate the island's Arab heritage, it did lead to the Moslems' diaspora. Arabs born and raised in Sicily were forced into exile to escape Christian "Infidels," those Norse invaders who suddenly seized the land of their forefathers and earned the greatest of Siculo-Arab poets' epithets: "wolves."

By 1061, when the Normans reached Sicily on their crusades, many native-born Moslems had already taken flight. But, in spite of the riches the exiles were able to tote along, they found no peace of mind abroad. These Sicilian Arabs had the most difficult time relocating in new countries precisely because of an obsessive nostalgia for the island. Such a feeling of regret is all we know about Al Mazzari, the Mazaran luminary of jurisprudence who sought asylum in Tunisia and whose tomb there in Monastir is still a holy site today.

It is to Siculo-Arab poets that we are indebted for the expression of the pain of eternal exile from Sicily. Chronicles relate that there were as many as 170 such refugee poets, all bent on evoking with profound feeling, passion and vividness the now distant *loci ameni* of the island and its halcyon days. In exile, Abu al-Arab from the court at Seville, the Agrigentine Ballanubi from Cairo, and Ibn Zafar from Syria all composed verses of heart-wrenching homesickness and grief.

But the most moving of exiled poets was the Syracusan Ibn Hamdis whose verses are dedicated to the land where his parents had died and were buried. His collection of lyrics are rich in images of Sicily and the Mediterranean:

Oh sea, you conceal my paradise
on your other shore . . .

I recall Sicily—in my soul
pain resurrects her image,
land of youth's mad joys,
now desert, once alive like
the flower of noble minds.

Driven from paradise
how can I bear witness to it?
If my tears were not so bitter
I could believe that they
were rivers of that holy place.

Ibn Hamdis—along with his Siculo-Arab colleague Abu al-Arab—was granted asylum at the court of Seville by Prince Al Motamid, who was also a poet. In Abu's works, the vision of a Sicily lost forever assumes pessimistic tones. Such sentiments compel Abu to reject the whole notion of roots in any land and to take a very modern stance as Citizen of the World: "I have sprung from earth, any land suits me, all men are my brothers, the world is my country."

While only fragments of this vast Arab *corpus poeticum* are extant, surviving parchments yet to be deciphered may disclose testimonies of a bygone era. At least this is the thesis of Professor Othman Kaak, curator of Tunis's National Library in the 1960s, who insisted that, by examining the thousands of parchments still lying in libraries and monasteries, scholars could unearth Arab texts beneath the layers of Greek and Latin script. Even without this kind of evidence, however, the Sicily of the Moslem conquest endures in the surnames of those Arab peoples living today in Cape Bon and other North African regions: Sikli, Scikli, Scikilli, Saqli—they all evoke the Sicily of the end of the first millennium.

## 5. Twelve Years to Reach the Gate of the Sicilian Córdoba

After the Arabs came the Normans. The Sicilian adventure of these warriors descending from the North lasted only about 130 years, from 1060 with Roger of Hautville's first raid for booty (arms and horses) across the Straits of Messina until the death of the last Norman king (Tancredi) in 1194. This year of the Normans' demise, nevertheless, was rife with significant occurrences: the German Henry VI, son of Barbarossa, was crowned Emperor in Palermo's Cathedral Christmas Day; and December 26, at Jesi, a small town in the Marches, Constance, the last scion of the Hautville family and wife of Henry VI, gave birth to Frederick II, the future Scourge of the World. As John Julius Norwich has observed, "the Norman spirit was still not dead and buried." In fact, in Frederick II, all the brilliance and talents of his Norman predecessors could be detected.

Let us backtrack, for the moment, to get an overview of Norman history in Sicily. It is a history rich in the exploits of a warrior people whose

**2. William II crowned by God. Monreale Cathedral. Palermo.**

crowning achievements are due to the courage and the diplomatic skills of the two Rogers. Moreover, these kings were eminently capable of shaping a policy that embraced enlightened tolerance and peaceful coexistence in a Sicily beleaguered by a plethora of complexities and conflicts.

The early years of the Norman Conquest, however, were arduous for those rugged knights enlisted by one of the emirs of eastern Sicily to crush his enemy (also an Arab emir) in Girgenti (Agrigento). In effect, this military aid to the Arab ruler of Catania and Syracuse was a pretext for an incursion by the Normans, who had already hatched the plan to be the liberators of those people in Sicily still professing the Christian faith after two and half centuries of Moslem domination.

In February of 1061, Roger and his brother Robert Guiscard mounted a second attack on Messina from the coast of Calabria. This time, they crossed the Straits with 2,000 footsoldiers and knights. Messina fell without resistance, so the Normans marched across the high plains around Castrogiovanni as far as the territory of Girgenti. The Arabs could muster no counter-offensive.

These first two Norman expeditions, nonetheless, were simply test-runs before the spring campaign of 1061 when Roger brought fresh troops back to Sicily with the expressed purpose of occupying the whole island. Only at that point did the Moslems, torn by internecine warfare, call for reinforcements from Africa.

An Arab expeditionary force arriving in the summer of 1063 tried to bolster the exhausted Saracen army that found itself dispersed throughout the interior of the island. Arabs and Normans engaged in a major battle around Cerami, ten kilometers west of Troina. The chronicler Malaterra estimated that the Arabs had "30,000 knights and an infinite number of foot-soldiers." The Normans were greatly outnumbered; yet, led by Roger, they succeeded in putting the enemy to flight, killing many and taking hosts of prisoners.

Thus the Normans secured their power over a vast area stretching from Troina to Messina. Then, in 1071, they infiltrated and conquered Catania. Subsequently, their goal was Palermo, the city whose beauty was reminiscent of Córdoba but whose pleasurable life promised even more sweetness. With its 250,000 inhabitants, Palermo was all gardens and fountains. By the middle of August, 1071, Roger and his troops had reached the gates of the edenic capital.

### 6. Al-Khalesa Falls and the Normans Enter Palermo

Before striking at Palermo, the Normans got a foretaste of the city's delights when, with no resistance, they swept through the gardens and citrus orchards of the outlying region near the Oreto River. As the chronicler Amato noted, the conquerors divided all the spoils, "palaces and everything else they found on the outskirts of Palermo; the nobles took the lovely orchards full of fruit trees and streams; their knights were regaled in this veritable earthly paradise."

The dog-days of August in Sicily could have tempted the Normans to tarry in this Eden. But duty beckoned. While expecting the arrival of the fleet captained by Robert Guiscard, Roger headed for Yahya Castle at the mouth of the Oreto, which had been built precisely to defend against the landing of hostile forces. Roger intended to take this strategic fort to facilitate Guiscard's landing; and he did so post-haste. Out of the 45 Arab soldiers stationed in the garrison, 15 were killed and 30 were taken as prisoners. On the spot, Roger renamed the castle Saint John and, in thanksgiving for his victory, consecrated it as a church. This sanctuary would be converted in 1150 into a leper hospital, called to this day Saint John of the Lepers. The inner walls of the monument are composed of the original Arab stones of the old castle besieged by the Normans.

The actual siege of Palermo lasted all of 1071. The city fell to the Normans, finally, in January of the next year. The old Arab capital had been a citadel defended from numerous towers linked by strong chains stretched across the bay to obstruct the entrance of undesirable fleets. To resist the Norman onslaught, the Arabs barricaded themselves in the city, managed to get reinforcements and thus prolonged the outcome of the pitched battle. But, ultimately, the Normans, with forces united from land and sea, succeeded in storming Palermo.

The Normans' first major attack was focused on the Al-Qasr Quarter — the Castle — the center of the city's bazaars surrounding the Great Mosque, which, in turn, was protected by an uninterrupted span of high walls with nine well-guarded gates. This quarter extended from the Royal Palace to Quattro Canti (the Four Corners) and from Castro Gate to Celso Street.

At dawn on January 5, 1072, the Norman infantry attacked. But Moslem resistance was surprisingly strong. The battle raged, long and bloody; and, even when the Normans managed to secure their ladders against the ramparts, they saw their ascent would be costly. A certain Arifredi did scale the walls and enter the city unscathed; but the battlements remained impregnable.

At that point, Robert Guiscard shifted the focal point of the assault. Stealthily, he led 300 soldiers to the walls surrounding the quarter of Al-Khalesa, the administrative center of the city, where he thought they would meet with less resistance. Robert was right. Positioning their ladders, the Normans entered Palermo, fought their way to the gates of the Al-Qasr and battered them down to let in their fellow-invaders.

Thus the Arab capital fell. But Robert displayed mercy to his prisoners of war, announcing that there would be no reprisals and that the Arabs' possessions and property would not be confiscated. It was clear, nonetheless, that, with the Normans' seizure of Palermo, the entire Mazzara Valley was in their hands.

**3. Cefalù's Norman Cathedral, begun in 1131.**

## 7. Roger I's Ill-Fated Widow, Entombed in Patti

While isolated parts of Sicily remained under Arab control, the fall of Palermo in 1072 signalled the end of Moslem domination on the island and the inception of that enlightened Norman era distinguished by conquests in the fields of culture and art. In the aftermath of this Christian triumph, Mazara surrendered (1077)—as Syracuse and Taormina did nine years later. Then, in 1088, the Normans took Butera, and, in 1091, Pantelleria and Malta. Possession of these latter two island territories subsequently facilitated safe maritime traffic through the Canal of Sicily and—thanks to the Normans' economic and political pragmatism—fruitful international trade with African coastal powers and negotiations leading to Good Neighbor agreements.

Roger, now Grand Count, also set his relations with the Church in order, establishing dioceses in the major Sicilian cities. He thus emerged, in the eyes of the Papacy, as liberator of Sicily from its infidel tyranny. But, more than an impetuous warrior who had drawn blood in many a battle, Roger developed over the years into a wise statesman. And when Pope Urban II conferred the honor of *apostolica legatio* on him (1098), Roger gained official recognition as the most capable and potent monarch in all of Italy.

Roger died June 22, 1101, at the age of 70, in Mileto (the town he considered his capital). He had married his third wife, the Countess Adelaide (given that name by classical authors even though her tombstone reads Adelasia), in 1089; and she had given him two sons: Simone (b. 1093) and Roger (b. December 22, 1095, when his father was 64).

At the moment of the Grand Count's death, his widow found herself in charge of two young sons. Called upon to provide a successor to the throne, she appealed to her relatives, the Marquis and Marquess Manfredi of Savona, for protection of Roger I's patrimony. When her first born, Simone, died on September 28, 1105, Roger, ten at the time, ascended to the throne as Count of Sicily.

We know little about the childhood of the person who was to become Roger II. Among the few relevant sources, the Abbot Telesino recounts how young Roger was boisterous and domineering, especially with his brother Simone. Roger did, however, reap the civilizing benefits of Palermo's courtly, cosmopolitan ambience. His tutors, both Greek and Arab, prepared him well for his adult life—when he would attend to affairs of state and govern in three languages: Latin, Greek and Arabic.

Before we delve into Roger II's character as a Prince and into the splendors of his court, let us return to his mother, Countess Adelaide. After Baldovino of Boulogne had been crowned King of Jerusalem on Christmas Day of 1100, the widow consented to marry him. Arriving in the Promised Land with undreamt of pomp and circumstance, Adelaide was described by a chronicle thusly: "She was escorted by two triremes, each carrying 500 warriors, and by seven ships laden with gold, silver, vestments of purple and scarlet, and enormous quantities of precious stones and splendid cloth— not to speak of arms, cuirasses, swords, helmets, shields . . ."

Delighted with this happy union, Baldovino neglected to inform his spouse that he had contracted another marriage. By the time his second wife discovered his duplicity, Baldovino had squandered all her wealth. Adelaide's last resort was to return to Sicily alone, in 1117. The following year, this noblewoman, mother of the great Roger II, died and was buried in the cathedral of Patti. In this church later dedicated to Saint Bartholomew, one can still visit her tomb set under a canopied arch. On the lid of this Renaissance sarcophagus, the reclining figure of the ill-fated countess is sculpted in gracious style.

## 8. For Roger II, Red Carpets in the Streets and Banquets on Gold Platters

In 1130, Roger, son of the Grand Count, was crowned King of Sicily in Palermo's Cathedral. Barely 70 years had passed since his father and his uncle Robert Guiscard had invaded the territory. In this brief period, Roger I had devoted all his energy to unifying his realm and guaranteeing to all his subjects, regardless of ethnic origin, an equality based on Law and the protection of the State. Sicilians, Normans and Arabs enjoyed equal rights and all major spoken languages—Greek, Arabic, Latin, Franco-Norman— were officially recognized. So much had been done, but there were still many things to do.

Roger's investiture as King of Sicily with the endorsement of the Anti-Pope Anaclete II had been a miniature, through risky, political coup. The monarch had managed to make the best of a bad situation: the discord within the Papacy that came to a head with one of its major schisms wherein Anaclete had been chosen pope by a splinter-group opposed to the selection of Innocent II. Exploiting this internal divisiveness, Roger had negotiated his own divine right to the crown of Sicily. Subsequently, this right was immortalized in the mosaic extant in Palermo's Church of the Martorana: Roger, in oriental garb, receives his crown from Jesus Christ Himself.

The actual ceremony making Roger king by divine right took place in the Coronation Chapel built for the occasion. What remains of this structure, integrated as part of the church erected later, can still be seen from Matteo Bonello Street.

A huge crowd attended the gala event and celebrated long into the night. The Royal Palace, Cassaro Boulevard and other major Palermitan arteries were carpeted with precious handlooms—as were the streets leading to the holy space where Roger was crowned. Alessandro Telesino states in his chronicle that the guests at the ceremonial banquet used plates and goblets of silver and gold.

Roger II, once crowned, embarked on new campaigns to bring southern Italy under his sway. It was during his return to Sicily from one such mission that the monarch's ship was caught in a violent sea storm. For two full days it seemed that his vessel would sink. Then, as the crew sighted Cefalù and its fortress, the waters miraculously grew calm. Roger took this as a sign from Heaven, a special act of Christ the Savior's grace on his behalf. Thus inspired, the king vowed to have a magnificent cathedral erected on Cefalù's bay. As the English writer John Julius Norwich asserts, "it is still one of the most beautiful churches in the world." Its mosaics, the finest of which is the majestic Christ *Pancrator* (Creator of All), were done by world-famous artisans brought to Sicily from Thebes and Corinth.

Roger summoned hosts of learned men to his court. Among the most eminent, the Arab geographer Edrisi was commissioned by the sovereign to write *The Utmost Pleasure of Traveling Around the World.* Better known as *The Book of Roger,* it is the most important work of geography in the entire Middle Ages. As an addendum to this volume, a disc-shaped map of pure silver two meters in diameter and 150 kilos in weight was included. Unfortunately, this artifact has not survived.

The great king died in 1154. He had reigned 24 years and conquered every land on Mediterranean shores as far as Algiers. His daughter Constance was born two months after his death.

### 9. After William II, a Throne Without Heirs

Forty years (1154-1194) separate the death of Roger II and that of Tancredi, the last Norman king. They also represent the final stage of Norman rule in Sicily before the period defined as the "Teutonic Furor," those violent times of Henry VI, son of Barbarossa, and Constance, wife of Henry and mother of the Sicilian/Norman-born Emperor Frederick II. These four decades marking the end of Norman Sicily are dominated by the presence of two Williams: I, branded the Bad, and II, dubbed the Good.

William I, born about 1120, had begun to reign in partnership with his father Roger II from 1151 on. Characteristic of William's reign were incidents like the assassination of his minister, Maione di Bari. Victim of a bloody conspiracy, Maione was stabbed to death by Matteo Bonello in front of the Archbishop's Palace. The hilt of the sword that, as tradition would have it, was used to dispatch the minister, is still wedged in the frame of that Palermitan monument's gate.

William I died in 1166 after ruling for twelve years and undergoing the constant anguish of public and private misfortunes. His first born Roger, heir to the throne, suffered an accidental death. And even though he laid the cornerstone of the Zisa, it was his successor who completed this impressive Arab-Norman structure and took all the credit for its edification. One historian wrote that a more appropriate name for William the Bad would have been William the Sad.

Virtually on the eve of his father's death, William II was crowned King of Sicily in the Cathedral of Palermo. But, due to his tender age, regency was assumed by his mother, Marguerite of Navarre. Enlisted into her services was her cousin, Stephen of Rouen, Count of Perche, who subsequently became Chancellor and Archbishop of Palermo. Aware of being a foreigner among native forces contending the throne, Stephen opted for withdrawal to the Holy Land. Thereafter the scepter was passed on to various exponents of warring factions and to the clergy represented by the newly-elected archbishop, Walter of Offamil, who was reputed to be the founder of Palermo's Cathedral.

In 1177, William II married Joan, daughter of Henry II of England. On the occasion of their wedding, English nobles, coming as guests to Sicily, were struck by the magnificence of the Norman court. This union brought prestige to the King of Sicily; but, unfortunately, it was barren. Furthermore, the couple's sterility led to the fall of the Norman dynasty. Judging from William's consent to the marriage of his aunt Constance and Henry of Suebia (the future Henry VI), this demise was regarded with resignation by the monarch himself. He thus helped to assure the Hohenstaufen ascendancy to the Sicilian throne.

Ultimately, William II's crowning achievement was the construction of Monreale's splendid cathedral. According to a legend embellished by the king himself, his father appeared to him in a dream, revealing the source of a secret treasure that William II could put to good use. This legend served to justify the enormous expenses involved in erecting the cathedral and commissioning its whole series of mosaics. As Kitzinger attests, this monument would embody "the last and grandest of the pictorial representations glorifying the Norman Era."

William II died in 1189 at the early age of 35. After a painfully embarrassing struggle among contending archbishops, he was buried in the Monreale Cathedral he had had erected. His death sans heir precipitated the end of Norman Sicily. Five years later a new epoch began in earnest.

## 10. A Teutonic Sovereign Closes the Norman Era

After William II's death and a long and fierce battle waged by the nobles in favor of Count Roger of Andria's right to the throne, Tancredi, Count of Lecce and illegitimate offspring of William I's son Duke Roger of Puglia, became King of Sicily. Coronated by Walter, Archbishop of Palermo, in 1190, Tancredi was, according to chronicler Pietro da Eboli, so incredibly ugly that he deserved the Latin epithet needing no translation: *"embrion infelix et detestabile monstrum."*

Signs of upheaval could be detected even before Tancredi ascended to the throne. Long gone was the epoch when the two Rogers, with their political vision and tolerance, guaranteed equality to all their subjects. Tancredi inherited, instead, a realm torn by communalism. A group of Christians allegedly ransacked the Arab Quarter of Palermo. The riot that ensued was bitter and bloody, especially since it was the result of the repressed tensions described four years previously (in 1180) by the Arab traveler Ibn Jubair: "Palermo's Moslems were hard-pressed to save the fast-disappearing relics of their faith."

Other clouds were gathering and rumbling in the already dark sky Tancredi surveyed. The very year he was coronated, Henry, husband of the Norman Constance of Hautville, had staked his claim to the throne upon the death of his father Frederick Barbarossa. Declared monarch, Henry immediately descended upon Italy, aiming to occupy Sicily and reclaim the island in the name of his wife Constance, daughter of Roger II. The pretender swept through the Land of the Midday Sun with breath-taking speed. Victorious at Naples, he rushed on to Capua. Then, at Salerno, he was stymied by Tancredi's troops. Constance herself was taken prisoner, but the last King of Sicily, on a generous impulse, paid the homage due blood relationship and set her free.

While Tancredi lingered in Salerno the news of his beloved son Roger's death reached him. Consequently he returned to Palermo posthaste. Overcome by grief, he never ventured forth again, for he was to die soon thereafter, February 20, 1194. His widow Sibilla briefly assumed regency in the name of her young son William III. But internal and external difficulties quickly brought the Norman monarchy to its dramatic end.

Henry VI climaxed his invasion of the South with his triumphal entrance into Palermo on November 20, 1194. It was here that he demonstrated all his ferocity, deporting Sibilla and all her children save William III to Germany. William's own end was more tragic: blinded and castrated, he was left to rot in a dungeon.

Chronicles report that, once he had conquered Palermo, the son of Frederick I Barbarossa did not hesitate to have Tancredi's tomb opened so that he could take possession of the last Norman's crown, scepter and other burial accouterments. Among the latter was the famous cloak, reputed to belong originally to Roger, that is found today in a Viennese museum.

In his work on Frederick II, the historian Kantorowicz, citing De Cherrier, notes that in 1195, "there arrived at the imperial castle of Trifels (in Germany) a caravan of 150 mules laden with gold, silk, gems and other precious objects. Word spread that this was only a small part of the spoils taken by the emperor from the Siculo-Norman realm." This "tribute" thus brought down the curtain of the Norman monarchy in Sicily. It was the last act in a drama so enlightening and yet so brief.

### 11. The Tombs of the Great Kings: Sacked and Desecrated

The vengeance wreaked upon Palermo and other parts of Sicily by the merciless Henry VI, son of the Suebian Frederick Barbarossa, made the extinguishing of the Norman monarchy all the more gloomy. But Henry himself did not survive his misdeeds very long and was unable to see his son, the future Frederick II, grow up.

Before dwelling upon the events following the demise of the Normans in Sicily, however, let us linger over the royal and imperial tombs of Palermo and Monreale. Beyond the hatreds incarnate in their history, even in their long sleep of death, those compelling personalities there interred still remind us of how Sicilian history was shaped.

Inside Palermo's Cathedral, the tombs of Roger II, his daughter Constance, her husband Henry VI, and Constance's and Henry's son Frederick II loom in all their simplicity and severity. A Roman sarcophagus along the wall encases the remains of Frederick II's wife, Constance of Aragon. In Monreale's Cathedral lie William I and II, the former in porphyry, the latter in marble.

The history of these tombs is strange and wonderful. Roger II, having the cathedral of Cefalù erected, fully intended to be buried there. In fact, he also had two porphyry sarcophagi sculpted in the church, one for his body and the other, as he stated, "in august memory of my name and for the glory of Christendom." Yet, nine years later, upon his death in 1154, Roger's wishes were not respected. Why not? Julius Norwich offers the explanation that in those nine years Palermo Cathedral had emerged as a metropolitan church while Cefalù's remained a bishopric. At any rate, the porphyry tomb Roger II had built was kept in Cefalù for sixty years awaiting the king's corpse, only to be moved, empty, to Palermo. Finally, it was the body of Roger's nephew, Frederick II, that was laid to rest in the sarcophagus.

Cefalù's clergy, consistently in favor of respecting Roger II's wishes, eventually compromised by asking that William I be entombed in its church. The request, however, was ignored, and Roger II's successor was buried in Palermo's Palatine Chapel. Later, his body was transferred to Monreale, where his son William II also lay.

In 1811, after a fire ravaged Monreale's Cathedral, the funeral urns of the two Williams were opened to see if their remains had been damaged. William I's corpse was surprisingly intact while William II's was nothing but a skull and a pile of bones. Was there any moral in this story of William the Bad's uncorrupt body and William the Good's hulk turned to dust?

Over the course of the centuries, the tombs in Palermo Cathedral have been opened twice: in 1490 (on the order of Viceroy Don Ferdinand of Acuna) and in 1781. This second inspection was reported in detail by Canon Rosario Gregorio: "Roger II's corpse was a pile of bones, ash and chalk dust ... Henry's was supine, with wisps of blond and dark hair still clinging

**4. The Palatine Chapel in the Palace of the Normans. (Palisi Collection)**

to his skull and traces of a moustache over his lip ... Constance of Hautville's bones could scarcely be detected amid the dust and ash ... Atop Frederick II's body two more had been laid. The one on the right—perhaps Peter II of Aragon—was covered in a regal cloak . . . The other was wrapped in a fraying mantle ... In Constance of Aragon's tomb only the largest bones remained"—with the imperial crown now housed in the treasury of Palermo Cathedral.

## 12. Building to Amaze Posterity

The greatest testimonies to the glory of the Norman Age were left by these men from the North in stone. While their reign lasted 130 short years, the Normans succeeded in constructing small churches and imposing cathedrals decorated with mosaics, proud palaces and fabulous villas with artificial lakes and fish hatcheries. As Denis Mack Smith has observed, the Normans concentrated Sicily's wealth predominantly in the coffers of their kings and created an opulence around them that was unsurpassed in all of twelfth century Europe. Whatever the case, it is true that the Normans erected many buildings as if they intended to amaze future generations.

**5. The Cathedral of Palermo, begun in the 12th Century.**

As we know, the Normans appeared on the Sicilian scene to reconquer the island for Christendom and the West. Precisely for this reason, they were inspired, even while waging war against the Moslems and laying siege to Arab strongholds, to usher in a renaissance of Christian architecture. These northern warriors, before they laid down their arms, started to build those temples that vindicated the monks of Saint Basil who had kept the Christian faith alive during the Moslem domination. Once conquered, the Arab capital of Palermo, which had struck Guglielmo Appulo, the chronicler of the Norman crusade in Sicily, as "a city subject to demons," impressed the rude defenders of the Faith as a City of Delights, a genuine terrestrial paradise to enjoy to the full. Following the example of their Arab predecessors, the Norman kings had themselves surrounded by palaces and courts conforming to Oriental tastes and dressed in a sumptuous style that made them forget their Nordic traditions.

**6. The Cloisters of the Cathedral of Monreale, 12th C.**

Architecture under the two Rogers was religious and courtly. Their reign saw the construction of cathedrals in Catania, Troina and Mazara and innumerable churches some of which, unfortunately, are today in ruins. All over Sicily, however, small Norman churches are still intact. Witness the gem of Saint Mary in Mili San Pietro (Messina Province) where a gravestone commemorates the burial of Giordano, Count Roger's son.

The list of major Norman religious structures is, indeed, amazing: the Palatine Chapel, the Chapel of the Incoronated attached to the earliest part of Palermo Cathedral, the church of Saint John of the Eremites done in the style of a mosque, Saint Mary of the Admiral so vividly described by the Moslem traveler Ibn Jubair; Cefalù's cathedral, so dear to Roger II; Messina's cathedral which, transformed later into an archbishop's palace, stood until the 1783 earthquake; the Church of the Holy Trinity of Delia, still standing in the countryside near Castelvetrano.

In and around Palermo, at the time of the two Rogers, the Arab Castle by the Sea was restored and reinhabited; an old Arab fortress was converted into the Royal Palace; Favara Castle was erected just outside the city walls and became one of the centers of urban life amenities; and, at Altofonte, an important chapel was built near the Park Palace, summer home of the king.

During this same period, around 1132, Admiral Bridge was ordered built by Admiral George of Antioch. The bridge, however, is more famous for having been the site of an 1860 battle between Garibaldians and Bourbon troops. While underground today, it is extraordinarily well-preserved.

Under the two Williams, the churches of San Cataldo (Palermo) and the Annunciation of the Catalans (Messina) were erected. The magnificence of these edifices was surpassed, however, by Palermo Cathedral and its rival in Monreale, so lavishly adorned with mosaics. Civic architecture also flourished. Witness the Castles of Scibene, Zisa, Cuba, Little Cuba, Sovereign Cuba, and the royal palaces at Monreale and Castellaccio. These buildings represent the last manifestations of a unique culture which had perfected its architecture to the point where, as Guido Di Stefano says, "its flower was beautiful in the extreme but not transplantable."

# Chapter II: The Age of Frederick II

## *1. A Four-Year-Old King at Palermo's Court*

The Suebian Henry VI, who in 1194 had desecrated the tomb of Tancredi, last king of Sicily, survived his evil deed by three years. He died in Messina on September 28, 1197, at the early age of 32, after catching malaria on a hunting excursion. Henry was buried at Palermo in the cathedral erected by Archbishop Offamil.

Constance of Hautville, his widow, took charge of their son Frederick, only three at the time. The future Frederick II had been born December 26, 1194, at Jesi, in the Marches. To dispel any doubts regarding a pregnancy that took nine years of marriage to come about, the forty year old daughter of Roger II had asked that the whole realm witness her labor. Consequently, her son saw his first light from under a tent pitched in   the   ,main market square. According to Constance's wishes, eight months' after Henry's death, the heir to an illustrious throne was crowned king on May 17, 1198. Frederick was not yet four.

That same year, however, tragedies struck. On January 8, 1198, Celestine III expired. Having entrusted her son to the new pope's protection, Constance died on November 27.

This Vicar of Christ, Innocent III, had specific political aims: to oppose all Teutonic influence on the Papacy and to reestablish the Church's authority and independence as antidote to what he considered the Holy German Empire's excessive power.

Constance of Hautville's last will and testament gave the pontiff his pretext to resist and perhaps block the union of the Empire with the whole realm of southern Italy. The pope, in fact, considered this territory the undisputed fiefdom of the Church. Fulfilling Constance's wishes, on November 25, 1198, Innocent III became regent of state and of the infant Frederick.

It took the pope little time before he realized, nevertheless, that the absence of an official king would unleash the power-hungry bent on the conquest of Sicily. One of Henry's most aggressive lieutenants, Marcualdo of Anweiller, emerged as such a threat when he marched his troops with Pisan mercenaries and insurrectionist Saracens toward Palermo. But he was defeated on July 21, 1200, at the Battle of Monreale. The following year, however, Marcualdo returned and, via the treachery of a castle-guard, entered Palermo and managed to capture the seven year old Frederick. Chronicles report that the Child King, upon seeing Marcualdo's emissaries, tore at his own clothes with such a gesture of noble outrage that his strong, authoritarian character was already manifest. The pope responded immediately to save his charge by sending reinforcements led by the brave French soldier of fortune, Gualtier of Brienne, who routed Marcualdo decisively. Subsequently, in 1208, Innocent III imposed order by forcing the barons to swear allegiance to Frederick at the Diet of San Germano.

Meanwhile, according to his mother's wishes, Frederick was raised in the Court of Palermo and "bred on Sicilian mores." By that year of 1208, he had reached the legal majority (fourteen years of age); and, thenceforth, he assumed all the responsibilities of rulership. Flanking him as advisors were papal favorites such an Cardinal Cencio Savelli (who would later become Pope Honorius III) and the "unknown quantities," Bishop Ruggero of Catania and "Master Francesco."

The following year, when Frederick reached fifteen, the pope married him to Peter II's sister, Constance of Aragon, who was the widow of the King of Hungary. Constance was a few years older than Frederick; but he was happy with this union and warmly welcomed her when she arrived escorted by her brother Alphonse, Count of Provence, and her retinue manning hundreds of ships. The wedding took place in Palermo Cathedral in 1209. Two years later, an heir was born to the royal couple and named after his paternal grandfather Henry.

The following year, however, Frederick was called upon to leave Sicily.

## 2. Struggles in Sicily and Conflicts with the Papacy

That same year his heir was born (1211), Frederick, upon the insistence of Pope Innocent III, had been chosen King of Germany. Thus, in March of the next year, Frederick left Sicily and established himself in Aquisgrana, where he was to be crowned on July 25, 1215. The son of the Suebian Henry VI and the Norman Constance of Hautville fully backed the policies of the Roman pontiff—up to this point.

But Frederick's compliant attitude would be short-lived. As he developed his own strong personality, he would be quick to take completely autonomous political stands and come into bitter conflict with the Church of Rome.

After eight long years of absence from Sicily, Frederick returned there as emperor in 1220. He was 26 years old—almost middle-aged according to the times—and was determined to carry out his own political programs in the South.

To understand Frederick II's actions in depth, we must back-track for a moment and review the period when the monarch was absent from Sicily. While certain events that took place during those eight years are not directly related to the island's history, these occurrences help to explain what happened when the emperor did return.

Immediately after being crowned at Aquisgrana, Frederick promised Innocent III that he would defend free papal elections and recognize the Papacy's temporal power in the Kingdom of the South. But the emperor was not to keep his word. At the moment when Francis of Assisi and Dominic of Guzmàn were emerging as great reformers, Frederick met and collided head-on with the Church.

Innocent III died in Perugia on July 16, 1216; and, as soon as the new pope had ascended to Peter's throne on July 24, Honorius III found in Frederick his main opponent. The emperor, in fact, was bent on carrying out a plan that he considered totally legitimate: the unification of the Reign of Sicily, which he deemed his personal inheritance, and the Holy German Empire.

The inevitable conflict with the Papacy resulting from Frederick's action became even more bitter and broad-based given the League of Italian Commune's open opposition to Teutonic domination. Nonetheless, via an adroit diplomatic maneuver, Frederick was able to convince Pope Honorius that he would never act against the interests of the Church. Thus, on November 22, 1220, Frederick II traveled to Rome with his wife Constance of Aragon, and was crowned emperor by the pontiff with due solemnity. But, while Honorius III fully intended to send Frederick on a crusade to the Holy Land, the emperor's only horizons were his lands in southern Italy.

May of 1221, at Messina, Frederick convened a council during which he made it perfectly clear that he meant to reestablish full authority in Sicily and wrest power from the Sicilian Barons whom he deemed usurpers. The edicts issued by Frederick from Messina were drastic: gambling and blasphemy were outlawed, and prostitutes were forbidden to frequent public baths so as to have no contact with other women. Furthermore, Frederick forced Jews to wear emblems recognizable to all other citizens and evicted the Genoese merchants doing business in Syracuse.

It was subsequently these Genoese merchants who, in retaliation for their losses, exploited Moslem discontent to form a coalition against the emperor. But Frederick acted decisively, defeating the leader of the revolt, the Emir Ibn-Abad, and sentencing him to death. Other Moslems who asked for amnesty were deported to Lucera, in Apulia.

In the midst of his battles, Frederick lost his faithful companion of thirteen years. His wife Constance died November 9, 1222. But exactly three years later (November 9, 1225), at Brindisi, he married Yolanda of Brienne, daughter of King John of Jerusalem. This wedding seemed to draw the emperor closer to the Holy Land.

### 3. *The Bloodless Crusade, Thorn in the Pope's Side*

After his marriage to Yolanda, daughter of the King of Jerusalem, Frederick devised his next strategies: to appease the pope, who was becoming more impatient about the emperor's hesitancy to wage war against the Infidels, and, simultaneously, to put into action the plan of expansion toward the East that had been the intention of the Normans.

A series of events soon convinced the emperor that he had no time to lose if he wanted to achieve his goals. March 6, 1226, the Lombard Communes, whose dreams of autonomy had already given Frederick sleepless nights, drew up a new 25 year charter for the League in defense of their ancient rights. Twelve days later, Pope Honorius, in the long run friend and ally of the emperor's in spite of their disagreements about the urgency of crusades, died. Honorius's successor, Gregory IX, while more advanced in years, was possessed of an extraordinary energy and an authoritarian character making him most difficult to resist.

Frederick, then, realized he could no longer put off his crusade. After weathering the heat for the whole month of August, he set sail from Brindisi with his troops. But an epidemic that broke out on the ship and his own raging fever forced the emperor to abandon the expedition. His army landed at Otranto.

As a result, the pope, feeling that he had been tricked, angrily launched his attack from the Cathedral of Anagni: the excommunication of Frederick II. Undaunted, the emperor responded with determination. Disseminating a manifesto to kings, he explained the objective reasons for his withdrawal from the crusade and lashed out against ecclesiastical power and "the shackles of those priests who would bind us all, milk us dry and, in the guise of lambs, play like rapacious wolves to subjugate us." The imperial manifesto, proclaimed *viva voce* from the Capitol of the Eternal City, struck Gregory IX as the ultimate challenge to his authority. In retaliation, he refuted it publicly and reconfirmed his excommunication of the emperor.

This situation, tense enough in its own right, was worsened by factionalism. The pontiff himself, hard pressed by Frederick's supporters, was forced to flee Rome and take refuge first in Viterbo, then in Perugia. The emperor, at this point, had the good sense to recognize that, in the long run, the Pope's authority could not be eradicated. Frederick therefore chose to depart on a new crusade.

But he did so without bellicose intentions. Undertaking a virtually diplomatic mission, he approached certain Moslem notables with extreme tolerance, above all, the Sultan of Egypt. The emperor made it known to the latter that the city of Jerusalem could be ceded to him in the event of its conquest by Christian forces.

True to this pact, which of course was challenged by the aging pope for its concessions to the Infidels, Frederick II occupied strategic outposts in Palestine and swept on to enter Jerusalem in triumph on March 17, 1229. In the meantime, the pope persisted in accusing the emperor of being an heretic rather than a crusader; and when Frederick landed back in Apulia on June 10, 1229, he was met by a hostile papal army. Enraged, the emperor enlisted his best troops and won another battle, this time on Italic soil. Subsequently, on July 23, 1230, Empire and Papacy signed the Peace Treaty of San Germano. Only then did Gregory retract Frederick's excommunication, but not without exacting a heavy price.

By that time Frederick, only 36, had become the ruthless and determined man history would remember. Now that his crusades were ended and his peace was made with the pope, he could concentrate all his attention on his southern Italian realms. In Sicily he would reassert his authority as absolute monarch via a document abolishing all feudal privileges and placing all power in his own hands. The rigors of these decrees would be somewhat mitigated, however, when Frederick set up the court at Palermo that would become the most refined in all of Europe.

## 4. Divine Origins of Imperial Power

The Peace of San Germano, which signalled the end of the crusades and the truce with the Papacy, was concluded in 1230. The following year, Frederick II articulated the fundamental points of his political vision in the *Liber Augustalis* or, as it is better known, the Melfi Charter. Inspired by the great law-makers of history, above all Justinian, and framed as an appeal to the majesty of Augustus, this testament of the New Caesar, Frederick II, represents the greatest edifice of medieval law. In solemn, theocratic language, Frederick sanctions imperial right, overrides the authority of feudal lords, and establishes the centralized powers of State in the emperor. At the same time, however, he proclaims the equality of all citizens in the face of the State's laws and emphasizes how his person, "overflowing with justice," will guarantee equity in the treatment of each and every one of his subjects.

Essential to Frederick's conception of politics is one seminal idea: as the origins of spiritual power are divine, so too the emperor's temporal power has its source in divinity. In effect, via the enunciation of such a principle, the *Liber Augustalis* created the conceptual structure of the secular State and, moreover, codified the laws and rights of such a governing body in diametric opposition to ecclesiastical jurisdiction. Practically speaking, this antithesis would take shape in the long and bitter power-struggle between the Empire and the Church.

The instrument via which authority was exercised in Frederick's realm was the Magna Curia. This body consisted of seven grand marshalls, two captains governing Calabria and Sicily, and eleven executors of justice. While any communal autonomy had been eliminated by a bureaucracy that placed itself above social classes and the whole feudal structure of society, favors and traditional privileges were granted to communities—though only thanks to the emperor's "benevolence." Cities did have a say in government, however, in that, twice a year, they could send two or four deputies to an assembly that met to examine subjects' denunciations of injustices allegedly suffered and to consult with the sovereign *in re* affairs of the realm.

This form of representation has been considered the foundation of the Sicilian Parliament that would later evolve. But the State of law and order designed by the emperor set off violent reactions. Messina revolted against the ban on electing municipal magistrates. Catania and Syracuse followed suit. Frederick's response to insurgency was summary and severe. He occupied Messina and had the leaders of the insurrection beheaded. The city of Centuripe was razed to the ground and its inhabitants were deported in 1233 to a new city named Augusta, in honor of the emperor.

Given Frederick's political conflicts with the Papacy, he had time to return to Sicily only sporadically (1240 and 1249). Yet, as we will witness, he managed to attract a host of scientists, scholars and poets to the island, thus creating an environment in which major cultural contributions to the Middle Ages were made. The sophisticated humanistic and scientific interests that motivated him were the bases for one among the many appellatives he earned: *stupor mundi*.

Let us return briefly to the emperor's European battle front. Frederick was called upon to suppress a rebellion organized in Germany by his own son Henry. On this occasion, in 1235, Frederick was his rigorous self. Divesting Henry of the title of King, the emperor had him imprisoned in Apulia.

Back in Italy, Frederick had to wage war against the Lombard Communes, that had enlisted his old enemy the pope in their ranks. In an act of good faith with his allies, March 24, 1239, in the Lateran, Gregory issued his second excommunication of Frederick. Once again, the indomitable emperor retaliated in kind via his "Letter to Princes" penned by his advisor Pier delle Vigne. The pope answered this appeal and challenge to the Council with a dictum in which Frederick was branded a "blasphemous beast."

August 22, 1241, the old pugnacious pontiff died. Celestine IV succeeded him but expired after 17 days in office. Long months of uncertainty ensued. Finally, on June 25, 1243, at Anagni, Innocent IV was elected pope.

As hostile to Frederick as was Gregory, Innocent backed the emperor's worst enemies and, on July 17, 1245, reissued his excommunication. The pope's declaration also included the denial of Frederick's imperial preroga- tives. The emperor, of course, was quick to protest, appealing to the Council. Likewise, the pope was fully prepared to rejoinder, this time with the admonition that "the two swords of power—temporal and spiritual—were entrusted to the head of the Church who had once conceded the temporal to the emperor but now withdrew it." Thus, the Papacy's new crusade against Frederick began. Furthermore, all of Germany rose up against him.

Things were going badly for Frederick in Italy as well. He lost some major battles and suffered serious misfortunes, including the tragic losses of his faithful advisors, Taddeo da Sessa and Pier delle Vigne. The latter, long-time trustworthy servant of the Empire, fell into disgrace, went to prison, had his eyes plucked out there, and apparently took his own life.

Having withdrawn to his Apulian Fiorentino Castle in ignominy, the emperor, beset on all sides, died on December 13, 1250. He was not yet 56.

### 5. A Light in the Dark Ages

Frederick II was convinced of the equal status of the "two swords," the one of the Church and the other of the Empire, and, with that conviction, he struggled against the Papacy until he was finally worn down by a ruthless conflict with no holds barred. As a man compelled to do battle on these two "fronts" all over Italy and Germany, Frederick, nevertheless, managed to devote time to issues of scientific and humanistic knowledge. According to Professor Antonino De Stefano, expert in the various achievements of the emperor, Frederick single-handedly turned the Sicilian court into "the most splendid cradle of secular culture glowing in Latin Europe at the dawn of the Modern Age."

As Roger II had done before him, Frederick II summoned to his Palermitan court a multitude of learned men of diverse cultural back- grounds, languages, races and religions and gave them the freedom to create, study and interpret infinitely varied works on science, nature and art. The emperor was the patron par excellence of this fervent intellectual activity because he himself believed in the universality and unity of human knowledge.

Frederick was himself highly skilled in the mechanical arts. His ingenuity and talents in these fields bore fruit in his designs of war machines and hydraulic and architectonic structures. His passion for hunting, and for the animal kingdom in general, drove him to write that treatise *De arte venandi cum avibus* that is considered his scientific and literary testament.

Frederick's life of the mind is highlighted by the scientific and philosophical issues that he, with true intellectual curiosity, raised with the experts at his court and all over Europe. Today, with hindsight, we can see how medieval, and perhaps naive, his spirit could appear vis-à-vis his investigations into "the foundations upon which the Earth rests as it hovers over the abyss." But most sophisticated medieval minds were, after all, still absorbed by questions related to the location of Hell, Purgatory and Paradise, the bitter taste of sea water, the fire and smoke emanating from volcanoes like Etna and Stromboli, the varying temperatures of water.

Between 1226 and 1229, when Frederick was mounting his crusades, his advisor, the Scottish encyclopedist Michael Scott, who had studied at the Universities of Oxford and Paris and had translated numerous scientific treatises from Arabic into Latin, tried to satisfy the emperor's curiosity by making all medieval knowledge available to him. The fact that Scott was held in such high esteem at Palermo's court attests to his success.

Frederick's interest in fauna was not only expressed in his world renowned treatise on hunting birds and falconry but also in his collection of rare species of living animals housed in his Lucera Castle and exhibited all over Italy. An eye-witness reports how the emperor came to Ravenna in 1231, bringing numerous beasts yet unknown to Italians: elephants, dromedaries, camels, panthers, lions, leopards, white falcons, bearded owls.

7. **Frederick II and the Falconer.** From the *De arte venandi cum avibus*, **Apostolic Library at the Vatican.**

In 1245, the monks of Verona's San Zeno Cathedral had to offer hospitality to Frederick and this menagerie.

Along with scientific endeavors, Frederick promoted the artistic. The first poetic movement in Italian poetry, the Sicilian School, originated from his court at Palermo. He also established a center of culture there, whence were emitted the first glimmers of Humanism in the Dark Ages.

Frederick II left traces in history characteristic of someone larger than life. Soon after his death, his legend grew to such proportions and spread like so much wild fire that people expected him to return to this world. The chronicler Brother Salimbene wrote that he would not have believed in Frederick's death if he had not heard the news directly from Pope Innocent IV's mouth.

### 6. Architect of the Suebian Fortresses of Sicily and Apulia

Frederick II's personality permeates not only the politics and culture of the Middle Ages, but also their architecture. His memory, carved in stone, abides above all in Apulia—where he spent a good part of his life to have

**8. Catania, the Castello Ursino, built by Frederick II in the XIII century.**

access to northern Europe—and, naturally, in Sicily.

Near Lentini, the proud remains of Murgo's Basilica, founded in the early 13th century, are an important testimony to the achievements of Suebian architecture in Sicily. In addition, Saint Mary of the Alemanni and Saint Mary of the Valley, both in Messina, and the Abbey of Saint Mary at Maniace, in Bronte, were erected during the Suebian rule.

Frederick II had to spend most of his time building an intricate system of castles and fortresses around the island to defend it from invasions and secure his power there, especially while he was absent for such extended periods. The Maniace Castle of Syracuse is the most ancient example of a Frederickan building. Constructed at the edge of Ortygia Island between 1232 and 1239, this proud *castrum* is one of the best preserved of the emperor's monuments—notwithstanding damages sustained during the earthquake of 1693 and from a 1704 explosion of its gunpowder magazine. Another major castle erected by Frederick can still be found in Augusta— though since 1890, when it was converted into a penitentiary, its structure has been radically altered.

The Castle of Catania, called Ursino in ancient times, was rebuilt by Frederick after the castles of Syracuse and Augusta. Nowadays, thanks to restorations completed in the 1930s, its primitive structure is still visible. It is a powerful edifice to which Frederick II devoted special attention, suggesting how its reconstruction should proceed: "The foundations should be built with rough stones and mortar; the lower walls, two meters high, should be done in cut stone, and the rest in masonry." The emperor even had the military architect in charge of the construction, Riccardo da Lentini, give him a detailed report of his architectural progress. Today, Ursino Castle, with its imposing walls more than two meters thick and its four towers resisting the ravages of time, stands as the noblest testimony to the Suebian Age in Sicily.

At Enna another structure, called Frederick's Tower, displays similar nobility in its architectonic details. This octagonal tower rests atop a hill that commands the entire landscape. Recent studies lead us to believe that this structure, erected upon older foundations, was used as a geodesic observatory. Given that Enna, dubbed the Umbilicus of Sicily, is geographically the center of the island, one can imagine how a defense system of towers could have been constructed along lines extended from the eight sides of Frederick's structure.

Experts claim that it is not certain if this tower was built during the reign of Frederick II of Suebia or that of Frederick of Aragon. Frederick's Tower, nevertheless, recalls in its style the specifications drawn up by the great Suebian emperor.

Among the other monuments to Suebian architecture in Sicily, Stefano Bottari includes the Salemi Castle which, "notwithstanding the irregularity of the floor plan, seems to be realized in Frederick's style," and the so-called Castle of Lombardy in Enna, which "is an imitation of Lucera Castle."

This latter structure and the Castle of Monte—so desolate and imposing on its vast plain—evoke the power of Frederick's sway over Apulia. Both are virtually intact—unlike the Fiorentino Castle, where the great emperor died unexpectedly on Saint Lucy's Day in 1250. Today the Fiorentino is nothing but a pile of stones strewn across a hillock invaded by weeds. These ruins abide only as a melancholy symbol of the decline of Suebian power.

### 7. For the Papacy, Better the French than the Suebians

Frederick II's death did not put an end to Innocent IV's war on the Empire and its titular head. Frederick's descendants were still confronted by a bellicose pope bent on exterminating the Hohenstaufen.

According to the emperor's last will and testament, Corrado, son of Frederick and Yolanda of Brienne, became King of Sicily and Germany and Corrado IV of the Holy German Empire. But, while Corrado was absent from Italy, Manfredi, the son born in 1232 out of wedlock to Frederick and Bianca Lancia, was nominated Vicar and Regent of the Kingdom of Sicily.

Fate, however, was ruthless in dealing with all the players in the game of imperial power. For when Corrado departed from Germany and descended upon Italy to seize the scepter in Frederick's southern realms, death cut his incursion short on October 10, 1254, less than four years after his father's demise. And while Corrado, dying at 26, had left a two year old heir, Corradino, this child's sad end would move historians and poets to tears. Frederick's grandson, in fact, was decapitated in Naples's Market Square on October 29, 1268—at the age of sixteen.

Manfredi was not to fare much better. Pope Innocent IV, more and more determined to wipe out Frederick's children, interrupted his six year stay in Lyon to return to Italy and implement his anti-Suebian policies in person. Meanwhile, in Sicily, at a crucial time of civil unrest, the turn of events revealed that the island's fortunes were on the decline. Pietro Ruffo, long-time trusted vassal of Frederick II and supporter of his last will and testament, became an opponent of Suebian power. Ruffo went so far as to try to establish a seignory with Messina as its capital and a federation of free city-states called by one of his contemporaries a "Republic of Vanities."

Manfredi, not surprisingly, was excommunicated by Innocent IV. But he found it expedient to make a compromise with the pope. On September 27, 1254, Manfredi agreed to be Vicar of the Church. But this accord was soon revealed to be founded on air when Manfredi led his troops, among whom were loyal Saracens, against the papal forces. After the papal army was defeated near Foggia (Apulia) on December 2, 1254, the pope himself, then in Naples, failed to weather such a storm and died a week later.

Shortly thereafter Alexander IV was elected. Following in the footsteps of his predecessors, the new pope took up the gauntlet to do battle against the Suebians, reconfirming Manfredi's excommunication in the Lateran on April 5, 1257.

Manfredi, nonetheless, considered himself the victor in the battle. Therefore, he moved south in assumed triumph. Believing the false reports of Corradino's death, Manfredi had himself declared King of Sicily—and was thus crowned in Palermo Cathedral on August 10, 1258.

All over the realm, confusion reigned and factionalism reached its peak. Meanwhile the Papacy pressed for its goal of choosing its own ruler for Sicily. From 1252 on, Innocent IV had supported Richard of Cornwall, brother of Henry III of England, for this hallowed position. This same honor had been offered, however, to Charles of Anjou, brother of King Louis IX of France. To add fuel to the raging fire, in 1254, Henry II had accepted the Sicilian crown on behalf of his son Edmund of Lancaster, who was eight at the time. But Edmund had been deposed by the new pope, Alexander IV, in 1261.

Charles of Anjou fared better. To usher him to the throne of Sicily, the pope was willing to spend countless ducats. So when Manfredi died during the Battle of Benevento against the French in 1266, Charles I of Anjou unexpectedly found the gates to the Sicilian realm wide open. The new pontiff, Clement IV, formally proclaimed him King of Naples and Sicily.

## 8. The Axe that Beheaded a Progeny

Charles, brother of the King Louis who was to become a saint, had made his mark during the crusades and possessed the title of Count of Anjou. Through his marriage with Beatrice, he had also become Count of Provence. Just forty years old, he was energetic, unscrupulous and cruel.

After the Battle of Benevento, he sent a missive to the pope, relating how the bodies of the enemy covered the whole field. As mentioned, Manfredi was one of those corpses. A two-day reconnaissance unearthed his mutilated hulk. The French troops that had opposed him and come to admire his courage wanted to give him a proper burial; but Charles of Anjou refused to do so on the pretext that Manfredi's excommunication barred him from hallowed ground. Consequently, the illegitimate son of Frederick II was literally ditched under a bridge. The French soldiers, one by one, deposited stones on top of the cadaver; and thus a tomb was erected as in ancient times. Charles, however, had the body disinterred from this place of honorable burial and cast on the banks of the Liri River at the crows' disposal.

Charles of Anjou, after sending news of his victory to the pope, attended to his revenge. Manfredi's young wife Elena was cast into a dungeon, where she died in 1271 at 29. Manfredi's four sons were also imprisoned. As Pasquale Villari wrote, "Manfredi's grandfather, the emperor Henry VI, had barbarously exterminated the Norman lineage, a house to which he was related by blood, chaining Sibilla, Tancredi's widow and her children up in the Castle of Caltabellotta. As nemesis, Charles, equally barbarous, had come to wreak vengeance by putting an end to the Suebian domination in Italy."

Corradino was all that remained of the Suebians. But fate also struck implacably at this last representative of their progeny. Corradino, a German by birth and an aspirant to the imperial crown, was called upon to lead an army against the French and the pope who had made their entrance into Italy possible. Crossing the Alps, Corradino descended with 3,000 men upon Verona on October 21, 1267. Then he entered Pavia and, in a successful alliance with the pro-Empire Ghibellines, Pisa.

At this point, the pope, recognizing Corradino as a serious threat, had him excommunicated and enlisted Charles of Anjou's forces against him. In spite of this resistance, the last of the Suebians prevailed for the moment, entering Rome via Sant'Angelo Bridge on July 24, 1268. Proceeding triumphantly to the Capitol, Corradino was proclaimed emperor. Then, on August 18, amid all the euphoria, he left Rome with his army. Five days later, six miles from Tagliacozzo, he met the enemy along the shores of Lake Fucino. Corradino's forces outnumbered Charles's and, in the first stages of the battle, the former had the upper hand. But Charles's reinforcements turned the tide. The death toll was considerable, as was the number of prisoners taken by Charles, who had them mutilated and burned alive.

Corradino, however, managed to escape and find refuge in the Maremman castle of Giovanni Frangipane. But, betraying his friendship with Corradino, Giovanni had the emperor handed over to Charles's men. Tried *pro forma,* the last of the Suebians was condemned to death along with twelve of his companions. On October 29, 1268, Corradino's head was severed from his body.

Charles proceeded to pursue a policy of fierce repression all over Italy. The repercussions of such a strategy also reached Sicily, where he was already hated implacably. The climate in which the Sicilian Vespers would take place was being prepared.

## 9. Corradino's Death, a Boomerang Returning to the House of Anjou

Corradino of Suebia's death at the bidding of the ruthless Charles of Anjou set off a chain reaction of dramatic historical events. First of all, the Suebian dynasty was extinguished. But, simultaneously, Corradino's execution acted as a boomerang that would strike back at the Angevins. Public opinion throughout Europe lashed out at Charles and the Roman court it accused of conspiring with him. The rumor spread that Clement IV himself had wanted Corradino put to death and responded to all doubters, "I do not ask for vengeance, but I will not shy away from justice." Clement pronounced this ambiguous sentence as he was strolling in his garden with Charles's emissaries and, at the same time, made the poignant gesture of plucking off the "heads" of some poppies in one of his flowerbeds. Perhaps the pope was too weak after a recent illness and too much convinced of his own political impotence to dare show any signs of righteous indignation at the death sentence Charles executed against Corradino and his nobles.

Whatever the case, the tragic death of the last of the Suebians was related in all its particulars by medieval chroniclers. The fact that Charles witnessed the execution from his balcony was the major cause of their horror. Corradino, the chronicles report, was informed of the sentence by an elderly French knight, Jean Bricault, Lord of Nancy, who came to his cell while he was absorbed in a game of chess with Frederick of Austria.

**10. Corradino at the Battle of Tagliacozzo. From Villani's *Cronaca*, Apostolic Library at the Vatican.**

Hearing the fatal news, Corradino and Frederick maintained their composure and merely requested three days' time to prepare themselves for a Christian death.

Their plea was granted, and Corradino set about making his last will and testament regarding his heredity and succession. The condemned also donated a considerable part of their wealth and property to German monasteries.

The dawn of October 29, 1268, a Monday, Corradino emerged from his cell and, with sure steps, climbed the scaffold erected in New Market Square upon the orders of Charles of Anjou. After the Notary Robert of Bari read the proclamation condemning him to death, Corradino turned to the crowd gathered, denied his culpability and asked pardon for his vassals. Then his head was severed from his body without ceremony. After cursing and sobbing at the sight of his decapitated friend, the Duke of Austria soon shared his fate.

Beyond the accounts of the real event of Corradino's beheading, legends emerged. It is said that the populace, at the moment of the execution, saw a royal eagle soar over the scaffold, swoop down to graze the mutilated body of Corradino, and stain itself with his blood. Another story goes that the executioner, having lopped off the head of a young and innocent prince, was stabbed to death by masked harbingers of Justice.

The chroniclers' reports, in any event, seem improbable. One of them wrote that Robert of Betunia, the King's son-in-law, mustered the courage to stab the notary who had read out the death sentence. Another recounted how Corradino, before he met his fate, managed to cast his glove into the crowd, thereby transferring his power as ruler of Sicily to the King of Aragon, son-in-law of Manfredi.

The body of the ill-fated Suebian was not granted burial in hallowed ground. Wrapped in a simple sheet, he was dumped in a ditch. Only later were the bones reputed to be Corradino's consigned to a proper resting place in the Church of the Carmelites. The death of this young prince stirred popular feeling so deeply that two years later, in 1270, many people believed a German impostor's claim that he was the resurrected Corradino.

# Chapter III: Between Anjou and Aragon

## 1. Charles of Anjou's Iniquities Backfire

As was to be expected, Corradino of Suebia's violent death upon the orders of Charles of Anjou did not bring peace to the Reign of Sicily. On the contrary, it unleashed all of the hatred Sicilians harbored against the Angevins. Furthermore, the rulers of this dynasty did nothing on the island to win over the natives. Instead, they pursued their goals of political vendetta all over Sicily and the rest of Europe.

One of the probable causes of Sicilians' hostility to the Angevins was the latters' policy of heavy taxation. Yet, the Suebians, who taxed the islanders just as onerously, were not hated like their French successors. Another, more plausible motive for Sicilians' particularly strong resentment against their French masters must be sought beyond mere economic matters: Charles of Anjou constantly offended Sicilians' sensibilities.

Indifferent to Sicilians' sense of pride as well, Charles of Anjou transferred his administration to Naples and installed foreigners, mostly French, in the highest courtly, bureaucratic and politically strategic positions of the entire realm. There in Naples—the city Benedetto Croce thought

11. Charles I
of Anjou.
Engraving.

Charles was "wise to choose" as his capital—the monarch even devoted much time to breeding horses and improving their stock. Meanwhile, in Sicily, the French aristocrats and functionaries in the service of the new king took possession of the estates, wealth and valuables of the native nobles killed in battle, executed and exiled.

Charles of Anjou was determined to root out and annihilate the Saracens who had been the Suebians' loyal allies. Consumed by his will to power and territorial dominion, the king took charge of the Guelph forces to prepare their military campaigns in Africa and in the Orient. When his brother Ludovico of Anjou—known better to history as Louis IX of France, the Saint King—undertook the Christian mission of new crusades, Charles supported him, advising first that he do battle with the Infidels in Tunis. Charles's aims, however, were opportunistic rather than religious. Tunis, under the sovereignty of the Kingdom of Sicily, had not been paying its due tribute to the crown for many years; and Charles obviously thought that via a crusade he could force Tunis to honor its financial obligations.

Louis, nonetheless, had very different purposes, convinced as he was that, by confronting the Infidels in Africa, he could reestablish the rights of Christianity. But, the torrid summer of 1270, the King of France, his sons, the nobles in his retinue and his soldiers found themselves in dire straits there in North Africa. A plague epidemic broke out and, when the king himself succumbed to the dread disease, Charles took charge of the expedition and won a decisive victory over the Tunisians. The treaty signed thereafter secured the financial and commercial benefits he was seeking. He even exploited the occasion of the storm that hit the fleet returning from Tunisia by seizing the ships that had belonged to those allies of his who had accompanied him on the invasion.

Meanwhile Sicilian nobles in exile all over Europe appealed to various courts for support in restoring the Suebian dynasty. The prime movers of this insurgency were John of Procida, a doctor highly esteemed in the Suebian court, and Roger of Loria (or Lauria), an able sea captain. They also collaborated to ignite the terrible Sicilian Vespers.

## 2. The Thunder-Bolt Annunciation of the Vespers

The Aragonese already had set their sights on Sicily when the Sicilian conspirators against Charles of Anjou sought an ally in their court. John of Procida had taken refuge there after the Battle of Tagliacozzo and the tragic death of Corradino to try to organize an insurrection against Charles. But John was not to find strong support at first. Aragonese King James I had married his first born Peter to a young woman of Sicilian blood: Constance, the daughter of King Manfredi. Due to this marriage, the ancient rivalry between the Angevins and the Aragonese, whose arena had traditionally been Provence, took on even broader dimensions. As Steven Runciman points out, even before Peter ascended to the Aragonese throne, Constance received the title of Queen of Sicily as Manfredi's direct heiress. Nor did Peter conceal his aspirations to be King of Sicily. His claim was not only his union with Constance, but also his position as the major exponent of Ghibelline authority.

Charles, in the meantime, pursued his policy of expedient alliances by courting the Papacy. But he was thwarted by the 1277 election of Pope Nicholas III of the House of Orsini, who was dead-set on supporting the conspiracy against the Angevin monarch. Nicholas, however, reigned only three years, dying on August 22, 1280. Shortly after the pope's death, a violent conflict arose over his succession, with contending Italian and French factions. Charles lost no time manipulating the Conclave to favor a French pope—or any other who would support his own policies.

Charles acted most astutely. The fact that the Conclave deliberated for six whole months—a delay which caused the impatient populace to take to the piazzas in protest—was a stroke of luck the Angevin king could exploit. On the pretext of quelling the disturbances, Charles sent his troops to Viterbo, where the Conclave was being held, and installed one of his men as mayor of the city and other trusted vassals as guards of the papal palace. True to the politics of the times, these guards refused two cardinals of the Orsini line entrance to the Conclave. Duly intimidated, on February 22, 1281, the other cardinals elected the French cardinal of Saint Cecilia, Simone of Brie, as Pope Martin IV.

This was Charles's choice for the papal throne. In fact, the new head of the Church of Rome, having served the Saint King Louis IX, was an old and trusted friend of the royal French house. After being made cardinal by Urban IV, Simone had been apostolic legate in France and had supported Charles's claims to the throne of Sicily. With such close ties to the Angevin monarch, Martin openly defended French interests in the Holy See.

Martin IV's preferences were clear from one of his first acts: the nomination of seven new cardinals, one English, two Italian, and four French. After an opportune meeting, Martin reconfirmed Charles as Senator of Rome.

Thus, all winds seemed favorable for Charles of Anjou. He seized the moment by seeking even greater glory on a new crusade. To attack Byzantium, the king mounted enormous expeditionary forces of 10,000 knights and more than 10,000 foot-soldiers. The pope backed him whole-heartedly. But, suddenly, lightning struck when Charles received news of the bloody revolt of Palermo.

### 3. The Day of Reckoning

The explosion of the Vespers had been prepared by Sicilian conspirators over a period of years. After the death of Corradino, illustrious Sicilian exiles were harbored at the Aragonese court. John of Procida was even nominated Chancellor of Aragon by Peter. It seems that John also went on a secret mission to Constantinople to seek aid and collaboration from the Byzantine Emperor Michael Paleologus. The moment, after all, was ripe. The Emperor's hatred for the Angevins had been spurred by Charles's threats of invasion. Moreover, there was constant contact, from 1268 to 1280, between Aragonese and Byzantine diplomats; and, from 1280 to 1282, Constantinople smuggled spies and arms into Sicily.

Yet the Vespers, in all their explosiveness, was a supremely popular uprising that, in one stroke, caused a conflict to erupt which otherwise would have dragged on with uncertain duration and outcomes.

Regardless of historical ifs, the facts of the Vespers are well known: they began the eve of March 30, 1282, the Monday after Easter, at Palermo, in front of the Church of the Holy Spirit. This Norman edifice is today in the center of Saint Ursula Cemetery, but in the Middle Ages it sat alone out in the countryside near the deep gorge of the Oreto River.

The traditional Easter Monday celebration had not yet begun, but the square was packed with Palermitans ready for the festivities. Groups of young people were singing. French soldiers were mingling with the civilians to participate in the ceremony and also to make sure the Sicilians were unarmed.

Perhaps it is best, in this context, to quote the great historian of the Vespers, Michele Amari, who narrated this crucial episode of Sicilian history in impassioned terms: "French and Sicilian hearts were throbbing. Then, a young Palermitan woman of rare beauty, noble bearing and modest demeanor, made her way toward the church with her husband and their party. Seeing her, a French soldier by the name of Drouette, wishing to offend or take undue liberties, stops the woman as if to search her for arms, manhandles her, and even touches her breasts. She faints into her husband's arms; and he, choked with rage, shouts: 'Death to the French, once and for all!' In a flash a young man bursts from the crowd, disarms Drouette, and stabs him through the heart . . . Such an act, finally, awoke those slaves awaiting their liberation for centuries. 'Death to the French,' the people roared. And, as the chronicles of the times report, that shout resounded like God's judgment, reverberating throughout the countryside, piercing every Sicilian's heart . . . The battle rages over Drouette's body, where the dead fall from both sides. The multitude clashes in chaos, scatters, regroups. Our forces, in grim desperation, employ all their weapons against men armed from head to foot: stones, canes, knives. Sicilians hunt down all Frenchmen, dogging them at every step, and tearing them from limb to limb . . . Horrid were the scenes on this stage set for a religious festival, and the banquet tables, spattered with blood, were in flames. The force of the populace, unleashed, overflowed. The skirmish was brief, and many of our people were massacred. But 200 Frenchmen had fought and 200 had perished."

The slaughter continued for several days. Sicilian women married to Frenchmen and foreign monks ensconced in convents were summarily executed. It is estimated that, in the course of one night and one morning, 2,000 French, men and women, fell. All Angevin flags were torn down and replaced with the imperial banner of Frederick II. Heralds were sent to towns and cities, in the vicinity and all over Sicily, to convey the news of the revolt. The Vespers conspirators seized control in Palermo; and the Corleonese rose up and declared their allegiance to the cause. The French Executor of Justice, Jean of Saint-Remy, and his loyal followers withdrew to the Castle of Vicari—only to be discovered and fall in another massacre. It took little time before the whole island was a sea of flames.

### 4. A Duel Between Two Kings with Sicily as the Stakes

In the first week of April, 1282, while in Naples, Charles of Anjou was informed of the fateful events that had taken place in Sicily via a message sent to him by the Archbishop of Monreale. Charles made the mistake, however, of underestimating the seriousness of the crisis, thinking of it, instead, as a localized problem that would merely delay his crusade in the Orient. Thus, his only response was to dispatch his vice-admiral, Matteo da Salerno, with four armed galleys destined for Palermo's harbor, whence punishment could be inflicted on a few upstart Sicilians. But at Messina, where the population had joined the Vespers rebellion after some hesitation, two of Charles's ships were captured in Sicilian waters, and the other two managed to escape to friendly seas. His aborted retaliation, then, led Charles of Anjou to grasp the enormous dimensions and the gravity of the revolt in Sicily.

But Pope Martin IV was still backing him. In fact, the pontiff, ever neglectful of his ecumenical mission and partial to the French, refused to receive a delegation from Palermo requesting the pope's protection in the name of the free commune established in the island's capital. Martin IV's only response was his bull of excommunication launched against the Sicilian rebels and the Byzantine Emperor Michael himself.

Martin, however, could do nothing to help Charles of Anjou regain his hold on Sicily. Furthermore, Charles's own measures, from flattery to threats to open warfare, were useless. Even when the fleet of his that was

**12. The court of Frederick II in a 15th century French miniature.**

supposed to embark for the Orient stationed itself at the Calabrian port of Catona, close to the Straits of Messina, and attempted incursions along the Sicilian coast, Charles found all his designs on the island thwarted.

Peter of Aragon, in the meantime, seemed indifferent to what was going on in Sicily and made it known that he was mounting a crusade for which he asked the pope's blessing. The prudent Peter, who inexplicably did not come to be known as the Temporizer, did, however, receive a Sicilian delegation informing him of the situation on the island. The delegates paid particular homage to his wife Constance, declaring that they and all their Sicilian compatriots considered her the legitimate Queen of Sicily. Impressed by their determination, Peter of Aragon, while he was aware that any favorable response to this claim would be interpreted as a direct challenge to Charles and Martin IV, made the momentous decision of embarking for Sicily.

On August 30, 1282, the Aragonese king landed at Trapani with a multitudinous retinue. Five days later, at Palermo, he was proclaimed King of Sicily. Hastily, Peter promised to respect the ancient Sicilian privileges enjoyed since the Norman times of William the Good. Then, Peter enlisted all able-bodied native knights in his army to go and meet the enemy at Messina.

King Charles, sizing up the situation and judging it rash to collide with Peter's forces head-on, abandoned the bridge head he had occupied at Messina and withdrew to the continent to wait for reinforcements from

France. Consequently, Peter could sweep across Sicily as far as the Straits without having to inflict a single wound.

That whole winter, a stalemate between the Aragonese and the Angevins prevailed. Then, at the close of 1282, Charles made a strange proposal to Peter: a duel between the two monarchs to decide who would rule Sicily. The challenge, strange not only because Charles, 56, was considerably older than Peter (41), was accepted, with one modification: each king would have 100 knights at his side. The date of this joust was set for June 1, 1283, at Bordeaux, within the King of England's domain. To play out the fate of Sicily, in effect, God's judgment was being invoked.

### 5. Another Frederick on the Much Sought-After Throne

The duel for Sicily between Charles of Anjou and Peter of Aragon never came to pass. It did not take place in part because the pope opposed it and demanded that Edward of England refuse to comply. But, just as importantly, the duel failed to materialize since, when all was said and undone, the whole thing was a farce.

Chronicles relate how, for this strange encounter, the date was set, but not the exact hour. Thus, that day, while both monarchs did show up on the field of battle with their portentous retinues, they arrived at different times! King Peter kept their appointment by coming soon after dawn. Waiting a couple of hours without seeing Charles, Peter decided—or so he feigned—that his opponent was not going to keep their date. The Aragonese monarch thence departed, affirming that the Angevin was a coward and that he was the victor by default. Charles followed suit when he presented himself in the late afternoon.

A bigger duel, however, was in the making. Its first inklings were evinced by the contentious Martin IV who, not content with merely excommunicating King Peter of Aragon, vowed to launch a crusade against the blasphemous and rebellious Aragonese. But the papal anathema did not stop Peter. Entrusting his Siculo-Aragonese armada to the able Roger of Lauria, Peter won major battles against his adversaries. During one of these encounters, the Aragonese succeeded in capturing the Angevin King's son Charles of Salerno (called the Lame due to his disability) on the high seas. Hearing the news of his capture, many Sicilians, in memory of Corradino's fate, demanded the execution of King Charles's son as revenge for previous Angevin atrocities. But, deeming that Charles the Lame would be more useful alive than dead, Queen Constance had him spared.

In the next few years, both Charles and Peter seemed to renege on their aggressive strategies and finally abandoned that battlefield that was southern Italy. Peter left Sicily in charge of his wife Constance, and Charles withdrew to Apulia, at that juncture an area untouched by war.

The Angevin was convinced that something important was bound to occur. So he worked feverishly towards that day. He spent the Christmas of 1284 at Melfi and New Year's at Foggia.

Then he fell sick and, sensing the proximity of death, made his last will and testament on January 6, 1285. Therein, he deposed that, if his son Charles of Salerno remained prisoner, his nephew Charles Martel would be his rightful heir. Regency would be entrusted to Robert Count of Artois, and the Captaincy would fall to Jean of Montfort, his High Courtier. The following morning, Charles of Anjou died. His corpse was taken to Naples post-haste and entombed in a splendid marble sarcophagus.

That same year, the deaths of both Martin IV and Peter of Aragon removed from the political arena of Europe the remaining protagonists in the continental struggle for domination in Sicily. On March 29, the pugnacious and partial Martin IV was lowered into his tomb, only then abandoning the intransigent approach that could have kept Europe at war indefinitely. Then, on November 10, Peter of Aragon left this world before being able to reap the fruits of his many triumphs.

According to Peter's wishes, Sicily passed into the hands of his second born James and Aragon was bequeathed to his first born Alphonse. For these heirs, luckily, times had changed, and the embattled moments of the Sicilian Vespers had transpired. Thus compromises were possible, as witnessed by the treaty signed in Paris in July of 1286 between France and Aragon. Two years later, when Charles the Lame was released from prison, he accepted this peace.

Sicilians, however, had to bide their time before gaining their freedom since the game of compromise between principalities and the Papacy was still being played behind their backs. In fulfillment of an ancient prophecy, another Frederick—the Third—emerged upon the throne of Sicily "to follow in the footsteps of Frederick II."

Frederick of Aragon was the third son of King Peter. When Alphonse III died suddenly in 1291, Frederick was chosen King of Sicily by his older brother James II. On December 11, 1295, the Palermitan Parliament accepted this decision publicly. Subsequently, Frederick III was proclaimed King in Catania on January 15, 1296. His reign, characterized by the political and administrative reorganization of Sicily, would be long and constructive.

## 6. The Subtle Games of Boniface VIII

Although he was Aragonese, Frederick III felt the fascination of his Suebian roots. His mother Constance, after all, was a descendant, via the "natural" links of Manfredi, of the great Emperor Frederick II. With such a sense of heritage, the 25 year old Frederick III, crowned King of Sicily early in 1296, appeared to his subjects as what Antonino De Stefano describes as "the ideal monarch, just and generous, and the accomplished man of arms and letters, knightly, intelligent, cultivated."

In his coronation speech, Frederick III passionately appealed to the political vision of his great ancestor. Once he had reaffirmed the divine right of kings, Frederick III then reminded all Sicilians how Charles of Anjou had been obsessed with subjugating their entire island. The Angevins, Frederick stressed, were the eternal enemy to confront. Shortly after this ceremonial oration, the new king further articulated his own designs. His letter of April 3, 1296, to his brother James stated categorically that he intended to reconquer the ancient parts of his realm still under the hated Angevins and, thereby, to avenge the death of the two great Suebians, Manfredi and Corradino.

Blocking Frederick's path, however, was Boniface VIII, who employed all his authority, flattery and threats to convince the young king to abandon Sicily. The pope's first step was to force Frederick's mother Constance to leave the island and come to Rome where, to honor an accord between James of Aragon and the Church, the elderly queen's daughter Yolanda was to be betrothed to Robert of Anjou. When this marriage took place in Naples in March of 1297, Boniface VIII retracted Constance's excommunication. But, thereafter, Constance herself, feeling the weight of such an overweening power play, decided to retire to the Convent of Saint Claire in Barcelona. Reunited with her son James, she died on April 9, 1300.

Once he had succeeded in uniting an Aragonese and an Angevin, Boniface VIII played another subtle game. Using all his prestige and economic power, the pope organized a crusade to Sicily to be led by none other than Frederick III's brother James. Boniface maintained that the ultimate goal of this crusade was, of course, the Holy Land; but, he added, the Holy Land could not be reached before Sicily was subjugated. The warrior pope's design herein was to turn the island over to the Angevin monarch whom Frederick III considered merely the Count of Provence.

The expedition was launched with an Angevin-Aragonese fleet that embarked in September of 1298 to invade the island. After his successful landing at Marina of Patti, however, King James was stalled in eastern Sicily at the siege of Syracuse. Then, near Cape Orlando, in the summer of 1299, the Angevin-Aragonese fleet commanded by Roger of Lauria, who in the past had always fought on Sicily's side, inflicted serious damage and injuries on the forces of Frederick III. The King of Sicily himself, showing his bravery in battle, was wounded. But he was saved when his own ship abandoned the battle and took flight. King James, perhaps because he did not want to do further violence to his brother, failed to pursue his victory to the bitter end. Even though the pope considered his withdrawal treachery, James returned to Spain. Undaunted, Boniface VIII appealed to Charles of Valois, brother of the King of France, in the hope of finding an ally capable of delivering the death blow to Sicily. Nevertheless, events did not transpire as the pontiff would have wished.

### 7. King of Trinacria Alone

Charles of Valois, brother of the King of France, for his service to Boniface VIII in the struggle against Frederick III of Sicily, received innumerable honors, privileges and political plums. Among the latter were the recognition of his right to the imperial crown of Constantinople, the Vice-Chancellorships of Romagna and Ancona, and the Dukedom of Spoleto. In addition, the warlike pontiff nominated him as Standard-bearer of the Church.

While Charles of Valois and Boniface VIII were relishing their apparently definitive victory over their common enemy, Robert of Anjou, by the beginning of 1302, was carrying on secret negotiations with the King of Sicily. Perhaps Robert was spurred to do so by his wife Yolanda, Frederick III's sister, who ironically had married Robert at the urging of the pope himself. At any rate, Frederick was happy to negotiate for peace, on two conditions: (1) that he could maintain control over Sicily and Calabria; (2) that he could marry a daughter of Charles II of Anjou, i.e., one of Robert's sisters. Robert accepted Frederick's terms and proceeded to seek the pope's consent to them. The pontiff, outraged, categorically refused to compromise.

The pope's recalcitrance was, in effect, a declaration of war. Consequently, Charles of Valois launched a massive attack on Sicily, but fate was working mercilessly against him. During his siege of the city of Sciacca, the plague broke out, decimating his troops and animals. A pragmatist, Charles of Valois himself initiated peace talks with Frederick III. Their Peace of Caltabellotta was signed August 31, 1302.

The pact stipulated that Frederick III, during his lifetime, would rule Sicily and the outlying islands, but that, after his death, these territories would belong to Charles of Anjou and his descendants. Frederick's heirs were to receive an indemnity in the form of another island, either Sardinia or Cyprus.

Frederick's marital intentions were fully satisfied via his engagement to the Princess Eleonore, Charles II of Anjou's daughter. The actual title that was Frederick's due, however, remained in doubt, pending Robert's decision to dub him "rex insulae Siciliae" or "rex Trinacriae."

Shortly after the Peace of Caltabellotta, Frederick III had taken a hard line regarding his status, proclaiming that "we possess the island of Sicily and we will remain its king." Nevertheless, he expediently acceded to the Angevin's future decision—at least for the moment.

Boniface VIII reacted violently to the secret accords made by Robert and Frederick. During a meeting held between the pope and Charles of Valois, Boniface lashed out with such vehemence and insults that Charles reached for his sword. Yet, when Boniface had calmed down, he accepted the treaty, with the proviso that Sicily continue to fulfill its duties to the Church. When clauses to that effect were added to the pact, Boniface was appeased and Frederick III was obligated to pay the Papacy an annual tribute of 3,000 ounces of gold, to arm troops at the Curia's disposition, and to provide foodstuffs the equivalent of 10,000 acres of grain for the needy in the Holy Land. The pope also resolved the issue of Frederick's title, preferring King of Trinacria to King of the Island of Sicily. This fine distinction satisfied Boniface because it did not contradict, in form, the Angevins' claim to the island.

The pope's clauses were appended to the treaty in the summer of 1303. At the same time, rumor had it that Boniface, playing both ends against the middle, had promised aid and new privileges to Frederick in the event that he broke the peace treaty and moved against Charles of Valois. But when Boniface VIII died on October 11, 1303, the truth of this matter was buried with him.

### 8. An Emperor, Ally of Frederick III

Once the warlike Boniface VIII was lowered into the tomb, the vise squeezing Frederick III from every side seemed to loosen somewhat. Thus he could attend to the most urgent affairs of the Kingdom of Sicily, namely, the reunification of its ancient territories (Calabria included) under his sway and, contrary to the wishes of the House of Anjou and the Papacy, the hereditary sovereignty of Sicily.

The truce granted by the Peace of Caltabellotta allowed Frederick III to develop his expansionist policies in Africa and the Aegean Sea, areas he considered strategic for Sicily's security. His invasion of the Tunisian island of Jerba met with success, and the island remained in his possession until his death. Setting his sights, then, on Constantinople, Frederick III aimed to win back that title of King of Jerusalem which had belonged to his predecessors but was now being contested by the Angevins. To pave his way, Frederick married his daughter Constance to King Henry III of Cyprus in 1317, and, when Henry died, to King Leo V of Armenia in 1331.

**Frederick's** politics constantly moved between two poles which he tried to counterbalance: his militant strategy inspired by his own proud spirit and a pragmatism demanded in his confrontations with Charles of Valois and the Church.

Toward the end of 1307, relationships between Sicily and the Papacy became particularly tense. On the other hand, ties between Sicily and Naples improved when Robert, succeeding his father Charles in 1309, tried to draw up new peace accords with Frederick. Other events, however, demanded their full attention, especially Emperor Henry VII's arrival in Italy in 1310. Generating new political alliances and new hopes and fears, this grand entrance was considered by Frederick III and the rest of the Ghibellines in Italy a real victory in and of itself. The King of Sicily also saw this occasion as the right moment to ally with Henry VII and wage war against the Angevins. Robert of Anjou, concurrently, threw his lot in with the Papacy and its ally, the Italian Guelph party.

Henry VII, who had come to Rome to be crowned Emperor, was blocked by Angevin troops as he attempted to pass through the gates of the walled Vatican City. Forced to withdraw to the Lateran Basilica to be coronated by just three cardinals, Henry never forgot the outrage. Thus, having reached an agreement with Frederick III, the emperor declared war on the King of Naples. Having committed *lése majestè* by stopping Henry's coronation in St. Peter's, Robert of Anjou was banished from the Empire. Furthermore, Henry ordered that all his possessions be confiscated and that his subjects be absolved from their sworn allegiance to him.

Strengthened by the alliance with the emperor, Frederick III went back to war with Naples in 1313, landing his troops in Calabria. Yet, once again, Frederick's dreams of recovery of his lost heritage collided with destiny. August 24 of that year, at Buonconvento, near Siena, Henry VII died so suddenly that poisoning was suspected and left Frederick without the only ally who could make victory possible.

Thus Frederick III decided to tempt fate by sailing with his fleet toward Pisa to see in what state the forces of the dead Emperor might be. Learning that they had disbanded, he headed his armada back toward Sicily. But violent sea-storms left it stranded for a month in the port of Cagliari.

### 9. Two Kings in Sicily: Challenges to Robert of Anjou

Everything seemed to conspire against Frederick III that autumn of 1313. Yet, as he waited in Sardinia for the seas to calm, he expressed his determination to endure in a letter to his brother James: "Better war than a dishonorable peace; with my sword and my blood, I will defend Sicily's freedom." Finally, Frederick managed to return to Sicily, landing at Trapani on November 11. There, he was received by Sicilians as a hero because what frustrated his plans were not other men but the forces of destiny and the elements.

Profiting from Frederick's absence from the island, Robert of Anjou had sent his fleet on raids of the Sicilian coastline and Lipari. These incursions, however, were merely test-runs before a major naval attack designed to deal Frederick his death blow. Robert's forces here consisted of 100 galleys, 220 troop ships, 3,000 knights and 3,000 footsoldiers. The cities of Venice and Genoa, hostile to the Empire, also sent armies to aid Robert against Frederick; and 800 Aragonese knights James had allowed to be mercenaries of the Angevins on condition that they would never be used against his brother Frederick brought up the rear of Robert's expedition.

By August 9, 1314, the Angevin armada had reached Sicilian waters near Carini and was ready for a landing. Successful there, it laid siege, from land and sea, on Trapani. Gathering whatever ships and ground forces he could muster, Frederick led them out to meet the Angevins on October 25. Yet, while some brief skirmishes occurred, there was never a decisive battle. Robert's army and navy were too weakened by disease, hunger and thirst to mount a major attack; and Frederick's fleet was caught in a gale that drove it back to Palermo for shelter. Finally, in December, a truce was declared that would last until March of 1316. Frederick even granted *laissez-passer* to Robert's navy so that his exhausted seamen could cross Sicilian territory on foot, reach Messina, and, there, sail across the Straits to Calabria.

Robert, however, broke the truce as soon as he could and, once again, invaded Sicily. In retaliation, Frederick reassumed hostilities. But the new pope, John XXII, foiled Frederick by declaring that the truce was in effect for three years more. This ploy enraged Frederick, and, informed that the pope and Robert were conspiring against him at Avignon, he sent a delegation there to announce to the pontiff and his guest that the war was still on.

John XXII flew into his own, holy rage, and thereupon excommunicated Frederick. The pope also threatened to pronounce anathema against any- and everyone who dared to oppose the Kingdom of Naples. Meanwhile, Frederick's actions received the unanimous approval of the Sicilian Parliament, which met on July 17, 1320, at Messina precisely to back their leader. As a consequence, for fourteen years, Sicilians were officially banished from Christendom. All their churches were shut down, all holy bells were silenced, and public prayer and processions were abolished.

In defiance of the Church, on Easter Sunday, 1321, Frederick crowned his chosen heir to the throne, his son Peter, as King of Sicily. The die was cast. Trying to eschew military strategies, Frederick III proceeded to seek external allies that would back his daring diplomacy. When Ludwig the Bavarian arrived in Italy, Frederick took the occasion to court him. Ludwig, at that point, seemed to be Frederick's last hope.

## 10. Forty Years to Establish the Rights to a Kingdom

The alliance of Frederick III and Ludwig the Bavarian resuscitated the ties between the Kingdom of Sicily and the Holy German Empire. As was the custom, this pact included a marital arrangement clause. Frederick's daughter Elizabeth was betrothed and eventually wed to Stefan, the Emperor's second born son and the future Duke of Bavaria. Thus the House of Aragon formed one more link, this time to the Bavarian dynasty.

It should be noted that in spite of John XXII's open hostility and condemnation of Frederick III, the latter never intended to challenge papal authority. Therefore, when Ludwig stooped to the grotesquery of declaring that John XXII was deposed on the grounds of heresy and criminal conspiracy and of coronating the Franciscan Heresiarch Pietro Rinalducci of

13. The Catania Cathedral where Frederick III is buried. The Fountain of the Elephant, called "Liotru" in Sicilian.

Corvara as Pope Nicholas V, the King of Sicily, going against the Emperor's wishes, refused to promulgate the deposition of the trial against John XXII on the island.

History justly credits Frederick III with using his authority to keep Sicily free of schism at this crucial moment. The king went so far as to prohibit anyone on the island from preaching against the deposed pope by instituting the death penalty for such "sedition."

No words or deeds, however, could put an end to the struggle between Sicilian and Angevin forces. Now it was Ludwig who entered the lists, with Frederick's support in the form of 600 knights, 50 galleys and his sons as the leaders of a new expedition. Their opponent, with the backing of enormous sums of money, was ready with a new armada and fresh troops. At one point the Bavarian, hard-pressed by the Angevins and tired of waiting for reinforcements, recrossed the Alps and headed for home. The Sicilian fleet commanded by Peter arrived to bolster the Teutonic attack precisely when the Emperor was on his way back to Germany.

Peter then decided to return to Sicily, though he lost a number of ships on the way in a gale. Thus, Frederick's major political objective—that of restoring the Suebian dynasty in Sicily with the help of the German Emperor—was not realized. With his dreams of expansionism in Africa and the Orient dashed to the ground, and with the weariness of endless combat against his implacable enemies, the Angevins, and their ever-faithful ally, the Papacy, Frederick III concentrated his remaining energies within the confines of Sicily.

Frederick's last hope of finding a way out of his quandaries came when his undaunting adversary John XXII died on December 4, 1334. But the French cardinal Jacques Fournier succeeded John as Benedict XII, promising to follow in the wake of the Church's political opposition to the interests of Sicily and the Sicilian people. In fact, the new pope immediately reconfirmed the interdiction against Frederick which the king himself, believing it to be the result of the preceding pontiff's personal animosity, had had revoked. Then, Benedict XII proceeded to help the Angevins launch another invasion of Sicily. Robert, however, while he hurled himself into the attack on Palermo with verve, was unable to claim victory and eventually withdrew once more.

A significant achievement for Frederick was the peace treaty made with Genoa. But after a reign of 40 years in Sicily, the only right he had secured on the island was that of ruling as long as he lived. He had fought his whole life against powerful enemies to defend the kingdom; and, while he had made alliances with foreigners, he had always done so to protect his subjects and their territory.

True to his principles, the great king succumbed on June 25, 1337, in the convent of the Knights of Saint John between Paternò and Catania. His body was transported to Catania's cathedral for temporary burial. The tomb, however, has remained there to this day.

## 11. Feudal Families and Sovereigns

Ascending to the throne of a Sicily at war, Frederick died leaving a still embattled island. This is the situation that best characterizes his long reign.

After Frederick's death, for about eighty more years, Sicilians would find themselves swept up by the convulsive circumstances perpetuated by the Angevins' struggle for power on the island, by the Papacy's continual support of the House of Anjou, by more frequent and more destructive interventions of Iberian rulers, and by the emergence and empowerment of an aggressive feudal nobility of Sicilian origin. Caught among these forces, Sicily, by the beginning of the next century, would lose its identity as a kingdom and become a vice-regency.

For the moment, however, it is useful to dwell upon the personality of Frederick III, last great king of a proud Sicily that aspired to autonomy. The king, in spite of his heavy commitments to military campaigns, managed to usher in a new and better order to govern the island. Frederick passed more just laws than Sicily had usually seen and administered them in that same spirit of justice with which they had been promulgated. Furthermore, he acted as a generous patron of literature, science, and art; improved the condition of servants and slaves; protected Saracens and Jews, integrating them into the Sicilian community; waged a moral war on gambling, black magic and luxurious excess.

Ultimately though, his major achievement is considered the Frederick-an Constitution. Issued in 1296 in the wake of the Norman-Suebian Age, this document established that the monarch could never abandon Sicily even if he took possession of another realm. Furthermore, the constitution provided for the restructuring of the Sicilian Parliament according to consistent norms. This governing body was to meet at least once a year, on All Saints' Day. All its members—prelates, barons, and mayors—were to attend in order to come to decisions regarding war and peace, public administration, legislative acts, foreign policy, and the distribution of honors, donations, grants and privileges.

While Frederick III was a man of his times, he had the kind of vision that could have laid the foundations for constitutional monarchy—were it not for some defects inherent in his political edifice. These defects can be traced to the very constitution of Frederick's parliament, a body numerically dominated by nobles who brought all their personal rivalries and conflicts to bear on the affairs of state. Imposing decisions in their private interest rather than for the people's welfare, these nobles, during but especially after Frederick's death, dominated the urban centers and controlled the public domain and the lands of the crown. In short, while the Normans considered feudal estates temporary concessions made to barons, the nobles, during the time of Frederick III, succeeded in taking possession of their lands and in having only formal obligations to their sovereign in the administering of private property.

Thus, in the fourteenth century new protagonists of public life emerged from a group of prominent families—the Ventimiglias, the Palizzis, the Chiaramontes, the Moncadas—exercising and struggling for power via rivalries, alliances, and marriage contracts. Testimonies to the splendor of their culture still abide in the imposing baronial edifices found all over Sicily. Witness the Steri and Sclafani Palaces in Palermo, and the various fortified castles of Agrigento, Naro, Bivona, Favara.

The Chiaramonte family commissioned architects so accomplished that their distinctive style came to be defined as Chiaramontean. This same family had the prominent local painters Cecco da Naro, Simone da Corleone and Darenu da Palermo decorate the carved-wood ceiling of its magnificent Palermitan abode. Emperors in miniature, the barons, within their palaces, wielded the power of dealing life or death out to their subjects.

### 12. Peter II, Also Laid in the Great Frederick's Tomb

With Frederick III dead, peace seemed to reign in Sicily. Peter, the son of the King raised to equal monarchical status by Frederick himself, ascended to the throne amid Catanese nobles whom chronicler Michele da Piazza described as "all dressed in the finest silks in the most elegant of fashions, all waving palm fronds to herald a time of peace."

But Peter's status as King of Sicily was a flagrant violation of the Treaty of Caltabellotta. In response, Robert of Anjou reclaimed what he considered his right, i.e., the reabsorption of Sicily into his realm, and called once again for papal intervention. Peter, meanwhile, tried to ingratiate himself with Pope Benedict XII, sending an envoy to Avignon to make it clear that, as King of Sicily, he would pay the tribute due to the Papacy. The pope, however, followed in his predecessors' footsteps, siding completely with the Angevins. As a result, war was bound to break out.

On this diplomatic-political chessboard, powerful feudal families now made their appearance, especially the Ventimiglias, Palizzis and Chiaramontes. This latter clan had done great service to the Aragonese crown. Manfredi I of Chiaramonte had fought many battles and total wars against the French on behalf of Kings Peter and James. And after Manfredi I died in 1321, his brother John I, who had been part of the 1295 delegation sent by the Palermitan Senate to Boniface VIII to gain papal consent to the nomination of Frederick III as King of Sicily, became the head of the Chiaramonte family. Subsequently, John I married Lucca Palizzi and, via this union with another powerful feudal clan, enhanced his prestige and gained the strength needed to confront his rivals, the Ventimiglias.

In a battle between these emergent pretenders to feudal power, a Ventimiglia fell off his horse and perished. His followers, in retaliation, turned to Robert of Anjou for help in defeating the Chiaramonte-Palizzi coalition.

Naturally, Robert was delighted to accept this "invitation" and made haste to send an expedition, headed by his illegitimate son Charles of Artois, against Sicily. In 1338, Charles's forces succeeded in occupying Termini. The following year, after King Peter had been excommunicated for having refused to fall into the trap of an audience with Benedict XII, another Angevin invasion resulted in the seizing of the fortress in Lipari's port and in the occupation of Milazzo.

As sheer chaos reigned, Peter II died, August 15, 1342. His death was so sudden that no proper tomb had been erected beforehand—so his body was laid in the porphyry sarcophagus housing the remains of the great Suebian Frederick II. When Peter's son Ludovico, only five years of age, inherited the crown, the Palizzis, who in 1340 had fallen into disgrace and gone into exile, took advantage of a delicate situation by rebelling against the authority of the realm and enlisting Angevin aid. During this emergency, however, Robert of Anjou departed from this world. His demise, in effect, made it impossible for the Palizzis to have their revenge and for the old but never quite satisfied designs of the Neapolitan dynasty on Sicily to be realized.

Strangely enough, these events led to a workable truce. In the name of young Ludovico, John, Frederick's fourth son, was to reign. Yet, in spite of his status as Marquis of Randazzo and Duke of Athens and Neopatria, John, for all his warlike spirit, was unable to woo fortune to his satisfaction. Nor did he improve the lot of the kingdom.

### 13. A Florentine's Support of the Angevins in Sicily

With John, General Vicar of a reign in shambles, Sicily passed through a turbulent period characterized by the most noxious form of feudal anarchy. John himself attempted to strike back at the Angevins by reconquering Lipari and Milazzo. But while he had some success, he was thwarted in the long run by the Chiaramontes and Peter's own widow, Elizabeth. Ultimately, John came to a premature end in 1340, when a plague raging all over Italy killed him as well.

John's death added fuel to the fires burning in the struggles among feudal families. The main contenders to Sicilian power were the Catalan nobles headed by the Grand Executor Blasco of Alagona, Count of Mistretta, and the Latin faction whose leaders were Matteo Palizzi and Manfredi Chiaramonte.

Without royal authority or a parliament at this time, Sicily experienced decadence. Barren fields and lack of work took a greater toll on those Sicilians who were already destitute, gave nobles the perverse incentive to pursue their own selfish interests and overweening power, and revealed the island's internal contradictions in all their nakedness.

Ludovico, in accordance with the wishes of his sister Constance (called the Abbess), moved his court to Catania to facilitate an agreement with Alagona. But the monarch's maneuver induced the Chiaramontes to seek Angevin aid. Again, following the same old script, the Angevins launched an attack on Sicily. Their fleet, commanded by the Florentine Niccolò degli Acciaiuoli, raided the coast around Milazzo, broke through the city's defenses and occupied it. From there, Angevin troops marched around the island, taking possession of Palermo, Syracuse, Trapani, Agrigento and Marsala. As Sicily was to be almost totally conquered by the Angevins, however, destiny came to the aid of its inhabitants once more. When Niccolò's services were demanded elsewhere, the Angevins left their occupied territories on the spot, intending to return the next year.

Meanwhile, Ludovico died on October 16, 1355, at the young age of seventeen. The powerful Blasco of Alagona expired as well. Subsequently, the reins of power fell into the hands, first, of Constance, then, of her sister Eufemia. As Isidoro La Lumia has observed, "the whole island was in decay and ruins, plunging into the abyss of anarchy."

The enemies of Sicily took advantage of this confusion. Via the treachery of Niccolò di Cesarò, the Angevins occupied Messina without having to inflict a wound. Niccolò of Acciaiuoli returned to haunt Sicilians; and the King and Queen of Naples, Louis and Jeanne, set foot on the island to survey their new conquests. Always the opportunist, Simone Chiaramonte seized the moment to seek the Angevins' support of his marriage to the Aragonese Princess Bianca, who was being held prisoner with her sister Yolanda in Calabria. However, not trusting Chiaramonte, the Angevins rejected this peace offering and sailed from Messina to lay siege on Catania, where young Frederick was now installed as King of Sicily. For the nth time though, the Angevins seesawed from crowning victories to defeats and, never delivering a decisive blow, demobilized—at least for the moment.

Meanwhile, Frederick, now in his majority, married Constance, daughter of Peter IV of Aragon. This marriage was, simultaneously, urged by the Catalans, especially Artale of Alagona, and opposed by the Latins, above all the Ventimiglias. In any event, the royal couple was wed in Catania in 1362; and, nine months later, Maria, the future queen, was born from this union. The following year, Constance died prematurely, struck down by the plague.

## 1. A Maid's Divided Realm

History remembers Frederick IV* as the Simple. His life, however, was not so, especially because of the growing influence, and interference, of Artale of Alagona and his followers.

During Frederick IV's reign, the Ventimiglias and the Chiaramontes did cooperate, ceasing to feud among themselves and working out a reconciliation. The king himself, after his wife's premature death, initiated peace talks with Jeanne of Anjou to put an end to the conflict that had meant so much bloodshed to both Naples and Sicily. With the support of Pope Gregory XI (the Frenchman Pierre Roger from the family of the Counts Beaufort), a treaty was signed on August 29, 1372. According to this pact, Frederick IV agreed to rule in Sicily alone as King of Trinacria—a title haughtily refused by his predecessor; the island was recognized as a fiefdom of Jeanne I of Anjou, Queen of Naples, to whom Frederick thus owed certain feudal obligations; Lipari remained part of her domain; and the pope was acknowledged as supreme sovereign of Sicily.

As if to sanction these agreements, which in a sense were humiliating, Frederick IV married a Neapolitan noblewoman, Antonia del Balzo of the Dukedom of Andria. Finally, a centuries-old battle was over, with Sicily at least potentially in Angevin hands.

Frederick IV, threatened by overweaningly proud barons, had made peace with his ancestors' enemies, thereby restoring royal authority to the island. But he would not live long enough to enjoy the tranquility. Dying on July 27, 1377, he was buried in Catania Cathedral. His fifteen year old daughter Maria succeeded him.

Given precedent, since the queen was still a minor, a regent had to be chosen. The position fell to the Great Executor Artale of Alagona, who acted as her tutor and governor. Yet this situation had its pitfalls. Peter IV of Aragon, appealing to Frederick III's own denial of women's succession rights and to the absence of any Sicilian male heirs, intervened to claim the crown of Sicily. But the pope challenged Peter's move and the barons categorically refused the Aragonese pretender, convinced that they were capable of ruling Sicily by themselves without any foreign supervision.

The times were, once again, troubled. The Great Schism of the West

---

* It seems fair to call Frederick the "Fourth," although some historians designate him as the Third, since he was the fourth Frederick to rule in Sicily.

cast an ominous shadow over a Papacy divided between Rome and Avignon. The Durazzos were contesting the Angevins for control of Naples. And the young Queen Maria of Sicily inspired, rather than a sense of peace and unity, the jealousies and appetites of the most powerful barons.

To complicate matters, Artale of Alagona, tutor and governor of the inexperienced Maria, decided to give certain aristocrats more access to power in Sicily. With this purpose in mind, he summoned the most prominent barons who might challenge his power to a meeting in Caltanissetta. From this "summit" emerged an agreement that Sicily would no longer be governed in a unitary fashion but, in the name of the queen, be administered by four autonomous Vicars representing the four major spheres of influence and zones of the island. The Vicariate would be collectively ruled by Artale, who made himself Feudatory of Catania; Manfredi Chiaramonte, now Grand Admiral of the Kingdom; the Count of Geraci, Francesco Ventimiglia, granted the powers and title of Grand Chamberlain; and the Catalan Duke of Randazzo, Guglielmo Peralta, John of Aragon's son-in-law.

At this point, Artale, engineer of this complex project, attempted to ward off any further influence the Aragonese might have on the Sicily of the Four Vicars by offering Queen Maria's hand in marriage to Gian Galeazzo Visconti, Lord of Milan. Visconti was willing because he already meant to expand south, but the stormy reaction of the Aragonese King Peter IV nipped the plan in the bud.

### 2. A Queen Abducted to Expel the Four Vicars

After Artale of Alagona made his offer, Gian Galeazzo Visconti seriously considered an armed intervention in Sicily. To that end, he launched a naval expedition to blockade the coasts of the island. That way, he calculated, he could disembark and easily take Queen Maria's hand. But certain spies among the many the Aragonese had in Sicily informed Peter of Visconti's plans; and the King expeditiously sent out a fleet to thwart the Milanese lord's designs.

Meanwhile, those Sicilian nobles excluded from the Vicariate were stewing with resentment. The most restless and determined among them was Guglielmo Raimondo Moncada, Duke of Augusta, who, in spite of his Catalan origins, was Artale's foe precisely because Alagona had passed over him in choosing Sicily's rulers. In retaliation, the duke proceeded to abduct Queen Maria from her residence at Ursino Castle in Catania. This daring exploit was performed, after meticulous secret planning, on January 23, 1379. Moncada conducted his prize first to Licata, where he met with envoys from the Aragonese king to account for his actions, then to his own castle in Augusta.

Artale naturally understood the significance of such a dramatic gesture which, given the absence of Queen Maria, negated any juridical bases the Vicariate might have had. Therefore, he resorted to every means available to rescue Maria from Moncada, including the siege of Augusta's fortress, where she was being held prisoner.

But the Grand Executor was check-mated. The ultimate victor in the game, it turned out, was Peter IV of Aragon. Providing safe-conduct for Maria, he then betrothed her to his nephew Martin, Duke of Montblanc and son of his second-born by that same name.

In Sicily, however, the Four Vicars remained in power. Then Peter IV died in January of 1387, leaving his throne to his first born son, John. Three years later, Martin the Young, according to Peter's wishes, married Maria.

**14. Guglielmo Raimondo Moncada kidnaps Queen Maria. Engraving**

Everything was proceeding in accordance with the Aragonese script—even to the point where the Vicars' power was on a down spiral. Artale of Alagona himself was on the decline and Manfredi Chiaramonte was re-emerging. The latter's influence was so great that he succeeded in marrying his daughter Constance to Ladislao of Durazzo, King of Naples.

Then, in 1390, the Count of Geraci, Francesco Ventimiglia, and Artale of Alagona died. One year later, Manfredi Ventimiglia gave up the ghost as well, to be succeeded by his son Andrea. This rapid turn of events

15. "Cristo Panto-
cratore" in Cefalù's
twelfth century
Norman Cathedral.

profoundly undermined the Vicariate's authority, revealing the fragility of its structure and favoring the Aragonese, who were still intent upon seizing Sicily.

With a sense of political expediency, the representatives of the Vicariate courted the Duke of Montblanc to entice him to return to the island with Queen Maria. In March of 1392, Martin the Young, his wife and father landed at Trapani and were duly received by a host of Sicilian barons. Only Andrea Chiaramonte refused to pay homage to the Aragonese, declaring that they were trying to usurp the crown of Sicily. But two months later, on May 17, 1392, Andrea, abandoned by his old friends and besieged at Palermo, found it wise to give up.

Andrea's surrender was his ruin. At first, Martin feigned magnanimity in acknowledging Chiaramonte's "repentance," only to have him subsequently condemned to death. The execution was carried out under the walls of the superb Steri Palace of Palermo whence Martin's ancestors had reigned.

### 3. Aragonese Rule and Sicilian Chaos

Historians call the brief return of the Aragonese to Sicily in the persons of Martin the Young and Martin the Old the Age of the Martins. The Young's rule was harsh. After the assassination—staged as a legal execution—of Andrea Chiaramonte, Martin gave his position of Grand Admiral to Bernardo Cabrera. This rich and bold Spaniard had sold his property at home to arm a large battalion he captained on the Aragonese expedition that accompanied the royal couple to Sicily.

Cabrera's rise to power was symptomatic of Martin's approach, which also included the squelching of the Peraltas' and Ventimiglias' authority and the ousting of Artale's brother Manfredi of Alagona from the position of Grand Executor. Guglielmo Raimondo Moncada, the nobleman from Augusta who had taken Queen Maria hostage in support of Aragonese designs, was installed in Manfredi's stead.

Having muffled the barons, Martin the Young thought he could govern in peace. But he had not taken into account the intricate web of internal and external interests and connections that both blocked and subverted the rule of any alien power in Sicily and would continue to do so in the case of the Aragonese. Martin, who had supported the anti-pope of Avignon, was branded a schismatic and constantly opposed by the clergy. And, even though the Vicariate no longer existed in fact, the pope campaigned for its return. Meanwhile, at Castronovo on July 10, 1391, the Sicilian barons, flattered by the pope's stance, signed an accord of mutual assistance with him "to provide for the security of the State."

At this point Martin the Old stepped in and tried to have this pact declared invalid. This astute statesman also pushed for the acceptance of Maria as Queen of Sicily. Yet, when she died without heir in 1402, Martin the Old forced his son to marry Bianca of Navarre. For seven years thereafter, Martin the Young and Bianca ruled Sicily. And when he died on July 25, 1409, his indomitable father took up the reigns instead of the Young's illegitimate son, Federico of Luna. Overburdened with responsibilities, however, Martin entrusted the supervision of the Vicariate to the queen.

When Martin the Old died on May 31, 1410, the kingdom was once again rent by strife. Many were the pretenders to the throne: Federico of Luna, who by now was the choice of Sicilians, the Duke of Calabria, the Count of Urgel, the Duke of Candia, and the youthful Ferdinand of Castille. Two strong factions emerged from the pack, one in favor of Bianca of Navarre as queen, the other for the Grand Executor Bernardo Cabrera, Count of Modica.

Threats of civil war loomed over the island. The Count of Modica, staking his claim to Sicily, launched an attack against Bianca's forces. Although his case was arbitrary, Cabrera gathered enough support to maintain that the queen had no legitimate authority. Ancient conflicts flared up once more. Nobles and municipal representatives all over the island split and did battle to decide whose claim—Bianca's or Bernardo's—was valid. The tragedy of civil war had its farcical moments. Notably, Cabrera fell in love with the hated queen and vowed to make her his.

### 4. Bianca of Navarre Saved and Cabrera Scorned

The tragicomic vicissitudes of the elderly Grand Executor Bernardo Cabrera, Count of Modica, and the lovely young Queen Bianca of Navarre are the subject of an early fifteenth century comedy known as *Master of the Fields*. This folk play, that highlights the farcical elements of the ill-fated love story, was performed throughout Sicily in that period in the squares of towns large and small. Extant today in Mezzojuso, this work can still be appreciated for its sense of the grotesque.

In a Sicily torn by anarchy, with the barons contending for divisive interests, the Grand Executor Bernardo Cabrera invalidated the claim to the throne of Bianca, Vicar Martin the Old's nominee. But Cabrera's thirst for power was thwarted by his own senile passion, that suddenly flared up in the old executor's heart. He went so far as to decide he would declare his love to the widowed queen and, by marrying her, rule Sicily jointly with her. In the summer of 1410, obsessed with his plan, Bernardo headed for Catania, which had risen up against the queen, to make his designs known to her. But Bianca, with no intention of receiving her ardent adversary when he arrived, had just boarded her escape ship. From the dock, nevertheless, Cabrera declaimed his passion, only to be bluntly refused. Even more determined, Cabrera pursued Bianca. When he laid siege to a castle at Syracuse where she had taken refuge, however, the bold Giovanni Moncada rescued her and escorted her to Palermo.

Refusing to accept defeat, Bernardo Cabrera, in January of 1412, tried to abduct the queen from her refuge, the Steri Palace. Forewarned, the queen managed to slip out of the palace in the middle of the night and, accompanied by a small retinue, reach the harbor where a Catalan galley awaited her. As the enraged Cabrera was approaching the port, Bianca's oarsmen challenged the waves and swept her beyond the rough shoals to the friendly ship that would carry her to safety.

Cabrera, now scorned, enjoyed the meager consolation of entering Steri Palace and viewing the room where the queen had been sleeping before she took flight. Physically and mentally exhausted, the grand executor could think of nothing better than climbing into her abandoned bed, caressing the still warm sheets, and expressing his dotage in sterile sobs. Emphasizing the ridiculous situation into which Cabrera had put himself, a chronicler observed that the man, "failing to nab the partridge, had to be content with its empty nest."

Bianca of Navarre reached Solanto Castle and was joined there, May 6, 1412, by Catalonian ambassadors and the Vicariate's and the Grand Executor's representatives. A decision was made that the queen would abdicate in favor of Bernardo Cabrera. But the supporters of the Vicariate refused to accept this "verdict." Consequently, war broke out again; and Cabrera himself was captured and punished for his follies.

In this climate of uncertainty, the battle over succession in Aragon added fuel to the fire. A parliament convened in Caspe (Aragon) in June of 1412 to determine who would succeed Martin the Old on the thrones of Aragon and Sicily. The Sicilians, aware that their island was at an historical turning point, proposed their own candidate, Federico of Luna. But on June 30, a choice was made disregarding Sicilians' wishes: Ferdinand of Castille, called the Just, son of the King of Castille and one of Martin the Old's sisters. Ferdinand himself communicated this decision to Bianca of Navarre. In short, it was the announcement of her end as ruler of Sicily.

### 5. Sicily as Vice-regency

The Aragonese parliament's choice of Ferdinand of Castille as King of Sicily meant, in effect, the island's total loss of independence. As Sicilian historian Isidoro La Lumia maintained, the Martins thereby ushered in Sicily's dark years as a vice-regency. La Lumia saw the Martins precisely as "the precursors and initiators of foreign domination by non-Sicilian rulers, ideologies and interests."

Recently, other historians have qualified this judgment. Libertini and Paladino, while acknowledging that "Sicilian independence was sacrificed to Aragonese thirst for power," assert that the Martins brought "order and peace to the island, resisted feudal anarchy with some success, and restored royal power to an extent."

In the long run, for years, Sicily had been battered by war and by the permanent conflict between native Sicilians and the Angevins. The latter, in turn, had been constantly aided and abetted by a Papacy deaf to Sicilian claims and even eager to use the weapons of excommunication and interdiction to subdue its opponents. Alternatives to this power struggle had never emerged in their own right; and the internecine struggles among Sicilian barons had shown that the island was "ungovernable from within." Meanwhile, the flickerings of the spirit of Sicilian independence that were periodically glimpsed never materialized into any effective movement.

One must add that Sicily was growing poorer and poorer. The latifundia system was in disarray—as vast stretches of barren fields testified. The people were always hungry. And the nobility attended exclusively to its own economic and social interests. Lacking a strong leader like Frederick

III, Sicily, exhausted after so many struggles, had no resources to combat the destroyers of its independence. The Parliament did meet in Catania on September 1, 1413, and manifest its sense of autonomy by sending ambassadors back to the new monarch with a message calling for "respect for all the Kingdom's ancient privileges, exemptions, liberties, charters and laws." But, basically, the representatives accepted the fait accompli of their loss of independence.

From that same parliamentary session, there emerged another request that ancient protocol be observed. Sicilians asked that Frederick III's proviso regarding permanent and unconditional residence of the king on the island be put into practice. Pragmatists that they always were, however, they proposed a compromise: the regency *in loco* of one of Ferdinand's sons, preferably his first born, Alphonse.

Ferdinand made a compromise in response, sending his second born, Duke John of Penafiel, to be Viceroy of Sicily. But when Ferdinand died almost exactly one year later (April 2, 1416), his successor Alphonse of Aragon recalled John and sent his vice-lieutenants, Antonio Cardona and Domenico Ram, Bishop of Lerida, to rule the island. John would later marry Bianca of Navarre, who, after her tragic and farcical Sicilian experience, had returned to Spain.

John's departure from Sicily and the installing of two vice-lieutenants in power crushed Sicilians' last hope of having their own king. The parliamentary session at Palermo in 1416 in effect acknowledged this fact. Alphonse had sensed this admission of defeat and recalled his viceroy—a man Sicilians were ready to accept as their sovereign. Ultimately there was little resistance to the affront of having two mere officers of the Spanish crown govern Sicily.

Autonomy had been lost definitively. Sicily, after so many struggles, so much suffering and blood, descended one more rung on the ladder of European power. The island was nothing but a vice-regency.

## 6. A Century in the Wake of Wars and Calamities

The first decades of the fifteenth century signalled the end of the political autonomy for which Sicilians had struggled so long and the beginning of their vice-regency in the orbit of Spanish power. Before dealing with this new and complex period of Sicilian history, however, let us look back at the 1300s via some general reflections.

Along with feudal strife and wars eliminating common people and nobles alike, famines and the plague of 1347-48 took their terrible toll on Sicily. Statistics expert Francesco Maggiore Perni calculates that, during the fourteenth century, the island's population was reduced by 400,000 inhabitants, hitting 1,150,000 in 1400. Palermo's decline in population was also considerable: from 165,000 in 1300 to 125,000 in 1400.

Architecture and city-planning reflected this decline as well. The brief and stormy Angevin domination left few architectonic traces on the island. In spite of his forty year reign being punctuated by so many wars, the Aragonese Frederick III had left upon Sicily, during the 1300s, a much more visible imprint of his reign.

In Palermo, the Church of Saint Augustine, erected by the Chiaramontes and the Sclafanis, still stands with its marvelous fourteenth century portal and rosetta window. While the churches of Saint Dominic and Saint Francis, built during the same period, have been transformed over the centuries to mask their original style, it can be appreciated in certain

16. The Chiaramonte Palace built in the 13th century and redone in 1488 at Favara, one of the centers of Chiaramonte power on the island.

monuments in Enna, Trapani, Agrigento, and the city on the slopes of Mt. Etna so beloved by the Aragonese, Randazzo.

For obvious reasons, military architecture was more developed than the civic or the religious during the century. Pioneers in the field of defensive structures, feudal families had superb castles constructed to glorify and bolster their power.

Most noteworthy among these families were the Chiaramontes. The edifices they had raised during the 1300s are even characterized as "in the Chiaramontean style," and can be found all over Sicily, at Modica, Misilmeri, Vicari, Siculiana, Favara, Mussomeli, Naro and Palermo.

Two other important fourteenth century castles are Caccamo's, site of key Angevin-Aragonese struggles, and Sciacca's, the fortress built toward the end of the century by Guglielmo Peralta, one of Sicily's Four Vicars. Also worthy of note is the Castle of Castelbuono, erected by the powerful feudal Ventimiglias and used, at the peak of their power, as a mint as well as a domicile. Within this imposing square structure, significant Gothic elements are still preserved.

The Aragonese, in addition, left stately towers constructed at strategic points outside city walls and in the countryside to guard against surprise attack. Their most impressive towers are intact today in eastern Sicily, around Paternò and Adrano.

As to Sicilian culture during the fourteenth century, there is little prose of significance and virtually no poetry. Chronicles have survived though— namely *The Rebellion of Sicily Organized by Sir John of Procida Against King Charles* and *The Norman Conquest of Sicily*. The latter was written by Simone of Lentini in the second half of the century. But literary language in general was of poor quality. Moreover, during the 1300s, official documents were written in a bastardized jargon, half corrupted Latin and half Sicilian dialect. Such a quasi-idiom was in itself a sign of uncertainty. Yet, as the dark age came to a close, signs of rebirth could be glimpsed.

# Chapter V: In Spain's Orbit

## 1. Eyes on Naples from Sicily

By the second decade of the fifteenth century, Sicilians found themselves ruled by two representatives of King Alphonse of Aragon rather than by one viceroy they would have "transformed" into their king. This vice-regency, furthermore, was set up with all the technical measures assuring that Sicilians' passion for autonomy would be truncated. Lip-service was paid to this dream, but its harbingers were all rhetoric without political clout. Those wielding power were, in fact, second-rate politicos whose goal was to solidify the administrative structures of Sicily as a vice-regency subject to the Aragonese crown.

The list of succeeding vice-regents is unimpressive indeed: Antonio Cardona and the Bishop of Lerida, Domenico Ram (1416-19); Ferdinand Velasquez and Martin of Torres (1419-20); and John of Podio Nuchi, Arnaldo Ruggero of Pallas and Niccolò Castagna (1421-23).

From this new situation, some positive aspects emerged. Since the Spanish regime was able to curb the ambitions of the barons, the island enjoyed a period of relative tranquility. The Aragon king, moreover, while he pressed for sworn allegiance and obedience among his subjects, promised to respect Sicilians' constitutional freedoms, sanctions and ancient privileges. Given that Sicily was also a prized possession for any ruler, the Aragonese monarch was wise enough to encourage the repopulation of his demesnes, to rearm his fleet, and reinforce his coastal defenses against Barbary invasions.

Alphonse himself made a concrete gesture of concern for Sicily on February 12, 1421, when he set foot on the island for the first time. His journey was also strategic because it was from Sicily that the monarch could best consider the moves he might make on the European chessboard.

Actually his stay was brief due to Queen Jeanne II's request for Aragonese aid to crush a rebellion in Naples. Without ado, in June of 1421, Alphonse convened the Parliament in Messina and enlisted men and arms to pursue his expansionist aims. Reaching Naples quickly thereafter, he was warmly received. The queen dubbed him Duke of Calabria, the title reserved for the heir to the Neapolitan throne, and granted him the right to collect the dukedom's tribute.

But the Aragonese did not proceed decisively enough to avoid certain intrigues in the Neapolitan court. Furthermore, it was feared that Filippo Maria Visconti would take the rebellion as a pretext for intervention. The Queen of Naples therefore decided to form an alliance with the Genoese, who were happy to strengthen their hand in the game of constant resistance to the Viscontis. Alphonse of Aragon, in this confusion of alliances, could see no better solution than that of returning temporarily to Spain.

The Aragonese king had left his brother Peter in charge of Sicily for the moment; but, when Peter could, he preferred to be in Naples. The position of Viceroy in Sicily subsequently fell to Niccolò Speciale, namesake of the chronicler. Speciale, serving from 1423 to 1429, imposed order on the island. He denied immunity to those clerics who had neglected the affairs of the Church and speculated in secular business matters. Furthermore, Speciale clarified the respective spheres of influence and jurisdiction of notaries, judges, lawyers, manor lords, constables and court clerks; and reorganized Palermo's customs house to expedite maritime commerce.

The Aragonese king returned to Sicily in 1432. Since his expansionist policies had not had positive results in the Tyrrhenian and since he could see no way to penetrate the European continent, Alphonse set his sights on the Tunisian island of Jerba. But, while he had been successful there eight years before in taking 3000 prisoners, this time the Aragonese monarch was foiled, as he had been in Naples, and forced to sue the Bey Abù Faris for peace.

## 2. Catania, Still Grateful to Alphonse of Aragon

Returning to Sicily after his Tunisian fiasco, Alphonse of Aragon remained on the island for about three years. This was a period when the king committed himself to administrative reforms. On January 12, 1433, from Palermo's Steri Palace—which he had chosen as his abode—Alphonse promulgated the Charters of the Kingdom. Herein, as absolute monarch, he delegated all powers, in case of his absence, to his viceroy. With solemnity, the king also confirmed "our royal wish" to maintain the autonomy of the "universities," i.e., the communes, and established the position of Presider over the Kingdom. This new governor was to exercise his full authority over all barons, whether they depended directly on the king or not. Thus, by drastically curtailing the barons' power, the Aragonese king could impose order in the granting of titles and call for a thorough investigation *in re* the legitimacy of their concession.

As compensation for the sacrifices he would have to demand in order to pursue his expansionist policies, Alphonse himself granted privileges and prebends with magnanimity. For example, Giovanni Ventimiglia, as reward for his pro-Aragonese deeds, received the title of marquis.

Furthermore, Alphonse demonstrated his sensibility to the kingdom's cultural development. On October 19, 1434, he founded the *Studium generale* in Catania, in recognition of that city's loyalty. In that same year, Alphonse also established the cultural foundation that, in the following centuries, would take on the name of *Siculorum Gymnasium* and be a major Sicilian center of research and scholarship during the Renaissance.

Once social and cultural matters were better organized in Sicily, Alphonse turned his attention to the Italian political scene. When Louis of Anjou and Jeanne II died within a year of each other (in 1434 and 1435 respectively), the time seemed ripe for Alphonse to stake his claim on the Kingdom of Naples. Thus, in 1435, the Aragonese king left Sicily—never to return.

His first move, however, was a blunder. On August 5, 1435, the fleet with which he intended to sail triumphantly into the Bay of Naples was intercepted near the island of Ponza by Genoese ships under Filippo Maria Visconti's command. The skirmish was a disaster for Alphonse. The king himself, and the Sicilian and Aragonese nobles in his service, were captured in this so-called Battle of the Barons. Only Alphonse's brother Peter managed to elude the Genoese ambush and return to Sicily.

In these dire straits, however, all the skill of the Aragonese king was displayed. Taken to Milan as a prisoner and left virtually at the mercy of his adversary, Alphonse turned a resounding military defeat into a satisfying diplomatic victory by convincing Duke Filippo Maria that it was expedient for the two of them to form an alliance and drive René of Anjou from Naples. Alphonse even succeeded this time in gaining the Papacy's support against the Angevins. He also abandoned his designs on Corsica, giving free rein to the Viscontis, who were determined to conquer north-central Italy.

Departing from Milan, where he had been imprisoned in a gilded cell, Alphonse of Aragon travelled overland to Portovenere. From there, he sailed for Gaeta, which had just been occupied by his brother Peter after the latter eluded capture. Embarking on February 2, 1436, the monarch took possession of the Castle of Gaeta, which would become not only his command post for the invasion of Naples but also a center of humanist culture.

Finally, fate seemed to smile upon the Aragonese king. After preparing himself with pomp and circumstance, he would take his next step: the entrance into Naples' magnificent Renaissance court.

### 3. Beccadelli, the Panormitan at the Court of Naples

For six long years, from 1436 to 1442, Alphonse of Aragon was engaged in an enervating and uncertain war before being able to make his triumphant entrance into Naples. During this period, he received providential assistance from two of the major humanists of the age: Antonio

Beccadelli the Panormitan and Lorenzo Valla. The former, who, as his nickname indicates, was from Palermo (Panormus was the Greek name for that city), had met Alphonse in Messina in 1434. Taken with the king's charisma, the intellectual courted him; and the monarch, in turn, developed a real liking for the humanist. Subsequently employed as the king's secretary, Beccadelli was at Alphonse's side at Gaeta, acting as friend and advisor. With this dual role that required the king's utmost trust, the Panormitan was sent on diplomatic missions and had other important political and administrative functions.

During those six years that he resided in the Castle of Gaeta, the monarch supported humanistic culture and its activities to the point that the Panormitan never forgot his generosity. Lorenzo Valla, equally grateful, fought hard to defend Aragonese interests; and the king, who in that period came to be called the Magnanimous, never betrayed Valla's trust.

Alphonse of Aragon took possession of Naples on June 2, 1442, entering the Gate of Santa Sofia via a surprise attack. But let us leave the king in his glory and return to the vice-regency of Sicily.

Among the island's many viceroys, Lop Ximen Durrea is remembered by history for his diplomatic skills and activism. It was Durrea who succeeded in negotiating with the Bey of Tunis and signing agreements with him that were favorable to Sicilian commerce. Durrea also intervened to put down the 1449 riots in Modica after the city rose up against Count Giovanni Cabrera's abuses of power. Once again, Durrea stepped in during

17. Beccadelli, known as "the Panormitan," an advisor to King Alphonse.

April of 1450 to deal with the disturbances in Palermo due to lack of provisions and the malfunctioning of the food distribution center. After the leader of this uprising, Pronotary of Trabia Leonardo of Bartolomeo, lost control of the crowd and the looters among it, Durrea used all his forces of repression to restore order and condemned the organizers of the revolt to death. Then, in 1451, with a velvet glove and an iron hand, Durrea obtained from the Sicilian Parliament the donation of 200,000 florins for his sovereign and, simultaneously, convinced Alphonse to grant certain concessions to Sicily, including the right to mint coins in Palermo.

For all the viceroy's power, nevertheless, discord still reigned among influential island families. In 1455, the first famous Incident of Sciacca occurred. The long-smouldering mutual hatred of the noble families of Perollo and Luna finally erupted in a blood bath. Pietro Perollo, angered at having lost a lawsuit to the Lunas, assaulted Antonio Luna during a religious ceremony. After Antonio had recovered outside the city, he returned to Sciacca with a band of armed men. Failing to find Pietro, he had all the Perollos he could track down slaughtered and their residences burned to the ground. In the aftermath of this massacre, the leaders of both families were banished from Sciacca.

In 1456, as a new Turkish threat emerged after the Fall of Constantinople, Alphonse requested further financial support from Sicily. The Parliament responded by providing the funds necessary for six galleys and two armadas, one Palermitan, the other Messinese.

In this period, to escape the Turks, the first groups of Albanians fled to Sicily and continental Italy. Establishing their own peaceful colonies, the Albanians would thrive in their cultural oases, preserving their ancient language, rites and customs to this very day.

### 4. Alphonse's Death and Sicily's Vain Search for a King

Alphonse of Aragon died on June 27, 1458, in Naples's Castel dell'Ovo. The day before, he had reconfirmed the wishes written into his last will and testament shortly after his conquest of Naples. This document stipulated that Alphonse's illegitimate son Ferrante would be Neapolitan monarch and his brother John, Duke of Penafiel, would rule Aragon, Sardinia and Sicily. At the same time, Alphonse left many problems unsolved: a large financial deficit, a war going on against Genoa, a hostile papacy, and recalcitrant Neapolitan subjects bucking at onerous fiscal burdens.

With Alphonse dead, Sicilians revived their hopes in a long-cherished dream: their own king. This time, they favored Prince Charles of Viana, son of King John and Bianca of Navarre. Paying homage to John, the Parliament formally stated this preference. But John, long at odds with his son, temporized. Then, summoning the prince, his father had him imprisoned and refused to release him until the Spanish *Cortes* swore that Sicily would always be Aragonese. Once again, Sicily's hopes for autonomy were dashed to the ground, and its people had to swallow the bitter pill of vice-regency.

The latter part of the fifteenth century was a time of famine and ferment. In 1464, the new administrators of the island had to quell riots in Messina that had broken out because of food shortages. Giovanni Mallone, leader of the revolt, was delivered into the hands of the new viceroy Bernard Requesenz and, after a mock trial, decapitated. Mallone's accomplices also paid with their lives. According to the custom of the time, once the rebels were hanged, their bodies were hacked to pieces and strewn in the central square as a warning to all citizens.

In spite of such repression, the turmoil did not cease, especially in Catania and Messina where there was a great deal of resentment against Palermo's being the Court of the Realm. Given this resistance, Durrea, a clever man who knew Sicily well and enjoyed enormous prestige on the island, was sent back to serve as viceroy. Indeed, he quickly took matters into his own hands. With the Turks threatening Sicily again, Durrea rigged new galleys, reinforced the island's maritime defenses and modernized its artillery with recently invented firearms.

18. Ferdinand and Isabella of Spain. From *Opuscoli palermitani* by the Marquis of Villabianca, Biblioteca Comunale, Palermo.

In the field of diplomacy, Durrea was also firm. Historians credit him with giving Sicilians a new sense of direction by convincing them to assist King John II in his campaign to regain power in Catalonia. Sicilian nobles, consequently, joined forces with the monarch's; and some of them—notably the Baron of Favara, the Marquis of Geraci and the Count of Cardona—went off to Spain to do battle at John's side.

As they had done so often in the past, Sicilians imposed taxes on themselves to support a king. The Messina Parliament, for instance, voted for a donation of 51,000 florins to the Aragonese crown.

John of Aragon died in Barcelona on January 19, 1479, leaving all his possessions, Sicily included, to his son Ferdinand II, called the Catholic. Ferdinand and his wife Isabel, Infanta of Castille, were, of course, the monarchs who unified Spain. With them a new age began—though it would still be dark for Sicily.

### 5. The Sicilian Inquisition

Ferdinand the Catholic, reigning from 1476 to 1516, lived those glorious years of the victorious battles against the Moors of Spain and the Discovery of America. The names of Ferdinand and Isabel are, however, associated not only with these grand feats, but also with the establishment of the Inquisition in all lands, Sicily included, that were under the Spanish crown. The skillfully masked political motives of this move were, of course, sanctioned by the claim that the Catholic faith had to be defended against any forms of "deviance." Such a justification won the Catholic King and Queen the pope's authorization to establish a permanent tribunal of the Holy Office of the Inquisition throughout his metropolitan territory.

The first Grand Inquisitor to be nominated was the Dominican monk, Thomas of Torquemada, who had been the king's father confessor for a number of years. The Inquisition's first edict was promulgated in 1481 to clear the path for its famous *autos da fè*. Over these acts of confessions of faith there loomed those terrible pyres fed, in the presence of frantic and frightened multitudes, by the bodies of "obstinate heretics."

When word reached Sicily that the Inquisition had been instituted, Sicilians reacted with tremendous anxiety. The supreme magistrates of the island and the viceroy himself appealed to Queen Isabel for exclusion from the Holy Office's jurisdiction. But in 1483 the Spanish Court relied on Pope Sixtus IV to assure Sicilians of the good aims of this institution set up to root out heresy, that "plague" spreading all over Christendom. The coalition of temporal and spiritual powers thus pulled off their *coup*, and the Inquisition had one of the bastions of its "faith" in Sicily.

Subsequently, in 1487, Torquemada, who had been nominated President of the Royal Council of the Holy Office, sent the Dominican friar Antonio La Pegna to preside on the island. That same year, on August 18, the first *auto da fè* took place in Sicily. A Jewish woman, Eulalia Tamarit, native of Saragossa, was denounced by the tribunal and burned at the stake.

As a direct consequence of the establishment of the Sicilian Inquisition, all Jews were expelled from the island. On March 31, 1492, Ferdinand had issued the expulsion edict throughout the Spanish realm. But the measure had particular repercussions in Sicily, since the Jews, long-time inhabitants of the island, were numerous and prosperous thanks in part to the usury they traditionally practiced.

The scholar Di Giovanni, who has written a fine study on the expulsion of the Jews from Sicily, recounts that during a 1481 religious procession in the commune of Castiglione di Sicilia, a Jew was so rash as to throw a rock at the statue of Christ Crucified, thereby breaking his arm. This sacrilegious gesture whipped the crowd into a rage, and two brothers rose up and killed the Jew. Afterward, they fled to Spain, where the king pardoned them. In response, the two brothers begged Ferdinand to expel the Jews from Sicily.

As one can imagine, this story was circulated all over the island to justify the deportation *en masse* of an ethnic group. The Jews, it should be repeated, represented a considerably large minority. In Palermo alone they numbered at least 5,000. While they observed their own laws and maintained their own rabbis and synagogues, the Jews paid heavy taxes imposed upon them by Sicily's rulers. When Alphonse was king, they offered his crown enormous sums of money to be left in peace to live their lives and do their business.

When the order of expulsion arrived in Palermo, many of its citizens signed a petition stating that the Jews of the city had never committed a single sacrilege and that even the Inquisitor La Pegna could attest to the Jews' righteous behavior. It was then decided that Jews who converted to Christianity, the so-called Neophytes, would not be expelled. The rest were driven out, eventually settling in Naples, Rome, North Africa and the Levant.

### 6. Laurana and Antonello, Giants of the Fifteenth Century

The 1487 establishment of the Inquisition in Sicily and the 1492-93 expulsion of the Jews brought the fifteenth century virtually to a close. Before passing on to the 1500s, however, it behooves us to take a look at Sicily's cultural, artistic and scientific achievements during the 1400s.

Perhaps the most significant cultural event of the fifteenth century in Sicily was the introduction of the printing press. In 1476, André of Worms opened a typographical establishment in Palermo. Encouraged and financed by the municipality, André, two years later, would issue the famous *Customs of the Gay City* collected by Giovanni Naso. In Messina, also in 1478, Heinrich Alding opened a press which published *The Life of Blessed Hieronymus*, the first of a series of fifteenth century editions. André of Bruges and Wilhelm Schomberger also became important publishers in Messina.

The birth of the book in Sicily helped to distribute knowledge and to give shape to the nascent humanist movement. The great humanist artist Francesco Laurana from Dalmatia thrived on the island, sculpting significant works like the bust of Eleonore of Aragon (still in Palermo) and that of Beatrice of Aragon (now in Berlin), several marble statues of the Madonna with Child, and numerous decorative structures like portals, chapel arches and altars. Domenico Gagini, first of the fine sculptors who came from the same family, clearly displays the salutary influence of Laurana.

The 1400s also witnessed the emergence of the great painter Antonello da Messina, characterized by the critic and essayist Stefano Bottari as "one of the finest masters of European art in the fifteenth century." Antonello created masterpieces preserved today in major museums of the world: "The Crucifixion" in Bucarest, "Saint Jerome in his Cell" in London's National

**19. Antonello da Messina's famous *Annuciation*, Palermo, Palazzo Abatellis.**

20. Francesco Laurana's delicate sculpture of Eleonora of Aragon. Palermo, Palazzo Abatellis.

Gallery, portraits in New York, Philadelphia and London museums, "Our Lady of the Annunciation" in Munich, "The Benson Madonna" in Washington, "The Soldier of Fortune" in the Louvre, "The Altar Piece of Saint Cassian" in Vienna, "The Crucifix" in Antwerp, and "Saint Sebastian" in Dresden.

Sicily houses some works of this artist whose compositional precision and classical sense of line and color were so exceptional. The witty portrait of the "Unknown Man" is found in the Mandralisca Museum of Cefalù; the splendid "Lady of the Annunciation" and the tryptic of Saints Gregory, Jerome and Augustine in Palermo's National Museum; the Saint Gregory Panels in Messina; and "The Annunciation" in the National Museum of Syracuse.

In architecture, Sicily experienced a Gothic revival. Emerging on the island during the Suebian era but eclipsed in the Chiaramontean period, this style took on Catalan overtones in the 1400s. But few architectural examples survive from this period. Most notable among them are the works of the artist from Noto, Matteo Carnilivari. In Palermo, one can still view the following buildings he designed in an imposing fifteenth century style linked to the history and traditions of the city: Judge Francesco Abatellis's Palace; the home of Ranieri Aiutamicristo, Lord of Calatafimi and Misilmeri; and the austere Church of St. Mary of the Chain (attributed to the artist).

# Chapter VI: Public and Private Vendettas

## 1. The Hated Moncada Driven From Steri Palace

The major political figure in the Sicily of the early sixteenth century was Ugo Moncada. Born in Valencia of an ancient noble family, he was related to the prominent Moncadas of Sicily. A courageous man-of-arms, Moncada had distinguished himself in many trials and, for this reason, he was held in high esteem by the king. Thus it was no surprise when, in 1509, Ferdinand chose Moncada as Viceroy of Sicily. Besides, the monarch wanted a man on the island who could wage war against the Infidels and rebuff their attacks on strategic Spanish possessions along the North African coast, among which Oran was a most important recent acquisition.

Moncada wasted no time in satisfying the king. By July 25, 1510, he had occupied Tripoli. Ferdinand the Catholic, in recognition of the prowess of his Viceroy/Captain General, designated Moncada Governor of Tripoli. As governor, Don Ugo instituted major reforms regarding commerce between Sicily and Africa and the most lucrative slave trade between the two geographical entities.

At that point, Spain attempted to reconquer the island of Jerba (lost in 1490), but the undertaking was mishandled by its Spanish and Sicilian organizers and ended in disaster. The expeditionary forces—all Spaniards—returned empty-handed and ravenous to Sicily where they virtually sacked the city of Palermo. When the Spaniards went so far as to molest women, the Palermitans retaliated immediately. The Spanish soldiers guilty of such an outrage were attacked by frenzied mobs and massacred on the spot. Shades of the Sicilian Vespers, albeit in miniature, were ominous. Moncada made haste to restore law and order.

But as artificer of this repression, Moncada came to be hated implacably by Sicilians. To fan the fires of this hatred, Don Ugo was the most prominent protector of Gian Luca Barberi of Noto, author of the charter via which the Spanish Court reclaimed its rights to feudal estates and ecclesiastical benefits. The nobles' fierce opposition to this document providing for the confiscation of their properties was naturally aimed at Moncada.

Don Ugo took further steps that made him lose favor everywhere and among all social classes in Sicily. For example, he allowed the Inquisition to occupy the Royal Palace and chose Steri Palace as his own residence.

The Palermitans' hatred for Moncada reached its bursting point when the viceroy had all base coins recalled and planned to send to the Messina Mint all available precious metals for the recasting of new coins. With their pride thus injured, the citizens of Palermo rebelled against Moncada's recall

21. Viceroy Ugo Moncada, driven out of Palermo in 1516. From *Ritratti della prosapia et heroi Moncadi*, by Agostino Lengueglia, 1657.

injunction and, citing Alphonse's 1452 establishment of the mint in their city, appealed directly to Ferdinand for satisfaction. Confronted by protests from Messina as well as Palermo, the Catholic King tried to reach a compromise by opening a mint close to Palermo, at Termini Imerese, that would be operated by the Messinese.

When Ferdinand died in 1516, all the Spanish stop-gaps burst. The viceroy took the risk of suppressing reports of the king's death in Sicily, afraid as he was of not being reconfirmed in his position. When the truth about Ferdinand emerged, the revolt, initiated by the aristocracy, spread rapidly to other classes. In Palermo, the popular insurgency was so strong that crowds stormed the tribunal of the Holy Office and routed the Inquisitor himself.

The viceroy had no choice but to flee. He took refuge first in Messina, where he still commanded respect. Then he joined the new king in Flanders. By that time news had spread that, along with popular uprisings against Moncada, a real conspiracy for his overthrow was being planned. Withdrawing, Don Ugo would leave the reins of power to a train of successors: Bernardo Bologna, the Marquis of Geraci Simone Ventimiglia and the Count of Caltabellotta.

### 2. The King's Iron Fist and Sicilians' Counterpunch

Viceroy Ugo Moncada's flight from Sicily coincided with the death of Ferdinand the Catholic. Expiring on January 26, 1516, at the age of 64, the king left the question of succession in a state of uncertainty that would have profound effects on Sicily. Having married Isabel of Castille in 1469 when he was seventeen, the king, upon her death November 26, 1504, had only one child, his daughter Juana. Married to Maximillian I of Austria's son, the Archduke Phillip the Handsome, Juana had been recognized by the Sicilian Parliament as legitimate heir to the throne of Sicily. Meanwhile, Juana and Phillip had had a son named Charles (who would be the future Charles V). After the death of his father in 1506 and the mental breakdown of his mother (gone down in history as "Juana la Loca," i.e., Joan the Mad), Charles was raised by his aunt, Margaret of Austria.

Ferdinand, at this point, tried to take advantage of his tenuous situation regarding succession by marrying Germaine of Foix, Louis XII's niece, in the hope of siring a male child who could disinherit his grandson Charles. But Germaine died childless in 1509; and, when Ferdinand the Catholic expired seven years later, Charles succeeded his grandfather in Aragon and Castille. Thus, the unity of Spain was once again secured.

The king Ugo Moncada met with in Flanders after his flight from Sicily was the sixteen year old Charles. The monarch had also summoned two Sicilian nobles, Count Golisano and Federico Abatellis, Count of Cammarata, to get an explanation of the motives for revolt on the island. Taking their advice into account, the young King Charles decided not to send Don Ugo back to Sicily. Making Moncada his Captain General, Charles then retained the two counts at his court. At the same time, the king wanted to set an example of how he dealt with insurgents. He thus banished from Sicily the two nobles, Simone Ventimiglia, Marquis of Geraci, and Matteo Santapau, Marquis of Licodia, who had assumed power during the rebellion without Spain's approval. Lastly, Charles installed his lieutenant general Hector Pignatelli of Monteleone as Viceroy of Sicily.

Sicilians, however, were not satisfied that the hated Moncada was gone. On the island, people suspected that Moncada might return on the political scene at any moment and that the Counts of Golisano and Cammarata were either imprisoned in Flanders or dead in some dark dungeon. In such a climate of suspicion, revolt once again broke out, this time organized by Gian Luca Squarcialupo, an urban patrician.

Having, on his own initiative, called a secret meeting in Antonio Ventimiglia's villa "a day's walk from Palermo," Squarcialupo succeeded in uniting dedicated conspirators, patricians and common people. The insurgents, then, drew up a list of about 70 representatives of the State— among them judges of the Magna Curia and the Royal Patrimony, the Tax Collector, other officials of the Crown and nobles loyal to Spain—to be eliminated when they all had gathered July 23, 1517 in Palermo Cathedral for the Vespers of Saint Christine.

The whole city was preparing for this festival, traditionally celebrated with the extravagance later to be witnessed during the Feast of Saint Rosalie, and Count Pignatelli was making ready to lead his own procession to church. But a monk appeared before the lieutenant general to reveal all the details of the conspiracy and the impending slaughter.

### 3. Squarcialupo's Ingenuous Stab at Rebellion

Gian Luca Squarcialupo had deceived himself into thinking the conspiracy could remain a secret. His fellow-conspirators were not disciplined enough to keep their mouths "sealed tight," and, when they returned to Palermo after planning the massacre, as Isidoro La Lumia wrote, "news of the plot began to leak out, and, as usual, the rumor spread like wildfire."

The friar's disclosure of the conspiracy completely deflated Squarcialupo's balloon. As a precaution, Count Pignatelli had the ceremony cancelled. But he took no further emergency measures, nor did he have the gates of the city garrisoned. Thus Squarcialupo and his fellow-conspirators were able to enter Palermo through New Gate.

After a brief rest in the Church of Saint James Màzzara (once situated near Papireto Ravine), the conspirators reached the cathedral only to find it empty. Disappointed that their targets had escaped, the insurgents hurled themselves at the one person they could flush out in the church. Trapped in a deserted nave, Paolo Cagio, City Archivist, met his end.

Squarcialupo's diminishing group of conspirators proceeded from the cathedral along Via Marmorea, trying to incite other citizens to riot—without much success. Tommaso Fazello, the future Sicilian historian who at the time was a nineteen year old novice, left his monastery cell to observe the progress of the insurgency. Later he would write: "When I got to Piazza Beccheria, I suddenly saw Squarcialupo, Barresi, Settimo, Rosa and other conspirators numbering about 22. The leaders were on horseback, the others on foot. From the Càssaro, they headed toward Merchants' Loggia, attempting in vain to have all of Palermo join them. Watching them closely, I was amazed at their temerity. It struck me as insane for a few men to attack a great city, and I almost broke out laughing at this mockery of a rebellion."

However laughable it might have seemed, this revolt of a few bold men, unopposed by the authorities, left some deep traces in Palermo. Even without the popular support he had hoped to muster, Squarcialupo, after a moment of bewilderment passed in the Church of the Chain, reached Steri Palace where Pignatelli, his court and the municipal authorities had withdrawn. The besieged made the attempt to calm the rebels down, but the latter would not give in. Instead, they spent part of the night awaiting reinforcements under the walls of this fourteenth century Chiaramontean palace. Finally, as the bells of a nearby church rang out, a mob suddenly emerged from the port-side alleys, brandishing their improvised weapons and hauling bundles of twigs. The reinforced conspirators proceeded to set fire to the main gate of Steri Palace and break in.

Overcoming the guards' resistance, the conspirators hunted high and low for their victims. Two judges of the Magna Curia were hurled from the battlements; and Pignatelli himself was taken prisoner and escorted to the Royal Palace.

The rebellion was then ignited in other Sicilian cities, notably Partinico, Alcamo, Trabia, Termini, Trapani and Agrigento. But a group of nobles was quick to organize a counter-rebellion. Via a secret accord with Pignatelli, these barons, to suppress the insurgents, granted special powers to Guglielmo Ventimiglia, Lord of Ciminna, as Captain of Justice, and to another noble, Pompilio Imperatore, as agent extraordinaire. Subsequently, Squarcialupo and many of his followers were eliminated.

Once Squarcialupo's ingenuous stab at overthrowing Sicily's centralized rule had ended in failure, the barons reaffirmed their loyalty to the king. Charles, in turn, proceeded with caution. After sending reinforcements to the island, he appointed a new Inquisitor to replace the one ousted during the uprising. Pignatelli himself was made Viceroy of Sicily.

### 4. The French Coup: a Monstrous Fiasco

A few years after Gian Luca Squarcialupo's revolt was ruthlessly suppressed, Sicily was the scene of another anti-Spanish conspiracy. The new plot, that was to bring Sicily under the protection of Francis I of France, was uncovered in 1523. It had been organized secretly in Rome for several years by the four Imperatore brothers—Giovan Vincenzo, Federico, Francesco and Cesare—relatives of Squarcialupo's assassin, Pompilio Imperatore. The aim of this conspiracy was to hand the Sicilian crown over to Marcantonio Colonna, Papal Embassador to France, and to turn the island into a French protectorate. Also involved in this plot was Cardinal Francesco Soderini of Volterra, an insidious man who had had a part in the attempted assassination of Leo X.

Throughout Europe at this time the imbalances of power were extreme. Beyond the bitter struggle between Charles V and Francis I, there loomed the Turkish threat and its concomitant Moslem territorial expansion. Moreover, Martin Luther was in the process of winning over new proselytes, thereby intensifying his challenge to Christian princes and the Roman pontiff himself.

Backing this new plot to overthrow the Spanish in Sicily was another distinguished conspirator, the Count of Cammarata. Residing in Bruxelles since his release in 1518 via Charles's pardon granted in exchange for a large donation from the Sicilian Parliament, the count apparently joined the rebels due to an unpardonable insult he had suffered. Offended because the County of Modica, in his estimation, was not duly recognized by the Spanish crown, he aimed to secure his right to Modica via the bloodline of a female Chiaramonte.

The intrigue was ultimately discovered by two Sicilians, Pietro Augello and Cesare Graffeo, who had won Francesco Imperatore's trust and then betrayed it. When they reported the conspiracy to Charles V's Papal Ambassador the Duke of Sessa, Francesco Imperatore, who was about to leave for France to confer with King Francis I, was detained and arrested. On his person he was carrying "letters written in a code so inept that even a fool could decipher it." It is likely that Cardinal Giulio de' Medici, the future Pope Clement VII, was happy to see Imperatore apprehended and the treacherous Cardinal Soderini of Volterra thwarted.

Tortured by the Duke of Sessa's men, Francesco Imperatore revealed the details of the plot and the names of the conspirators. But somehow he managed to send his nephew Claudio off secretly to warn his Palermitan allies of their new danger. Pignatelli, also informed of the conspiracy, left Palermo as a precautionary measure and established himself in Messina. Among the loyal Messinese, in a city where law and order prevailed, Pignatelli felt safe in issuing the writ of banishment against the conspirators. In addition, he offered the reward of 500 gold ducats to anyone who succeeded in capturing the fugitives from justice.

Not to be bested by Messina, the Commune of Palermo swore allegiance to the Spanish crown and promised a reward of 100 ducats for any conspirator's head. The city-fathers, in this instance, were also sensitive to popular feeling that, since the Vespers, was clearly opposed to the French and would surely judge the idea of annexing Sicily to France as "monstrous."

One by one, the fugitive conspirators were hunted down and brought to Messina, where, before their trial, confessions were exacted via torture. Gian Vincenzo, Francesco and Federico Imperatore, Girolamo Leofanto, Giovanni Sanfilippo, Jacobello Spatafora, and the Count of Cammarata were all convicted of conspiracy and treachery and condemned to death. Some of them were executed in Milazzo, others in Messina—where the plague would soon cut down 17,000 victims. The estates of the condemned were, subsequently, confiscated by the Spanish crown. Their skulls, enclosed in iron cages, were displayed along the upper walls of Steri Palace, where they remained, as a grim warning to potential rebels, until the eighteenth century.

## 5. More Sciaccan Victims of an Implacable Hatred

During Hector Pignatelli's vice-regency in Sicily, the second "Incident at Sciacca" took place. Exploding in 1529 and giving vent to ancient resentments, this violent act, on the one hand, destroyed the city's two most powerful families, the Lunas and the Petrollos; and, on the other, it wounded and deeply scarred an entire community, leaving it demoralized and isolated for centuries.

The spark that ignited the violence seemed small indeed. Apparently, a band of Turkish pirates, having kidnapped a Sicilian noble, asked the city of Sciacca to ransom him. When the pirates accepted the Perollos' money instead of the Lunas', the fury of ancient vendetta was unleashed.

Isidoro La Lumia reported the facts of the matter as follows. One morning, along Sciacca's coast, a Turkish ship appeared, carrying a pirate in the service of Barbarossa. This pirate had captured the Baron of Solanto in the waters near Trapani and now, having raised a white flag, was asking for ransom money. The Count Sigismondo of Luna went out to meet the ship in a small boat and offered the pirate a certain sum in gold coins that allegedly was not sufficient. Vexed, the count came ashore, muttering curses under his breath. Meanwhile, his rival, Baron Giacomo Perollo of

22. Charles V receives ambassadors from the Sicilian Parliament. From the *Regni Siciliae Capitula*, Messina, 1526.

Pandolfina, had started to approach the ship. On reaching it, Perollo not only produced the desired ransom, but also, in a grand gesture of prodigality, lavished coins and refreshments upon the crew. Amazed by the baron's generosity, the pirate showed he could be a gentleman as well by freeing his hostage without collecting ransom and by declaring that Giacomo's friendship was ample payment. Finally, the pirate vowed that he would no longer raid the Sicilian coast stretching from Cape Bianco to Cape San Marco.

Back on land, Giacomo was greeted by the people as their hero and escorted in a triumphant procession to his castle. Sigismondo's only reaction was dire hatred and envy of his old adversary. From then on, the Lunas and the Perollos fought tooth and nail in a battle for which the followers of both families paid vis-à-vis constant vexations and injuries. A common occurrence in Sciacca in those days was to find a Luna or Perollo along one road or another, bleeding to death.

The decisive encounter, however, did not take place until the night of July 18, 1529, when Sigismondo Luna, with 300 armed men and other accomplices, besieged the fortified castle of the Perollos. Artillery was employed by both sides. Yet the old Norman edifice where the Perollos were barricaded held up under the Lunas' bombardment. Finally, though, the Lunas set fire to a gate and stormed the castle. Giacomo Perollo managed to climb down a wall and disappear. But the castle itself was sacked and the Perollo women were carried off and treated like slaves.

The Baron of Pandolfina, escaping momentarily, asked a municipal gunner for asylum and was hidden in a grain cellar. He was flushed out, however, by a Luna spy patrol. Surrounded by the Lunas' armed men, the baron was transfixed by a sword. The deed was performed by Giovanni Lipari of Trapani. The feud had inspired so much hatred that Perollo's corpse was tied to a horse's tail and dragged through the whole city.

In Messina, the viceroy received the news of the incident and immediately sent 600 Spanish foot-soldiers and other armed men to restore order in Sciacca. In the meantime, Sigismondo fled to Rome with his aged father. Prostrating himself at the feet of Pope Clement VII, Luna asked for papal absolution and a pardon from King Charles. The pope not only absolved his ally on the spot, but also argued his case before Charles V. The latter, however, could not be moved. Consequently, Sigismondo despaired, ran through the streets of Rome like a man possessed, and drowned himself in the Tiber.

# Chapter VII: Charles V, Pirates and Inquisitors

## 1. A Triumphant Expedition to Tunis

Hector Pignatelli, appointed five times in succession as Viceroy of Sicily, died in 1535, on the eve of the great expedition led by Charles V against Tunis and climaxed by the decisive victory of the coalition of Christian forces and by Spain's acquisition of that North African territory. Strengthened by the alliances and friendships that he had wisely made throughout Europe, the king-turned-emperor had acted with determination to meet the Turkish threat in the Mediterranean head on. Charles V's undertaking, while it entailed serious risks, brought him the prestige and credibility as defender of Christianity and Christendom that would substantiate his claim to rule by divine right.

In 1530, Charles V had already laid the foundations for his mission by conceding the African city of Tripoli and the islands of Malta and Gozo to the Knights of Saint John and Rhodes. The Emperor fully construed this concession as an outright gift to the Grand Master of that chivalric order. The only gratitude Charles expected of the Maltese was a formal act of submission to the crown of Sicily to be performed once a year in Palermo, on All Saints' Day, via the donation of a falcon.

**23. The Porta Nuova in Palermo built in honor of Charles V**

*97-Chapter VII*

In recognition of this gift, when the expeditionary forces of all Christendom were amassed in 1535, Maltese warships joined those of the Genoese, Pope Paul III (Clement VII's successor), the Neapolitans and the Sicilians. Sicily, moreover, made a point of adding to their regular fleet two galleys from the Palermo Commune, two from Messina, and two from John of Aragon, Marquis of Terranova. All in all, the armada that turned its prows toward Africa was composed of 400 ships, 26,000 soldiers, an imposing arsenal, enough food to feed its abundant army, and a multitude of horses.

As the Christian fleet was crossing Tunis Channel, it was met by about 80 galleys flying the Crescent flag. Though sustained by a volley of Moslem cannons, the Turks could not stop the Christians from landing near the ruins of ancient Carthage. On shore, the battle raged, with attacks and counterattacks. The Christian troops were ambushed and suffered heavy losses when a mine planted by the Turks exploded.

Finally, La Goletta was taken by the Christians, thanks to a company of 200 Sicilians commanded by Salvo Bugarella of Eryx. Bugarella led the charge on the Turkish bastions and was the first man to plant the Christian king's banner there. Later, Charles would reward him with a medal of honor and a title and privileges that his descendants would inherit. Soon after King Mohammed Hassan of Tunis came himself to the Emperor Charles V's tent to surrender formally and offer his help

Charles's African campaign had not yet ended. Four miles from Tunis, the pirate Barbarossa had attracted a crowd with his harangue against Hassan, whom he accused of being a traitor. This throng hurled itself at the Christian troops, but they closed their ranks and prevailed. Barbarossa withdrew onto the high seas; and Charles's army was able to free 7,000 Christian prisoners that had been taken previously by the Turks. As the pirate made his way in defeat toward Bona and then Algiers, Charles V relished his victory in the form of the booty of an entire Ottoman fleet. The after-effects of his triumph, however, were even more significant. For Spain had conquered another land, Tunis was opened to Western trade, and new Christian churches could be built on African soil. Although he found himself in economic straits, Charles could not be more satisfied. Hoisting his banner of purple and gold, he set sail for Sicily.

## 2. Palermo's Celebration for the Emperor

Charles V's African triumph was celebrated with solemnity in Palermo. Although this was the Emperor's first and last visit to Sicily, Sicilians relished it to the utmost.

Toward the end of August, 1535, after skirting Pantelleria, Marettimo and Favignana, Charles V landed at Trapani with his fleet. Here he discharged his galleys and army, retaining only his most trusted followers, namely the Duke of Alba, Don Ferrante Gonzaga, his secretaries Accades and Uries, the Prince of Sulmona, and the Papal Nunzio. After a few days in Trapani, he headed for Palermo, stopping briefly in Partinico Forest to meet the official cortege sent to pay him homage and led by Simone Ventimiglia, Marquis of Geraci and Presider of the Kingdom, with his train of nobles elegantly attired and accompanied by blueblood mounts, squires and pages.

Charles V was gracious with the Palermitans, but he did not drop his grave countenance the rest of the trip to their city. There was one more stop, however, at Monreale, where the emperor rested in the ancient Norman cloisters while some of his hosts went on to Palermo in order to prepare for his grand arrival.

Eight days later, on September 13, Charles V entered Palermo through New Gate (now the Gate of the Sun) riding a magnificent white horse given to him by the municipality and leading a solemn procession of knights and dignitaries. The entrance through this gate, which was soon thereafter rebuilt with Charles's coat-of-arms engraved in stone to commemorate his African triumph, was all the more dramatic for the presence of a host of Christians liberated from slavery in Tunis and now parading dressed all alike in fancy clothes. At the cathedral, the sovereign was received by the clergy. Once inside the church, Charles laid his right hand on the Bible extended to him by the Bishop of Mazara. Solemnly, the emperor vowed to defend and respect the laws, charters, and privileges of Sicily and the prerogatives of Palermo. Following this ceremony, Charles V proceeded on horseback, moving up Via Marmorea under a canopy of gold brocade in the company of the highest dignitaries of the city, including Magistrate Guglielmo Spatafora and Chief Executioner Pietro d'Afflitto. As the populace thronged around the emperor, people waved their banners decorated with scenes of his glorious deeds in Africa. Finally, the procession reached Guglielmo Aiutamicristo's palace (on what is today Via Garibaldi) where Charles was to stay. For the next three days in the nearby Piazza Fieravecchia, the most valiant knights of the age competed in jousts.

On September 16, however, the festivities were interrupted and the Parliament met in the great hall of Steri Palace. In the center of the room, a throne had been set upon an enormous platform reached by seven steps and covered with purple velvet. Charles ascended before his hushed audience, the representatives of the three Branches of Parliament: the Demesnial, the Ecclesiastical and the Military. The sovereign then sat and listened as Pronotary Ludovico of Sanchez requested the cooperation of the three Branches in making "an exceptional and generous gift" to the Royal

Treasury. Once the rite of confirmation was performed, Charles departed immediately. Later, he would be happy to learn that the Parliament had allocated him 250,000 ducats in return for his "extraordinary service."

Charles stayed another month in Palermo, hearing many Sicilians ask that the Inquisition be abolished. Then, deciding to suspend Holy Office activity in Sicily for ten years, he left for Messina. Received there with triumphant processions, festivals and gifts, Charles named, as Viceroy of Sicily, Marquis Francesco II of Mantua's third born son, Don Ferrante Gonzaga, who had distinguished himself in the conquest of Goletta and who was particularly dear to the emperor.

### 3. Bastions Against Pirates

Charles V's African victory, so gloriously celebrated in Sicily, had ephemeral effects, for it did not stop Barbary pirates from ranging far and wide throughout the Mediterranean or the Turks from invading Christian-held territories. Given both threats, the emperor and his young viceroy, Ferrante Gonzaga, were particularly preoccupied about Sicily.

Therefore, the Spanish crown rigged a new fleet to challenge the growingly audacious pirates and fortified major Sicilian cities and other strategic areas of defense along the coast with modern offensive weaponry. Many of Palermo's ancient proud towers punctuating the city walls were demolished to make way for more up-to-date structures resistant to recently developed siege techniques and artillery.

The architect of this conversion project was the brilliant Bergamascan Antonio Ferramolino, considered in his times "a magnificent engineer." Ferramolino had been with Charles on his 1535 African campaign precisely during the assault on the fortified city of Tunis. Remaining in Africa to secure Goletta's fortifications, the Bergamascan then joined Charles V in Palermo. Apparently, the military architect participated in the city's celebrations, processions and jousts honoring the emperor. But once Charles had departed for Messina and beyond, Ferramolino set down to designing and building a permanent defense system for Palermo. Later, he did the fortifications for Messina and Trapani.

Antonio Ferramolino not only designed bastions, but also supervised their construction. Furthermore, when duty called, he joined the ranks of those fighting on the walls to keep abreast of the concrete applications of his designs and to give advice to combatants on the basis of his profound knowledge of military art. Antonio was both a military genius and a man of action. His death in 1550 attests to this latter quality: he was killed while leading Christian troops against pirates barricaded in the African fortress of Mahdia.

From Charles's departure from Palermo in 1535 until Ferramolino's death fifteen years later, the architect built fortifications in Sicily for the emperor. In Palermo he erected a system of ramparts that would have withstood the ravages of time were it not for the negligence of human beings. These marvelous structures stood, for instance, at Carini Gate (also called the Gate of Aragon) until they were recently demolished to make way for the Palace of Justice.

In addition to these ramparts, Ferramolino built the bastions of Saint James at Papireto, Saint Agatha Gate, and Spasimo. To construct the latter, he converted the Church of Spasimo into a municipal warehouse. Parts of these fortifications are extant today and can be seen near Via Lincoln, facing the Botanical Gardens.

These costly projects were realized via the emperor's direct financial contributions and his subjects' sacrifices, i.e., new taxes and free manual labor. Moreover, to build Messina's fortifications, no less than 175 houses and a number of churches were demolished.

The indefatigable Ferramolino also constructed rampart systems around Milazzo, Syracuse, Catania, Augusta and Lentini. His projects required a collective effort justified by the continual threat of pirates. This "insurance policy against fear" was paid for dearly by Sicilians.

## 4. Danger Throughout the Mediterranean

The construction of ramparts and fortifications all around Sicily was dictated, as I have said, by the century-long threat of Barbary incursions. Such a menace can be traced to a major error made by Charles V in 1535: i.e., his failure to exploit his Tunisian success by crushing the Turks once and for all. Indirectly, Charles's victory had a disastrous effect throughout the Mediterranean, for, thereafter, the famous pirate Barbarossa and his lieutenant Dragut, considered for his ferocity "almost another Barbarossa," were more determined to control the seas and thwart every effort of legitimate powers to restore order in the area.

Sicily's inhabitants could not be content with defending themselves behind Ferramolino's new walls. On the contrary, they would often be forced to go on the counter-attack, venturing out to sea to destroy pirate bases and outposts.

Many campaigns did not end in Sicilians' favor. In 1541, for instance, during the vice-regency of Gonzaga, the invasion of Algiers turned out to be a fiasco when the fleet commanded by the viceroy was decimated by the fury of the elements.

Ten years later, Sicily organized a more ambitious expedition to eradicate Dragut by attacking Mahdia where his forces were docked.

Leading this invasion was Viceroy Giovanni de Vega, a man who had earned prestige by governing Sicily with great intelligence. Among his many achievements, Vega had conducted an accurate census on the island and created a network of watchtowers around the coast through which trustworthy guards could alert all of Sicily to the approach of unidentified ships.

Vega's first attack on Dragut was unsuccessful. Consequently, a new commander, the valiant Don Garcia of Toledo, was chosen from the distinguished members of the fleet. Garcia, leading his forces to victory in the conquest of Mahdia on September 11, 1550, would become Viceroy of Sicily. As a tangible sign of his triumph, the young condottiere had the heavy iron gate of Mahdia's fortress carried off on his ship. When the fleet landed in Palermo, Garcia had his prize installed under the arch of the Gate of the Greeks, where it remained until 1864.

Following this victory, however, Charles lost Tripoli in 1551. That left Goletta as his only outpost, an insufficiently protected one at that, on African soil. To plant colonies there again, the emperor sent another expedition against Jerba, which resulted in a temporary occupation. But the enemy fleet mounted a vicious counter-attack on the island; and most of its defenders were put to flight, leaving a small nucleus of brave combatants to hold off the Turks.

Among these Christians, a few hundred of whom were Sicilian, was one Sebastiano Pulleri. Tradition has it that Pulleri, during the siege, was clever enough to distill sea water into a drinkable form so that he and his companions would not die of thirst.

Nonetheless, the fortress defended by the Christians fell, and the Turks celebrated their victory by enslaving 300 captives. But even in chains some of these prisoners displayed their valor. Giorgio Montisori, for example, on board a ship carrying him to Constantinople to be sold into slavery, managed to set it afire and escape with a number of fellow prisoners.

Sicilians also distinguished themselves in battle in the 1565 defense of Malta against Turkish forces, cutting Dragut himself down with a well-aimed cannonball. But Sicilian combatants would shine even more during the decisive Battle of Lepanto in 1571.

## 5. The Sicilian Contribution to the Victory at Lepanto

The Battle of Lepanto, fought on October 7, 1571, was a crucial moment for Europe and the West. This event of legendary proportions meant the virtual end of the increasingly relentless Turkish expansion threatening the Mediterranean and the European continent. Prior to their crushing defeat at Lepanto, the Turks had not only terrorized the sea's coastal populations but also made Belgrade and Vienna tremble.

When Constantinople forced Cyprus, the last Venetian stronghold in the Levant, to surrender on July 1, 1570, all Europeans, with the exception of the pro-Turkish French, faced the gravity of the Ottoman threat. When the Turks invaded Cyprus and took this remnant of European and Christian power in the eastern Mediterranean, Spain responded quickly by forming and heading that league of Western nations which would counteract Ottoman aggression. With the Spain of Phillip II were allied, most notably, Venice, the Papacy of Pius V, the Savoy dynasty, and the Knights of Malta. As supreme head of these forces, the Spanish monarch chose his stepbrother Don Juan of Austria who, born February 29, 1545, was then 26 years old.

The League's armada congregated at Messina. The Venetian fleet was the first to arrive, in June of 1571. Two months later, on August 23, the Spaniards joined the Venetians, delaying their arrival deliberately so that their allies could grow weary and not contest Spain's claim as Lord of the Mediterranean.

Overcoming a series of organizational difficulties, the imposing armada of the now dubbed "Christian League against the Turk" set sail for Cyprus on September 16. On the way, these expeditionary forces received the news that Famagosta had fallen to the Ottomans and that all Christian survivors had been tortured and slaughtered—including the commander of Famagosta's fort, Marc'Antonio Bragadin, who had been flayed.

The encounter between Christian and Moslem forces took place sooner than planned because the two powerful armadas happened to meet by chance on October 7. But death and destruction were inevitable.

The Christians boasted 203 regular and six super-galleys. One hundred eleven of them were Venetian, 79 Spanish (though most were manned by Neapolitans, Sicilians and Ligurian mercenaries). With 13 ships from the Papacy, three from the Savoyards and three from the Knights of Malta, the armada was complete. On the other side, the forces were equally impressive: 208 regular and 63 super-galleys, many of which came from the Barbary Coast of North Africa.

Once the armadas had sighted each other, they both split into three squadrons. The imposing Venetian galleys, armed with cannons, were the first to attack. With their fire power, they created havoc among the Turkish ships and opened a breech in the enemy's left front. The central Christian fleet led by Don Juan of Austria also broke through the Ottoman defenses and succeeded in capturing the Supreme Commander of the Turks, Alì Pascià. Only the Christian squadron on the right failed to make successful maneuvers, thus allowing the famous Calabrian pirate Ulug Alì to escape.

Seven hours later, the Christians emerged victorious. Both sides had fought courageously, with the League losing 7,800 men and twelve galleys, and the Turks 30,000 men and every ship save the thirty Ulug Alì had led off in his retreat.

Sicily had contributed to this resounding victory with its ten well-armed and generously provisioned galleys carrying 500 arquebusiers under the command of Don Diego Enriquez, one of Spain's foremost masters of ground battle. Numerous Sicilian nobles were among the island's forces, including Baron Francesco Omodei of Vallelunga and the Palermitans Marquis Giovanni of Aragon and Avola and Don Cola of Bologna, son of the Marquis of Marineo. In recognition of Sicily's contribution on that glorious day at Lepanto, Don Juan of Austria, on the way back to Spain, docked in the port of Marsala and donated the standards, received from Pius V, that he had flown on his galley "The Royal" during the battle.

### 6. The Arquebus that Killed the Baroness of Carini

Let us return to Sicily and clarify an episode in its history that would have resonance for centuries to come: the case of the Baroness of Carini. It relates to the death recorded in the parish register of Carini, Palermo Province, on December 4, 1563, of one Donna Laura La Grua.

The story is well-known throughout Sicily. In the Castle of Carini, Don Cesare Lanza, the feudal lord who exercised absolute power over his lands in Trabia and Castanea, discovered his married daughter and her lover, Ludovico Vernagallo, in a compromising situation and killed them on the spot. Chroniclers of the times observed the code of silence regarding this bloody episode for fear of feudal retaliation, but the case inspired popular imagination. Thus, the death of the Baroness of Carini became the subject of poetry and music, retold and sung in various versions full of vitality, compassion, outrage and candor.

The news of this horrible crime resounded in its many variations from every corner of the island to the regions of continental Italy and the rest of Europe. Even the great Neapolitan poet of the nineteenth century, Salvatore Di Giacomo, was inspired by the tragedy of the Sicilian baroness to write one of his masterpieces, *Fenesta ca lucive,* in which he laments the cruel fate of a certain Nennella.

Via tenacious Sicilian oral tradition, the tragedy has been transmitted in folk poetry expressing pity for the victim. In the nineteenth century, the Sicilian folklorist Salvatore Salomone-Marino patiently collected in-numerable versions of the story; and recently another scholar, Aurelio Rigoli, has discovered several more. All in all, about 400 variations on the theme are extant, most of them in Sicilian dialect verse focused on that

**24. The Baroness of Carini, slain by her father.**

dramatic moment when the unfortunate baroness's father draws his sword to strike her down.

Folk tradition has it that the Sicilian noblewoman was killed with a sword. The legend has also come down that the baroness, before she expired under further onslaughts of her father's rage, braced herself with one bloodied hand against the bedroom wall and left a stain demarcating her collapse. Popular imagination also insists that the scarlet smear, having faded over the centuries, miraculously reappears under the light of the moon.

But the case of the Baroness of Carini is the subject not only of folk poetry and legend. It can be verified by documents in the State Archives of Palermo that authenticate the evidence of a real crime perpetrated in Carini during the second half of the sixteenth century. While folk poetry and legend coincide *in re* the particular weapon that killed Laura La Grua, the archival material provides no details beyond the fact that "both the woman and her lover were murdered."

In recent years, ancient documents found in Spanish archives, have clarified the facts of the case. A document drawn up in response to Phillip II's orders by the Council of Italy (the "supreme court" of the Spanish monarchy in its Italian territories) contains the information that Don Cesare Lanza killed his daughter and her lover with an *arcabuz*, that is, with an arquebus. Apparently, a firearm, not a steel blade, was used to punish these adulterers. Such is the most probable version of the truth surrounding the tragic death of the Baroness of Carini in sixteenth century Sicily.

## 7. A Lighter "Pagnotta" and Riots

The case of the Baroness of Carini was not the only dramatic episode occurring in Sicily during that second half of the sixteenth century. Under the vice-regency of the Duke of Medinaceli—a man who, undistinguished as a warrior, was considered an excellent statesman by Phillip II—riots broke out all over the island to protest food shortages and famine. While these uprisings were quickly and bloodily suppressed, they confirmed how tense Spain's relations with its possession always were.

Disturbances first erupted in Palermo on September 23, 1560, while the viceroy was at his residence in Messina. As Giovanni Evangelista Di Blasi recounts in his chronological history of the viceroys, "crop failures that year meant a low grain supply and soaring bread prices." In dire straits, the Palermitan Senate, that functioned as a food distribution office and was therefore responsible for purchasing enough bread to meet the population's needs, proposed to reduce the weight of the city's "pagnotta" (a round bread) rather than raising prices. This proposal, made by the Magistrate of Palermo, Girolamo del Carretto, and backed by the aristocracy, met with tremendous popular resistance. Moreover, the Consuls of the Arts and representatives of the lower classes organized a vociferous protest in the very hall of the city council. At that meeting, a commoner grabbed a "pagnotta" and threw it across the room, shouting that it was light enough so there was no point to making it even lighter!

Subsequently, riots took on the dimensions of open revolt. The Notary Cataldo Tarsino, a native of Calabria, led an angry mob through the streets of Palermo. When the City Captain, Baron Gastone del Porto of Sommatino, led his armed forces on horseback to restore law and order, he was stoned and wounded. The crowd, spurred by this "victory," roamed the city, breaking into houses and taking possession of weapons. The authorities fled to safety in the Castle by the Sea.

When this first popular outburst had subsided, the magistrate consulted with senators and nobles. It was decided that Count Vincenzo del Bosco of Vicari, "a most prudent knight who had the people's trust," would make official contact with Cataldo Tarsino, the leader of the revolt. Vincenzo del Bosco's hand was strengthened because he was the godfather of one of the notary's sons. The Count of Vicari was able to convince Tarsino not to hurl himself into a thoroughly risky undertaking and to take refuge that very night in his native Calabria.

The notary took the count's advice. Disoriented without a leader, his followers were vulnerable. On the same night he left, his men were dragged out of their houses and, as Filippo Paruta reported in his *Diary of the City of Palermo,* "they were hauled to the port and drowned, so that, the morning after, the sight of their bodies floating by the shore frightened many people."

Once again in Sicily, brutal repression of insurgents quelled a riot. Notary Cataldo, meanwhile, remained in his home town Paola. But then he was imprudent enough to return to Sicily, assuming the disturbance he had fomented had been forgotten. Totally mistaken, he was arrested the moment he set foot on the island, detained in prison for three years, then condemned to death by a Messinese tribunal. His judges also chose the methods with which to dispatch him. One of his hands was lopped off. Then he was drowned and hacked to pieces. Thus a rebel met his end in August of 1566.

Unfortunately Cataldo was not aware, when he decided to come back to Sicily, that Phillip II's 1561 amnesty granted to insurgents had specifically excluded him. In effect, the notary, returning to the island, signed his own death warrant.

### 8. Victor at Lepanto = Viceroy in Sicily

Some of the names of Sicily's viceroys in the second half of the sixteenth century are associated with the reconstruction and beautification of major cities, especially Messina and Palermo. Garcia of Toledo was perhaps the most prominent of such "urban renewers." The son of Neapolitan Viceroy Peter, Garcia was nominated Viceroy of Sicily by Phillip II in 1565 as reward for his services in the war against the Turks. To confer this honor upon Garcia, Phillip, in fact, forced the Duke of Medinaceli to leave his post one year before his term expired.

Garcia, once installed as viceroy, proceeded energetically, fortifying the Sicilian coastal cities most vulnerable to Ottoman invasion. At the entrance to Augusta's port, he had two fortresses built—one of which was named Garcia, the other Victoria, after his wife.

A practical person clear-headed enough to know young men had to be trained to defend fortifications, Garcia founded, on January 20, 1567, the Military Academy of Palermitan Knights and housed it in Aiutamicristo Palace. The trainees, "armed to the teeth," drilled near Admiral Bridge. For this reason the academy took, as its insignia, the figure of Horatio depicted on that bridge.

Ultimately, Garcia of Toledo is best known for the urban renewal of Palermo and Messina. For instance, inducing the Palermitan Senate to allocate enormous sums of money to compensate citizens whose houses had to be demolished, he had the entire Cassero district redone. The result was the long, wide Toledo Boulevard, named, like the Augusta fort, after him.

As his major project in Messina, Garcia had the Arsenal, with its adjoining prison, built. Even when his term as viceroy ended, he continued to work in Sicily. As a case in point, in 1574, he had Pretoria Fountain, which had been constructed for his father's villa, relocated in front of the Senate House of Palermo.

The other prominent viceroy during the late 1400s was Marco Antonio Colonna, Duke of Tagliacozzo and Grand Prosecutor of the Kingdom of Naples. By the time his term began in January of 1577, Colonna was already famous for having commanded the papal fleet in the Battle of Lepanto. After this triumph, Palermo duly honored him by erecting a *retablo* in the bay depicting his glorious deeds.

During this period, 1575-76 to be exact, Palermo had lost many of its citizens to the plague. In response, the viceroy's first step, once he was in office, was to eliminate all possible breeding-grounds of the disease. He thus imposed rigorous health standards on merchants who were suspected of selling infected wares and on doctors who failed to report cases of the plague and other infectious diseases.

Colonna was equally severe in the administration of justice. He had the death penalty imposed when due even on persons of high rank; and when notables would appeal to him on a condemned man's behalf, Colonna would withdraw to the Monastery of Saint Martin until the sentence was executed.

Like Viceroy Garcia of Toledo, Marco Antonio Colonna beautified Messina and Palermo. In the latter city, Colonna had Toledo Boulevard lengthened from the point where Garcia had brought its reconstruction all the way down to the port. It was also his idea to erect another portal in the walls near New Gate. Naming the gate Felice after his wife, Colonna had its first stone laid on July 6, 1580. Upon his orders, six silver-plated medallions were walled in the gate's foundations. Later, the viceroy had a second row of columns attached to New Gate to make it as grand as Felice Gate. Finally, he beautified the street that led from New Gate to Monreale and had the road to Saint Erasmus Square paved and named Colonna, of course, after him.

The life of this industrious viceroy, however, came to an unhappy end. Recalled to Madrid, Colonna did not pay his due respects to the king. In disfavor, he retired to Medinaceli, dying in March of 1584 at the age of 49. Poisoning was suspected, allegedly as revenge for his affair with a married Sicilian noblewoman.

### 9. A Robin Hood

Sicily's gravest problems in the second half of the sixteenth century were epidemics, banditry in the countryside, and grain shortages. Neverthe-

**25. John of Austria at the battle of Lepanto. Engraving.**

less, the Spanish rulers managed to fatten the royal treasury via tribute exacted from Sicilians themselves. Diego Enriquez of Guzmán, Count of Albadalista, who succeeded the mysteriously dispatched Marco Antonio Colonna, was a master at such exaction.

Arguing Spain's case before all of Sicily, the new viceroy emphasized that Phillip II was heavily committed to maintaining a strong armada in the Low Countries and was bleeding his own treasury to block the English monarch from fomenting rebellion in Flanders. On May 17, 1586, for another, more down-to-earth purpose, the viceroy convened an extraordinary session of the Sicilian Parliament to request subsidies for the dowry of Phillip's daughter, Infanta Caterina, who was betrothed to Duke Charles Emanuel of Savoy. The Parliament decided to allocate 200,000 scudos for that occasion.

During the vice-regency of Diego Enriquez, new public works were realized in Palermo. The dock was extended; and Monte di Pietà was re-installed in a seat more befitting its charitable operations. The viceroy also blessed the city with more fountains, notably the Garaffo and the Garaffello.

Enriquez's successor, Arrigo of Guzmán, Count of Olivares, appointed in 1591, had to confront a new problem in Sicily: brigandage. In the Valley of Demone, the feared Giovan Giorgio Lancia roamed with a band of about 200 men. The fact that Lancia was a kind of Robin Hood who stole from usurers and the rich to give to the poor did not mitigate the circumstances for the Spanish crown.

The new viceroy, determined to put a stop to Lancia's forays, appointed, as Vicar General, Prince Francesco Moncada of Paternò, who vowed to extirpate all brigandage from the island. Thus, Moncada granted amnesty in advance to any outlaw who killed a fellow bandit. Via this diabolic stratagem, Lancia's band was soon undermined because of defections and the suspicion eroding it from within.

Subsequently, Lancia fled to Naples, only to be apprehended. His death was atrocious: with his four limbs tied to galleys moving in different directions, he was quartered as a great crowd watched in awe.

Chosen in October of 1596, Bernardino of Cardines, Duke of Maqueda, succeeded Enriquez. Two years later, Phillip II died. Shortly thereafter, the news reached Messina, where the new viceroy was residing. He thus ordered his whole court to deck itself out in black. But when Phillip III was crowned King of Spain, mourning yielded to the pomp and circumstance of celebration in his honor.

In Palermo it happened that the festivities for the new monarch preceded the funeral of the defunct. In 1598, as Evangelista Di Blasi observed, a grand cavalcade in homage to Phillip III took place in which 272 knights participated. Only in the following year were Palermitan funeral rites performed for Phillip II.

The Duke of Maqueda is remembered for having emulated Garcia of Toledo and Marco Antonio Colonna vis-à-vis urban renewal. Maqueda had the street that still bears his name cut, dividing the city into its four main quarters. The dedication ceremony for the initiation of this new Palermitan artery was performed with great solemnity on July 24, 1600. In the presence of senators and nobles, the viceroy himself "crushed the first stone with a silver hammer." Twenty years later, in 1620, Piazza Vigliena would be completed at one end of Maqueda Street.

### 10. The Inquisition, Backed by Phillip II

In treating Sicilian history in the second half of the sixteenth century, one should not fail to mention Phillip II's repressive policies applied via the instrument of the Inquisition. As Helmut Koenigsberger points out, the king exercised his authority in Sicily not only through viceroys and ministers but also through his Grand Inquisitors. According to the Sicilian scholar Vito La Mantia, an expert on the Inquisition, Phillip was "a relentless persecutor of heretics, attempting to exterminate these enemies of God and the king."

Another expert in these matters, C. A. Garufi, calculates that, between 1537 and 1572, Sicily witnessed nineteen *autos da fé*, with 664 trials and

660 convictions. Among the latter, 22 people were burned at the stake, 38 were released, 325 were reconciled to the Church after torture, and 274 were tortured and condemned to slave labor on royal galleys.

As one can surmise, the Inquisition did not often resort to the death penalty. This was reserved solely for "impenitent heretics." However, at first, a goodly number of Jews and Moors were burned at the stake. With these heretics eliminated, the cases of capital punishment diminished.

In a period when the fear of Protestantism was intensified by official propaganda, inquisitorial activity was fervent in Spain, especially in Valladolid, the center of Spanish Lutheranism. Here, thirteen people, condemned to death separately, had their sentences executed together so that festivities held in honor of Phillip II, who was particularly fond of *autos da fé*, could be more glorious. As ancient chronicles report and as a print of the epoch shows, Phillip II, from a platform surrounded by 200 spectators in the center of a square, watched the macabre ceremony totally transfixed. It is said that, among the victims, there was a young aristocrat with whom Phillip was personally acquainted. On his way to the stake, this youth stopped under the royal platform and called out to the king: "How can a noble like you have one like me burned?" Characteristically intransigent, Phillip retorted: "If my own son was guilty as you are, I would carry the firewood to the pyre myself."

In 1562, a popular protest against the Inquisition was organized in Palermo. But nothing stopped inquisitors from performing the duties of their Holy Office. Moreover, they found it convenient to settle in Palermo, occupying a house acquired for them by Phillip II, on the Piazza of Holy Quaranta. This dwelling was presumably chosen because it had a dungeon.

In 1573, the Inquisition in Sicily issued a ban on the teaching of Latin by foreign and "other suspect" schoolmasters. In 1584, the sale of books considered heretical was prohibited. People were, upon occasion, tortured for being suspected of reading books contrary to religion. That way, it was thought, their souls would be cleansed.

Confronted by flagrant abuses of inquisitorial authority that clearly exceeded the limits of the Office's jurisdiction for political reasons, Sicilians asked King Phillip to intervene. His reply was simply, "my intention and my wishes have always been, and are, that the Holy Office have preference and honor for the infinite fruits it has borne."

*Autos da fé* were announced by town-criers who invited the faithful to witness the spectacles and thereby receive indulgences. At one of these tribunals on August 15, 1573, the viceroy made a special point to attend with representatives from the Senate of Palermo and from the city's patrician families.

The Inquisition's death penalty during the 1500s was not reserved to natives of Sicily. According to Vito La Mantia's compilations, a number of Venetians and Piedmontese and a Frenchman branded as "an obstinate Luteran" also burned at the stake.

In Sicily, inquisitors and viceroys often came into conflict. But the former always had the upper hand, given their weapon of excommunication. Nor was it rare that the Inquisition could sway the Parliament to bend to its will.

## 11. The Decline of the Spanish Armada and the Resurgence of Piracy

I have touched upon the major events and phenomena in the Sicily of the late 1500s: the actions and achievements of the viceroys against the backdrop of food shortages, natural disasters, banditry, popular uprisings and the dire effects the Inquisition had on the development of civil society. But let us back-track for a minute and deal with the aftermath of the Battle of Lepanto. Doing so, we can have a better overview of Sicily's history as it relates to the Sicilian people themselves and to the international arena circumscribing their island.

Center stage in this panorama is Phillip II, the king forever burdened by the loss of his father Charles V's title of Emperor. In reality, however, Phillip II found himself the head of another empire more vast than his father's, a domain concentrated in America and its prodigious resources, rather than in the Old World. In acting as sovereign of this empire, moreover, he was considered prudent. While he was less brilliant than his father, he was more circumspect. Although he was a stickler and a bigot, Phillip had an enormous capacity for work and even for statesmanship.

Phillip's only great military success, achieved through the League headed by his step-brother Don Juan of Austria, was the Battle of Lepanto. But, asks the historian Fernand Braudel, how far-reaching and consequential was this victory? Braudel maintains that the crushing defeat dealt to the Ottomans by the Christian League did not give the latter an ultimate strategic advantage. Having suffered serious losses and being threatened by inclement weather, the winners were not able to pursue their retreating enemy. With winter approaching, the Venetians returned to the Adriatic, failing to seize the moment and reconquer Cyprus.

Don Juan of Austria himself was tempted to organize an expedition to occupy the Dardanelles and block the strait. But then he acceded to Phillip's original orders, returning to Italy to dry-dock his galleys for the winter.

While the Christian forces did not totally succeed in routing the Turks and eradicating their power in the Mediterranean, the victory at Lepanto seemed to the West the end of a nightmare, a moment when it could bask in euphoria. To harmonize this dream world with reality, Pope Pius V began to plan a crusade to reconquer the Holy Land and Constantinople. This grant design came to naught, nevertheless, when Pius V, one of the major architects of the League, died the Eve of Saint Bartholomew, and Venice withdrew its support of the alliance.

A positive offshoot of Lepanto, however, was Don Juan of Austria's reconquest of Tunis on the first anniversary of the battle. With modest forces, he departed from Marsala, regrouped on Favignana for a few days, then headed for Goletta. With him came 13,000 Italians, 9,000 Spaniards and 5,000 Germans. But, when Tunis surrendered, there was virtually no bloodshed. And Don Juan, who was on his way back to Europe when orders came from Madrid to destroy the harbor fortresses, left Tunis intact.

It was destined, nonetheless, that Tunis be lost once again (as it was in 1574) and that the resurgent Turkish forces continue to haunt and menace the inhabitants of Sicily. In fact, in 1593, Turkish ships were sighted in a cove along the Calabrian coast and seemed to be turning their prows toward Sicily. This maneuver, however, was a diversionary tactic to prepare for the Ottoman sack of the outskirts of Reggio.

Sicily and Naples struck back at the Turks, probably in 1595 according to Braudel, by raiding Patras with their galleys. But by then the Mediterranean was no longer the theater of great maritime wars. In 1588, Phillip II's Invincible Armada had shifted its focus, ploughing through the waves of English seas. As is well known, this new offensive would be the beginning of the decline of the Spanish Empire.

## 12. The Great Gian Filippo Ingrassia of the "Fin du Siécle"

Phillip II's death and Phillip III's ascendancy in 1598 to the Spanish throne were the major events marking the end of the sixteenth century. It was an age during which Sicily participated, as a dominated yet still documentably proud *nation,* in the great political, diplomatic and military game on the European chessboard.

The *fin du siécle* revealed a Sicily with all its resources, human and otherwise, exhausted—as were its dominators' after pursuing the aggressive policies that took their toll in the sacrifice of human lives, in general material impoverishment, and in the lack of development of the island's potential. Yet the sixteenth century in Sicily, in spite of a bankruptcy leaving the island's social and economic problems unresolved, left significant traces in the sciences, arts and letters.

While there was no painter in the Sicily of the 1500s to match Antonello da Messina, Sicilian architecture evolved significantly from the persistent forms of Catalan Gothic to the early baroque. This latter style, of course, reflected a new sense of artistic taste ushered in with the Counter-reformation and developed, with native originality, by architects like Giorgio Di Faccio, Giuseppe Spadafora and Giuseppe Giacalone in their churches and palaces that still grace Palermo today.

In the field of literature, the sixteenth century in Sicily produced no great names. Worthy of note in literary history, however, are the Sciaccan Tommaso Fazello, chronicler of his own times, and the Messinese Francesco Maurolico, who continued Fazello's work. Maurolico was determined to dispute many of his master's claim, which were decidedly pro-Palermitan, by presenting an apologia pro Messina and its contributions to Sicilian history.

But it would be short-sighted to consider Maurolico merely a chronicler. This intelligent and talented writer was also a true Renaissance man. Well-versed in physics and astronomy, he was consulted by the Spaniards before the Battle of Lepanto for advice as to the right moment for setting sail from Messina.

Other literary talents of the 1500s who deserve mention are the chronicler Rocco Pirri of Noto, who penned a sacred history of Sicily highly praised by Muratori; Vincenzo Colacasio, who sang of Viceroy De Vega's victorious African campaign; and the poet Antonio Veneziano, who was admired by Tasso and called "the Sicilian Petrarch." The latter, a free spirit, for his caustic verses exposing the authorities to ridicule, was imprisoned in the castle of Castellammare. There, he died tragically on August 19, 1588, when the powder-magazine happened to explode.

During the 1500s several academies were founded in Sicily. Notable are those of the *Solitari*, the *Accesi*, and the *Risoluti*. In 1591, under the auspices of Phillip II, Sicilians also saw their first university opened—in Messina.

Finally, it is appropriate to mention here the great scientist of Regalbuto, Gian Filippo Ingrassia. A brilliant doctor as well, he earned the nickname of the Sicilian Galen, linking him to the island's Greek heritage. Pupil of Fallopio and Vessalio at the Universityof Padua, Ingrassia held the Chair of Anatomy in Naples. His major contributions to medical science were his description of how the stirrup of the human ear functions and his discoveries in the field of infectious diseases. His treatise on the plague, that "obnoxious malady" that struck Palermo in 1575-76, is also rightfully famous.

# Chapter VIII: The Viceroys Between Famines and Revolts

## 1. Coin Shavers Condemned to Death

At the dawn of the new, seventeenth century, Sicilians still had to face their ancient problems: banditism, famines, corruption, epidemics, revolts. And, with Phillip III (1598-1621), nothing changed on the political scene to make them think things would be otherwise. This king, much less competent than his father, had inherited a Spain slouching toward political and economic decline. Naturally, he sent a series of viceroys to rule Sicily, but few and far between were the dynamic ones among them. Most of Phillip's viceroys made Sicily feel the weight of being a dominated land and reduced the powers of the Sicilian Parliament considerably. Furthermore, Madrid's only coherent strategy in dealing with its possession was to use it as a frontier to defend between Christendom and the ever-menacing Turkish Empire.

One of Phillip III's first Sicilian viceroys was Juan Fernandes Pacheco, Marquis of Vigliena and Duke of Ascalone, who was serving as Ambassador to the Court of Rome when Madrid nominated him. Reaching Palermo in December of 1606 to assume office, he was ceremoniously received. Disembarking from a galley, he rode on horseback through Felice Gate, where an arch of triumph had been erected in his honor.

The first problem Pacheco had to face thereafter was the shortage of bread. Messina was buying high priced northern Italian grain to feed the crews of the ships docked in its port. Palermo fared no better, having to sell bread at a municipality-controlled price of six grains per day and to ration out daily amounts of this staple. To expedite matters, the Marquis of Vigliena devised ration cards for all Palermitans so that no one could exceed his limit.

Another problem besetting Sicily at the time was the "shaving" of silver coins. Speculators of all classes were amassing fortunes by shaving metal off the precious currency that passed through their hands in daily transactions. This stratagem reduced the weight and value of the available coins; but the "shavers," given a law of the kingdom that stipulated that even the shaved coins could be exchanged at banks for their original worth, could cash them in and make profit hand over fist.

The new viceroy saw the weakness of this bank law and devised a way to stop the speculation it facilitated. In short, he proposed that all coins made obsolete by this questionable practice be recalled at face value and that new monies be minted. While this was an excellent proposal, the coins could not be redeemed because the silver needed to mint new ones was not available and people would not turn the old coinage in without the guarantee of a fair exchange.

Political obstacles also blocked Pacheco. Messina, having been granted the privilege of operating a mint by Phillip II, was intransigent when the viceroy suggested that, given the emergency, Palermo could produce coins as well. During Pacheco's sojourn in Messina at this time, its citizens staked their claim to this exclusive right on no uncertain terms by staging a riot in which a knight whose name is not recorded by history was killed. When the Marquis of Vigliena learned that the knight and his squire were shaving silver coins in the city, the viceroy had them immediately brought to trial and condemned to death.

But Messina, irked by the Marquis's behavior, appealed to Madrid for redress. In response, according to protocol, Phillip III convened his Council of Italy. This governing body, although it was headed by the Palermitan John of Aragon, decided in June of 1608 that Messina's right to coin monies was inviolable and that the City of the Straits would have Sicily's only mint. It took two more years, however, before coinage operations could be resumed in Messina.

## 2. The Vice-Regency's Advocate of City-Planning Booed in Palermo

The Marquis of Vigliena was a strong partisan of Palermo. Consequently he delayed the execution of Madrid's orders to institute a single mint at Messina as long as possible. But, constantly pressured by Spain and Messina, the viceroy decided early in 1609 to promulgate a decree by which he recalled enough silver to coin new currency—including the "shaved pieces" he commanded the banks to cash in for the time being. When his decree had little effect, he proceeded to enforce it with a heavier hand, resorting to the assistance of the archbishop, his ecclesiastical authorities, and the Inquisition. Nuns were hence prohibited, under the threat of excommunication, from hoarding silver objects in their convents. Such a device allowed the viceroy to amass and send to Messina a considerable amount of the precious metal, three galleys full of 140,000 scudos in old coins, to be exact.

Once this problem was solved, an old one re-emerged: piracy. In response, Phillip III sent Captain Antonio Scarlai to Sicily to arm ships, conscript soldiers and organize campaigns against the pirates. These operations, of course, required funding. So the Marquis of Vigliena, without consulting the Royal Council or the Parliament, resorted to taxation once again. This time, the taxes were imposed on notaries and bailiffs, who were, in turn, forced to double the fees for their services to the public. When the Mayor of Palermo and several parliamentary deputies protested against the viceroy's measures, Vigliena had them incarcerated immediately. But after the Messinese sent a delegation to him to back the protest and the Vicar of Monreale threatened him with excommunication, the marquis relented and eliminated this unreasonable tax.

The bitterness of this political defeat, ignominy for the viceroy, was compounded with grief in his private life. A ship transporting money and precious objects from Sicily to Spain was captured by Moslems; and the Marquis's stepson Diego Fernandez, who happened to be on board, was sold into slavery.

When Vigliena transferred some of his operations from Palermo to Messina, the ship carrying the royal archives sunk in a storm, and irreplaceable documents were lost. Totally disheartened, the marquis left the affairs of State to his subordinates and, shortly thereafter, asked the king to relieve him of his duties. The monarch accepted his resignation and installed the Lieutenant of the Kingdom Giovan Battista Doria, Archbishop of Palermo, as viceroy. On September 12, 1610, as the Marquis of Vigliena was crossing the Cassero on his way to the ship waiting to return him to Spain, he was resoundingly booed by the people in the streets.

Ironically, two years before, Vigliena had been applauded when he broke ground for the piazza to be named after him. This square, a beautiful octagon reached from Maqueda Street, was also called Piazza of the Sun because, from dawn to dust, the sun's rays illuminated, alternately, the four magnificent buildings constructed there and decorated with fountains and statues. Leanti, describing this square of the Four Corners in 1761, asserted that "its equal could not be found in all of Europe."

### 3. A Seventeenth Century Fiscal Sting

The Archbishop of Palermo, after replacing Vigliena, did nothing to placate Sicilians or bring peace to the island or its major cities, Palermo and Messina. He even managed to rub salt into the Messinese's wounds by abusing his power.

When the Marquis of Monte Maggiore, chief military commander of Messina, died, its citizens duly expected Madrid to nominate a successor to the post second only in importance to that of the viceroy's. Without consulting the Messinese, Archbishop Doria proposed one of his men for this key position. When the citizens of Messina refused to accept his chosen man, the viceroy summoned the major opponent of his decision, a Messinese judge, to Palermo, and imprisoned him for such "disobedience." Once again, the Messinese appealed to Madrid. This time, Spain responded by removing Doria from his post and issuing the order that the judge be freed—along with three senators incarcerated in Milazzo for similar disobedience.

Scarcely was the new viceroy, the Duke of Ossuna, installed in 1611, when he went directly to Messina to carry out the royal orders. Satisfying the Messinese, Ossuna then headed for Palermo with his wife. There he was received in triumph at the gates, given a horse by the city and escorted in a cavalcade up the Cassero to the cathedral. After being sworn in as viceroy, he was accompanied to the Royal Palace.

Although he was only 31, Ossuna demonstrated excellent judgment. Perhaps *too* conscientious in performing his duties, he could never be doubted as to his commitment. Since the city at the time was infested by thieves, murderers, hired assassins and plunderers, the Duke of Ossuna took extreme measures to remedy the situation. He literally drove out the most shady of characters and issued a ban on the bearing of arms. Determined to set a severe example from the outset of his vice-regency, Ossuna then incriminated the entire Senate of Palermo in the scandal involving the failure of the Table, the city's public bank. The Duke made the senators personally responsible for its heavy losses suffered when its cashier, Francesco Gatti, fled with enormous sums of money. Furthermore, the viceroy detained the mayor of the city and its senators in Termini Prison, pending the capture of the cashier, dead or alive, within eight days. If Palermo's other officials had failed to comply or to have this fugitive from justice apprehended, its whole governing apparatus would have suffered a four year banishment from the Kingdom of Sicily. Fortunately, Gatti was quickly flushed out and taken into custody, and the mayor and senators were released.

A chronicler reported that the young viceroy, in the company of a trusted attendant, was wont to go out at night disguised as a soldier, beggar or a servant, and get into casual conversations with Palermo's underworld figures in taverns, warehouses, and dens of iniquity. Gaining the confidence of his interlocutors, the Duke would have all the information he needed to strike at vulnerable officials when necessary.

Ossuna is also remembered for having introduced new onerous "gift-giving obligations" in the community. Sicilians saw this action as a genuine "sting"—"pulled off" to balance Sicily's treasury.

The Duke imposed heavy excise duties on silk, taxes which hurt Messina most since it had enjoyed exemptions granted by Madrid in this industry for many years. Again the city rose in protest, appealing to Phillip III. Ossuna retaliated in his authoritarian way, having senators, judges and the Messina tax officer arrested and brought to Palermo in chains.

This struggle lasted until 1615. Finally, Messina backed its appeal for justice with a gift to the sovereign of 150,000 scudos. The city's case was heard. Phillip III ordered the viceroy to repeal the tax on the crude silk that Messina produced in large quantities.

## 4. The Duke of Ossuna's Popularity

The Duke of Ossuna, trying to recover from his political defeat of having to repeal the silk tax, sought glory on the high seas still infested by pirates. His first step, taken in Messina deliberately, was to have a "captain galley" built with 32 rowing stations. Launched in April of 1613, this ship was accompanied by smaller, but well-armed boats. The light weapons for his forces, upon the Duke's orders, were requisitioned from the citizens of Messina themselves.

When the fleet docked at Malta, the commander, Octavio of Aragon, learning that Biserta was defended by forces superior to his, prudently beat a hasty retreat. Undaunted by this failure, Ossuna sent another expedition to the Levant. This time, the action turned out well when the Sicilian galleys crushed a Turkish fleet and liberated a thousand Christian prisoners.

Gregorio Leti, the dispassionate biographer of the Duke and other important historical figures, portrays this viceroy as one whose spirit was rare for the times. Leti relates how Ossuna, upon visiting the cathedral of Catania with his wife, was invited to kiss the reliquary supposedly containing Saint Agatha's breasts. The viceroy turned to his wife and quipped: "Lady Catherine, if you, without being jealous, will allow me . . ." Isidoro LaLumia, reporting the same episode, notes: "The devout crossed themselves, evil-doers trembled, and the people were in awe, feeling, against their will, a strong attraction for that new and singular ruler." Such an observation helps us understand the popularity that the duke enjoyed, especially in Palermo.

Chroniclers record another instance of Ossuna's witty blasphemy. While being escorted through Messina's cathedral, where the Madonna's *Letter* is presumed to be, he stated breezily: "If the Blessed Mother had sent us a letter of credit, she would have graced us more. Thus, I could afford to attack the Turks in their hideouts and keep us safe from their raids."

Like his predecessors, this viceroy was committed to beautifying Palermo. After completing Piazza Vigliena, he helped finance the Church's construction of Saint Joseph's nearby. Subsequently, Ossuna had the Senate Palace enlarged and decorated with friezes. He was also responsive to the inhabitants of the Capo Quarter, who asked that a new gate be opened in the walls so that they need not go out of their way through Carini Gate or New Gate. When the monks of the Monastery of the Annunciation seconded this request, the duke complied. Finished on February 4, 1613, this new structure was named Ossuna Gate. Atop this portal, an eagle, with its wings spread wide, was sculpted. On one side was etched the insignia of the city of Palermo, and, on the other, the duke's coat of arms. Designed by the architect Mariano Smiriglio, this gate survived the first post-Unity demolitions and urban renewal. But, in 1872, like many other monuments to sixteenth and seventeenth century Palermo's walled structure, it was knocked down.

The Duke of Ossuna left Sicily in 1616 to become viceroy of Naples. But, overtaxing his subjects as usual, he was denounced to the king and forced to go to Madrid in order to exonerate himself. There, Ossuna succeeded in convincing Phillip III of his innocence. Phillip IV, however, reopened the case. Convicted and incarcerated in Almeda Castle, the duke died in 1624. "Causes of death, unknown," wrote Ludovico Antonio Muratori in his *Annals of Italy*.

## 5. Saint Rosalie Drives Out the Plague

From 1616 until 1646, a series of Sicilian viceroys tried to combat the ills of the times, notably, banditism, luxurious excess, and pestilence. Then, in 1646, a raging famine caused riots all over Sicily that would bring the goldbeater Alesi into the limelight.

First let us review that 30 year period. The new viceroy Francesco of Lemos, Count of Castro, had a temperament very different from that of his predecessor, the Duke of Ossuna. After serving a six year term, the count, according to Di Blasi, "became bored with worldly affairs," and retired to a Benedictine monastery. The count is still remembered in Palermo, however, for Castro Gate, which, in 1620, he had constructed and named after him.

Succeeding Castro as viceroy of Sicily was Prince Emanuele Filiberto of Savoy. Cousin of Phillip IV, he had served as an admiral in the Spanish navy. Installed in Palermo toward the end of 1622, this viceroy promoted sciences, arts and letters.

But Filiberto had to contend with the plague that was spreading across the island. According to the most valid sources, this disease arrived with an African ship that had landed at Trapani with a boatload of Christians just freed from slavery. Apparently, the municipal authorities, suspecting that some of these men were infected, first refused to let the ship dock. But, finally, the prince's secretary, aware that there was a precious carpet on board destined for the viceroy himself, insisted long enough to convince the authorities to yield. From Trapani, then, the plague took its toll all over Sicily. The viceroy and his imprudent secretary succumbed to it as well.

It was in this period that the cult of Saint Rosalie emerged. By 1624, the pestilence was ravaging the Sicilian capital. During religious processions, when numerous saints were being implored to stop the dread disease, the citizens decided to transport the bones that, discovered under a pile of stones on Mount Pellegrino, were allegedly Saint Rosalie's. After a group of medical and ecclesiastical experts had examined these bones and attested to their "authenticity," Church authorities exhibited them and officially recognized the cult of this hermit virgin of Quisquina. Subsequently, the plague epidemic began to subside.

Another important Sicilian viceroy was Francisco Fernandez de la Cueva, Duke of Albuquerque. In 1630, the duke dedicated Scipione Li Volsi's statue of Charles V in Palermo's Piazza Bologna and the statue of Phillip IV in Palace Square. La Cueva also initiated the construction of the grain warehouses near the wharves.

Succeeding him in 1638, Francisco del Mello of Braganza, Count of Assumar, is remembered for his proscriptions against luxurious excess promulgated in 1640. These measures outlawed the use of gold to adorn carriages, litters, halls and tapestries. But artisans who depended on the gold industry suffered from these decrees; and, through the intercession of

**26. Saint Rosalie, with map of Palermo. 17th C. Engraving.**

Cardinal Doria, they were revoked. The count's banning of the use of tobacco met the same end—though, when legalized, this commodity was taxed. Finally, under this viceroy, September 9, 1641, a Palermo tribunal of the Inquisition ceremoniously burned at the stake a declared Calvinist Frenchman, a Christian embracing Moslemism, and a madman claiming he was the Messiah.

La Cueva's successor was Pedro Fuxardo Zunica e Requesens, Marquis of Los Veles. Under him, in 1646, a serious famine occurred, leading to one of the most violent revolts of the century.

## 6. Famines, Uprisings, and Less Bread on the Table

The lugubrious specter of hunger loomed in Palermo toward the end of 1646 as the result of two decades of serious grain shortages. The authorities suddenly realized that emergency supplies did not exist and that there was not even enough grain to sow for the next harvest. In Messina, where demand greatest due to its large influx of seamen, they took the drastic measure of reducing the weight of the "pagnotta" while maintaining normal prices. Chroniclers disagree as to whether it was a poor woman or "a wretched little fellow" who rose up in protest. Someone, it seems, stuck a pole through a "pagnotta" and brandished it over a crowd in the streets. This protest was the spark that ignited the revolt.

Viceroy Los Veles came immediately to Messina to quell the riot. Once the City at the Straits was pacified, he rushed back to Palermo where he feared similar disorders. Although the bread basket's weight there had not yet been reduced, Los Veles did have to deal with hosts of starving people who were swarming from province to city every day in search of food.

On May 19, 1647, the retailers in Palermo decided to offer, for the usual price, bread rations weighing two ounces less. While they were responding to an order issued by the Spanish crown to get the senate out of debt through the sale of bread supplies at a high price, the people, unappeased, reacted violently. There are no records of any further motives spurring the actions of the government or those of Palermitans. What is clear, though, is that, blinded by rage, groups of demonstrators reached the Senate Palace fully intending to burn it down. There, the protesters were pacified by priests reminding them of the risks they were taking. Still, the disorders continued throughout that night. Vicaria Gate was set afire and the inmates in the adjacent prison were thus able to join the insurgents.

As the rebel forces grew rapidly, they tried to burn down the houses of the officials in charge of rationing, whom they considered responsible for their hunger. The viceroy, fearing the worst possible outcome, ensconced himself in the convent of Saint Antonino. At this point, the authorities learned who the insurgents' leader was: a certain miller by the name of Antonino La Pilosa. With the help of the Artisan Consuls of the Arts guarding the only city gates left open after a state of emergency was declared, he was captured a few days later. Then, on May 22, La Pilosa and a number of his fellow conspirators were summarily condemned to death.

The situation seemed to be returning to normal. The artisans who had assisted in quelling the riot were compensated via the nomination of two people's jurors to the previously four-noblemen body. Furthermore, these popular officials became members of the Palermitan Senate.

But the authorities were not completely convinced that these measures would suffice. The viceroy himself summoned more armed troops to the city; and the nobles, sensing the tension within Palermo's walls, took refuge out in the countryside on their feudal estates.

As the revolt was ostensibly ending in Palermo, it flared up elsewhere, from Agrigento to Syracuse, from Alcamo to Randazzo, from Bronte to Sciacca, from Lentini to Mazara. All over Sicily, the houses of the rich were looted, archives were burned, jails were opened, excise taxes were abolished. Only Messina, capital and bastion of Spanish rule, remained calm. The Messinese authorities even offered their assistance to counteract these assaults on royal power.

July 1, Palermo's Senate, in response to the popular jurors' proposal, levied new taxes in order to liquidate its debts and sell bread at subsidized prices. Since these taxes were imposed only on the wealthy, the populace was satisfied, and calm seemed to descend after the storm. But embers were smoldering under the ashes.

## 7. The Cost of Alesi's Revolt: Life

Sicilian insurgents were further encouraged by an incident taking place in Naples on July 7, 1647. New taxes levied by the Duke of Arcos spurred the popular uprising led by the fishmonger Tommaso Aniello. Better known as Masaniello, this commoner enjoyed tremendous prestige among his fellow-citizens and became the people's Captain General.

According to popular tradition, one night in a Palermo tavern, the goldbeater Giuseppe Alesi, a belt maker and two tanners were heatedly discussing Masaniello and his deeds. Talking and drinking, these four artisans got excited over the prospects of emulating Masaniello by "shaking off the ministers' yoke" in Palermo. They proceeded, then, to draw lots to see who would lead the revolt. Alesi won—so to speak—and the conspirators set the date for the uprising: August 15, a day when many nobles and city officials were in their country retreats. The ultimate goal of the revolt was nothing less than disposing of the viceroy, the noblemen and the ministers.

In spite of attempts to keep the plot a secret, there were leaks. A conscientious inquisitor by the name of Trasmera, duly informed, passed the news of the conspiracy on to the viceroy. But Los Veles did not believe that danger was imminent. When he learned the names of two of the conspirators, he had them summoned to his palace and tried to use reason, warning them of the damage that would be done to the city and to the rebels themselves. Other conspirators, however, believing their two comrades were to be executed by the viceroy, began to riot in the streets. Seeing violence erupt, Los Veles had the two insurgents released in the hope of restoring the peace.

**27. Giuseppe Alesi, leader of the 1647 revolution in Palermo. Ink drawing. Biblioteca Comunale of Palermo**

But no gesture could root out the profound popular discontent that was the rebels' "powder keg and fuse." Armed insurgents swept through the city and reached the Royal Palace. The few Spanish guards at the gate opened fire on the crowd, killing three men and wounding dozens more. A brief pause in the fighting did allow the viceroy to escape with his family on his captain galley, leaving the palace unguarded and ripe for looting. At this point Alesi set up his sentinels to prohibit further pillage.

On the following day, August 16, Alesi was proclaimed Captain General by the populace. Even the Senate complied, sending him an official letter in which it asked for his collaboration in finding an honorable solution to Palermo's bankruptcy. Swelling with pride, Alesi called all citizens to a meeting in the Church of Saint Joseph of the Teatini. Special invitations were expressed to every senator, the Judge of the Monarchy and Inquisitor Trasmera.

Alesi failed to understand that, from the moment of the uprising, Trasmera, from the Palace of the Inquisition, had been deliberating on the method, the time and the place to strike him dead. The inquisitor had stopped at nothing, not even bribes, to find ways and means to wipe out the naive and imprudent goldbeater.

At Trasmera's instigation, Alesi was counselled to demand for himself many privileges, the post of Mayor-for-Life with an annual income of 2,000 scudos and an entourage of 70 armed men to be paid by the community to boot. When Alesi accepted such honors and granted amnesty to his foes, including the viceroy whom he had invited back to the Royal Palace, calm seemed to be restored to Palermo. But, suddenly armed officials and nobles took over the whole city.

Alesi saw everything coming too late. He tried to flee, but the city gates were all guarded. Turning back, Alesi hid in the home of a tanner friend. Discovered, he was decapitated by a nobleman, Alessandro Platamone, on the spot. His head was then displayed high on a pole for the populace to see.

## 8. Three Naive Rebellions Against the Spanish

At least eleven of Giuseppe Alesi's companions lost their heads with him. But the revolt was not totally in vain. At least it taught the viceroy something, notably that the people, having obtained representation in the Senate, would not rest after this hard-won gain. In fact, on August 23, the viceroy himself was forced to sanction as permanent certain charters he had granted temporarily to the people. Moreover, the two popular jurors were securely in their seats.

Alesi's revolt was the last one in Palermo to be spurred by popular protest against the high price of bread and the lack of adequate representation in the Senate. But other cities all over Sicily were rocked that very same year by rebellions. In May of 1647, Catania experienced a people's uprising precisely over the issue of their say in government. Similarly, the populations of Patti, Bronte, Randazzo, Syracuse, Modica, Castelvetrano, Agrigento and Sciacca rose up to demand abolition of onerous taxes and to have official representation in their governing bodies.

Other revolts and conspiracies flared up in Sicily throughout the seventeenth century. But they differed from Alesi's in that they were predominantly anti-Spanish riots aimed at overthrowing one regime in favor of another. Many of these insurgencies, it should be said, were of little significance. On September 23, 1647, for instance, young Carlo Ventimiglia, stepson of Giovanni Ventimiglia, Knight of Malta, nailed up a manifesto in Palermo's Loggia of the Merchants inviting all citizens, in the name of an unidentified "Liberator of Our Country," to unite and march to Piazza Marina where a Knight with "the shield of three lilies" was waiting to free them from oppression. Captured, Carlo confessed, under torture, that the whole plot was his idea alone. In spite of his penitence, he was hanged in the public square.

In November of 1647, the Calabrian Francesco Vairo, who had served in Octavio of Aragon's navy and, during Alesi's revolt, had saved the viceroy's wife, hatched the plot of assassinating the late Veles's successor, Cardinal Trivulzio. Di Blasi, in his chronology of the viceroys, points out that Vairo wanted "to seize the capital and set up a government there that, whether democratic, oligarchical or aristocratic, would flatter him by giving its promoter a post of distinction." Vairo envisioned as head of this "republic" the ex-Jesuit Francesco Baronio of Monreale, who at the time was under arrest in an Inquisition jail. The conspiracy was quickly uncovered, and its four advocates were disposed of post-haste. After Vairo was strangled, his body was brought to the Four Corners where it was hung by the feet from a gallows.

In the winter of 1647, Gabriello Platenella da Bivona, a clerk at Palermo's Grand Hospital, sued the Governor of Marseille for French aid in fomenting a rebellion to drive the Spanish from Sicily. But strategic blunders cost Platenella his life.

A more concerted effort by the Messinese resulted in anti-Spanish riots which, starting in 1674, drove their dominators from the city. Messina, declaring itself free, then requested French assistance to defend against possible retaliation on the part of the Spaniards.

# Chapter IX: French Designs on an Island in Flames

## 1. Messina in Revolt and the Intervention of Louis XIV

Although the Messinese had remained loyal to Madrid in opposing all of Sicily's anti-Spanish insurrections during the seventeenth century, including the famous revolt of Giuseppe Alesi's at Palermo, the viceroys had dealt with these faithful subjects in heavy-handed fashion. The Spaniards never even considered compensating Messina by respecting the ancient privileges it held dear.

Compounding the Messinese's general feeling of discontent with their governors, a bitter struggle broke out between the city's patricians, banded into the Malvizzi party, and the plebeians, organized by the Merli faction. The latter, backed by the Jesuits and, secretly, by Madrid, also won the public support of the military commander of Messina, Luis del Hojo, who, in response to recurring food shortages, accused the nobles of being responsible due to their egoism and insensitivity.

In the city, disorders erupted, with mass looting and arson. On May 30, 1672, the Merli, to the cry of "long live Mary and the King of Spain," poured through the streets setting fire to the houses of senators and patricians. Informed of these incidents, Viceroy Claudio Lamoral, Prince of Ligny, quickly made his way from Palermo to Messina to order that all property seized by the Merli be returned to violated domiciles. The prince also commanded Hojo to leave the city.

The Malvizzi reclaimed their territory in Messina, but the truce did not last. Two years later, after senatorial elections won by their party, fighting broke out again. Trying to crush an armed populace, the new viceroy, the Marquis of Baiona, met with the resistance of heavy artillery. As the insurrection reached its peak, Spanish fortresses had to surrender. In that dramatic year of 1674, the Messinese suddenly realized they were free to govern their city as they chose to do so.

According to popular tradition, it was one Carlo Giacinto Ferrari, a Bolognese knight, who enlightened the Messinese as to the possibility of seeking French aid to drive out the Spanish. In a conversation with a parish priest who was hosting him, the Bolognese let it be known that, through his friendship with the French Ambassador to Rome, he could request the direct intervention of Louis XIV. Not incidentally, the King of France, in a prolonged war with Spain, took the opportunity to deal a serious blow to his enemy. When Louis's forces arrived in Sicily on September 27, 1674, the Messinese were reinforced enough to occupy the Spanish fort of

Salvatore and to stop an Iberian fleet sent by Barcelona from surrounding the City of the Straits.

At this point, as heir of Charles of Anjou, Louis XIV seriously considered the possibility of reconquering all of Sicily. To pursue his goal, the king lavished aid on the Messinese and waged a relentless war against the Spaniards on land and at sea. Messina's Royal Palace and Castellaccio fell to him. Then, near the island of Stromboli, the French won a major naval battle over a Spanish fleet.

Striking while the iron was hot, Louis XIV decided to choose his own viceroy for Sicily: the imposing figure of the Duke of Vivonne, brother of the sovereign's favorite, the Marquess of Montespan. But the duke, received in Messina with the erection of a triumphal arch, was quick to betray the trust of its citizens.

## 2. Madrid's Punishment of a Rebel City

The French Viceroy of Sicily, the Duke of Vivonne, looked like a merry giant and behaved as such. Unfortunately, the Messinese were bitterly disappointed with his behavior, realizing that France's representative on their island was a great lover of women, good food and wine, and, above all, idleness. The real maker and breaker of things Sicilian was, instead, his rapacious secretary Autiège, who seemed bent, first and foremost, on satisfying his master's whims.

Galatti, the author of a detailed account of the subsequent revolt in Messina, tells an anecdote revelatory of the character of this jester of a viceroy. On a given day when the Duke of Vivonne was to meet with the city's senators, after having spent the night in certain festivities, he was still sleeping at the appointed hour. Therefore, his secretary was obliged to wake him up and drag him to the Senate notwithstanding the duke's threats of beheading for the insolent rogue who had dared disturb his peace.

The French continued to record numerous naval victories against the Spanish and their allies, the Dutch. On April 22, 1676, during a long and hard battle near Augusta, the Dutch Admiral Ruyter was mortally wounded. Then on June 2, the French fleet emerged victorious in the vicinity of Palermo. But, while they took Taormina on October 10 and Scaletta on November 10, they failed to consolidate a united anti-Spanish front.

By 1677, Louis XIV had realized that his acts of war in the Mediterranean might cause England to change its policy of benign neutrality. So, rather than pitching new battles to occupy all of Sicily—as the Messinese hoped they would do—the French thought it expedient in 1678 to extricate themselves from the island and leave Messina at the Spaniards' mercy. About 16,000 Messinese who had thrown their whole lot in with the French were able to escape thereafter. But the rest of their fellow-citizens awaited the inevitable revenge of the Spanish reconquest. Meanwhile, some turncoat Messinese, to display their "age-old devotion to our true and legitimate, loving master," looted the houses of those notables who had openly backed the French.

The Spaniards were welcomed back by Messina with a *Te Deum* in the cathedral and bonfires in the streets. The new Spanish viceroy, Don Vincente Gonzaga, promised to be merciful—although he issued an edict of clemency only to those Messinese who had not fled. Ordering that the properties of all traitors be confiscated, he immediately took possession of the hated enemies' patrimony. In the next few days, 3,000 Spanish soldiers invaded the city—in an act which seemed to the Messinese an evil omen.

Ultimately, the Spanish punished Messina severely. First of all, the city was deprived of its most jealously guarded prerogatives won over the centuries from kings and emperors. The position of Military Commander was abolished; the academies and the university were shut down; and priests were forbidden to preach without royal authorization. The crowning insult, however, was the recasting of the bronze cathedral bell for the equestrian statue of Charles II. This statue, the work of Giacomo Serpotta and Gaspare Romano, depicted the king's horse in the act of trampling a hydra, symbol of the hated revolutionary forces. In 1708, Phillip V had the hydra removed from the pedestal. And in February of 1848, Charles II and his horse were destroyed by an angry mob rebelling against Bourbon tyranny.

### 3. The Great Earthquake of 1693

The century, near its end, was full of dramatic events. This time, Mount Etna entered the scene as protagonist. The volcano first erupted in 1669; and in 1682, 1688 and 1689, more lava gushed and descended from its craters. Etna's major eruption, however, came in 1693, this time accompanied by an earthquake that caused major damage throughout eastern Sicily, its outlying islands, and even Lipari and Malta.

Giovanni Evangelista Di Blasi described the cataclysm thus: "Sicily, in 1693, suffered irreparable calamities at the hands of an enemy much more potent than the King of France. The morning of January 10, around 4:30, the whole island felt a tremor heaving with all its strength from the Valleys of Noto and Demone and reaching, with diminishing shocks, all the way to Mazara Valley. People were terrified—more so, naturally, because the night was pitch-black. Abandoning their houses, they streamed into the piazzas and the fields, only to be exposed to the freezing temperatures of winter. Finally, when dawn broke, they were further disheartened by the sight of gaping cracks in what was left of their homes. But this earthquake was merely a prelude to the more terrible one occurring at nine in the evening of January 11. Then, the whole earth seemed to split open and pour forth its viscera. Magnificent edifices crumbled and abysses swallowed people up alive. Center stage in this lugubrious scene was the city of Catania, which, in an instant, became a pile of stones."

**28. An image of the devastasting 1693 earthquake.**

Twenty-three Sicilian cities were completely destroyed, notably Catania, Noto, Lentini and Avola. Syracuse, Modica and Mineo suffered severe damages—as did at least 19 other towns. The death toll was 59,700, 18,000 in Catania alone. A list of the names of all the victims was meticulously compiled by Mongitore and sent to the viceroy.

In Catania, the 9,000 survivors of the earthquake would live the rest of their lives with images of those terrible hours and days flashing before their eyes. As one of the survivors attested, "all the weapons of this Earth could not produce a boom like the one we suddenly heard." Catania was scourged not only by this natural disaster but by a man-made one as well. "Jackals" swarmed from the outlying countryside into the city to loot houses and churches and carry off objects both profane and sacred. For months, the

Catanese wandered aimlessly through an uninhabitable city deprived of the water that had stopped flowing from the springs and of the bread that had been buried under the rubble of the grain deposits. An inscription in the wall along a major artery of Catania still commemorates those awful times when jackals roamed the shambles of a city.

Viceroy Uzeda, responding with a swiftness not seen in the cases of present day earthquakes, sent his representative, Duke Giuseppe Lanza of Camastra, to assess the extent of the damages and begin the reconstruction immediately. Oral tradition paints a portrait of this nobleman as he went on horseback from city to city, redesigning their urban layouts. This enlightened official was also responsible for the subsequent re-edification in the baroque style of Catania, Noto and other important Sicilian cities destroyed by the earthquake.

### 4. Jousts and Bullfights in Seventeenth Century Sicily

A portrait of seventeenth century Sicily would not be complete without the inclusion of some of its joyful aspects. The Count of Santo Stefano, viceroy at the time when Messina's revolt was crushed, had supervised the construction of the Citadel that would defend the city against further threats from within or without. He then returned to Palermo to organize a grand celebration on the occasion of the marriage of Charles II and the Duke of Orleans's daughter, Maria Luisa of Bourbon. On that day, March 15, 1680, and in the following month, two jousts were held that were described in Mongitore's *Diary* and Di Blasi's *Chronological History of the Viceroys* and depicted in Pietro Maggio's book of illustrations. For "these two beautiful royal jousts so strange and wonderful to behold in all their splendor," twelve noble knights were chosen; and "a superb, oval-shaped theater, 624' x 240'," was built in Piazza Marina facing the fourteenth century Steri Palace. On the lower tiers of this theater, the seats for the common people were set up. On high, the nobles sat comfortably in specially designed boxes. Naturally, the viceroy's box was particularly "superb."

The knights displayed their skills extravagantly. Once the joust had ended and the prizes were distributed, the viceroy, flanked by the victorious knight, led a candlelight cavalcade.

The following year (1681), since it was evident that jousts were good entertainment for all social classes, a permanent enclosure was built on the Piazza Saint Olive to host such events. Place-names in the area today still recall this activity.

During this period, a dispute arose between the Dominican monks of Saint Cita and friars of other orders regarding precedence in a religious procession. Both sides appealed to Archbishop Giacomo Palafox and to the viceroy, who, in turn, disagreed as to which order(s) would be favored. As was often the case in Sicily history, the pope was then consulted. After he excommunicated the viceroy, the dispute dragged on for three more years. Finally, the ecclesiastical authorities prevailed; and, while Archbishop Palafox was removed from his position in Palermo, he received the more prestigious position of Head of the See in Seville.

New jousts took place in Palermo's Piazza Marina in April and May of 1690 to celebrate the marriage of Charles II (who had become a widower the year before) to Princess Maria Anna Neoburgh. The festivities also included a spectacular fireworks display held in the Piazza of the Royal Palace. During this spectacle, a mechanized giant supported a globe decorated with the signs of the zodiac.

Toward the end of the century—on October 10, 1696, to be exact—a "bull game" was held in front of the Royal Palace to celebrate Charles II's recovery from an illness. For this occasion an enormous cart was built to carry musicians, who played to the king's health as it was drawn through Palermo's main streets. When they reached Piazza Vigliena, they threw coins to the crowd and performed a number of comedies. In this climate of collective jubilation, Spain was unconsciously celebrating its inexorable decline.

### 5. The Age of Rocco Pirri and Giacomo Serpotta

The age upon which Galileo left his indelible mark gave birth to experimental scientists in Sicily as well. Among them, most notable were the physicist and mathematician Carlo Maria Ventimiglia, whose works are still preserved in Catanese manuscripts, and the astronomer, physicist and naturalist Giovan Battista Odierna, author of a treatise on the origin of typhoons and compiler of an almanac based on his study of heavenly bodies.

Sicilian culture during this century was also distinguished for its scholarship. Rocco Pirri's *Sacred Sicily,* for instance, provides an overview of the Church's role on the island. Continued by Mongitore, this work is a goldmine of information. Mariano Valguarnera, the polyglot and man of letters, did an in-depth study of his native Palermo and published his *Discourse* on the origins and ancient heritage of the capital. The Messinese Antonio Amico, Phillip IV's royal historiographer, produced numerous historical pieces. Filippo Paruta, an expert in numismatics and medal collecting, is best known for his *Sicily Illustrated Via Medals.*

Special mention should be made of Pietro Carrera, a strong-willed man who excelled as historian, poet and courtier. A native of Militello in Catania Valley, he was famous during his times not only for his poetic and historical works but also for his singular book on chess. Appearing in 1617 in the small town of Militello, this volume was printed in a shop set up by Prince Branciforte.

The artists Pietro Novelli and Giacomo Serpotta were dominant cultural figures during the seventeenth century. The former, called the Monrealese after his native city, was noted for his creative gift, which he applied under the influence of Caravaggio and via his Sicilian eclecticism. Born in 1603, Novelli succumbed in 1647 to a wound suffered during the abortive Palermo uprising led by the goldbeater Giuseppe Alesi. Pietro's paintings can still be found in churches all over Sicily, especially in Palermo.

The sculptor and stucco-worker Giacomo Serpotta is remembered for the plasticity of his cupids (*putti*), the modelling of fine allegorical female figures, and the vitality of his stucco decorations in churches and oratories. His equestrian statue of Charles II, commissioned by the Spanish government after the revolt in Messina, also gives Serpotta a place in the history of Sicilian art. His relief model of the famous Battle of Lepanto, glorifying that Christian victory of the sixteenth century against the Turks, can still be viewed in Palermo's Oratory of Saint Cita. The two youths molded at the base of the model, for their compositional beauty, represent the heights of this great Sicilian sculptor's powers.

29. An allegorical figure by Giacomo Serpotta in the Oratory of San Lorenzo, Palermo.

## 6. Spain in Sicily: A Controversional Assessment

To round out any discussion of seventeenth century Sicily, it is necessary to offer an assessment of the Spanish domination of the largest island in the Mediterranean and of the Mezzogiorno in general. This is an arduous task, especially because the pros and cons of Spain's rule of Sicily have been, and still are, the subject of heated debates.

Many subjects of Spanish rule provided one judgment by rebelling against its centralized government in the name of bread. Others witnessed the aberrations of Madrid's domination by undergoing inquisitorial persecution. And all Sicilians felt the heavy hand of their viceroys, who were more often bent on avoiding a Spanish king's displeasure than on satisfying their subjects and who were mainly concerned about their own posterity vis-à-vis what roads, squares and monuments they had built. Finally, no Sicilian could forget one of the most painful events in the island's history: the revolt of Messina that brought the wrath of Madrid down upon Sicilians in an egregious way never seen before in the long period of Spanish hegemony.

In the Sicily governed from Madrid, nobles reaped most of the benefits. But even common soldiers, if they were Spanish, enjoyed special privileges. A famous case-in-point of such an abuse of power occurred in 1680, when a rural guard by the name of Casanova, in charge of a clean-up campaign, arrested some thieves. It turned out that among those robbers whom Casanova had apprehended and who were subsequently punished with a thrashing and ten years in jail was a Spanish soldier. In protest, the military authorities representing Spain on the island pressured the viceroy to remove from office the presiding magistrates of the Grand Court and the lawyer who had favored the sentence. The judges and the lawyer were, as a consequence, deported to Tusa, Cefalù and Lipari.

This was not an isolated case during the times. Yet, traditionally, historians have tended to treat the Spanish presence in Sicily with kid gloves. Echoing Benedetto Croce's benevolent view of Madrid's domination of the island, Francesco De Stefano emphasizes how Spain governed Sicily for three centuries "without disrupting the course of the island's history or eradicating its particular character." De Stefano further stresses how much Spain did, especially in the 1500s, to keep Sicily in the European orbit. This is true: while Madrid acted in its own strategic, political and military interests, it cannot be denied that, by pursuing policies best articulated in the Battle of Lepanto, Spain assured that the island would stay within the Christian sphere of influence.

The historian Virgilio Titone is even more emphatic about the many merits of Spanish rule in Sicily. He goes so far as to affirm that the claim

**30. Naval battle in the Straits of Messina (1719)
between English and Spanish ships. Engraving.**

that Sicilians' problems were due to Spanish malgovernance is a "trumped up alibi."

Titone's thesis is vehemently challenged by another historian, Gabriele Pepe, who refuses to spare the ruling class in Sicily during the 1500s and the 1600s. As Pepe argues, "those in power on the island, whether barons, Spaniards, clergy or lay intelligentzia personnel, were the worst administrators of justice that one could possibly imagine . . . One could count the honest Spanish viceroys of the period on one hand . . . The nobles were servile, cowardly, ignorant, cruel, avidly corrupt . . . The clergy, though, was the worst sector of the elite. Rather than setting a moral example for Christians to live by, the priests acted the villains just as well as the barons or the viceroys."

## 7. The Shadow of Louis XIV Looms Once Again

Charles II, who had spent the last decades of the seventeenth century crushing Messina's rebellion, died without heir in Madrid on November 1, 1700, ten days before he reached 40. Thus, the new century began in mourning, an evil omen for all of Europe.

Before dealing with the consequences of the Spanish monarch's death, however, let us focus on how the events taking place in Madrid at that crucial moment were perceived in Sicily, especially from its capital. Due to his poor health, Charles II had already made his last will and testament toward the end of 1698, designating as his heir Joseph Ferdinand, the son of the Elector of Bavaria, Maximillian II. Charles II's decision was in part the result of his resentment against Louis XIV, who had committed himself to dividing Charles's inheritance before the fact of his death. These motives notwithstanding, the sudden demise of Joseph Ferdinand on February 6, 1699, forced the Spanish monarch to make a new will. On October 2, 1700, Charles did so, relenting and naming Louis XIV's 16 year old nephew Phillip of Anjou as his successor. It was later revealed that this difficult choice had been the outcome of Louis XIV's own intrigues in Madrid, where he had convinced the Spanish king's father confessor, Cardinal Portocarrero, to support this young French noble.

After making this thorny decision, Charles II fell ill once again. But immediate medical care seemed to restore his fragile health. A dispatch from Madrid to Palermo, arriving on November 3, brought news of the king's recovery and caused the city to erupt with joy. Mongitore's November 3 entry in his Palermitan *Diary* underscores this reaction: "By chance, the King of Spain suffered an illness that rendered him mute for seven hours. Yet, by the grace of God, his health was just as suddenly restored. When this news reached Palermo, the city celebrated. A public proclamation ordered that the streets be illuminated to express his subjects' happiness."

The festivities lasted three days with their jaunty cavalcades, shooting blank cannon salvos, fireworks displays, and religious ceremonies in the cathedral with the relics of Saint Rosalie displayed especially for this occasion. But while Palermo was celebrating Charles's regained health, Madrid was performing his funeral rites. The king had, in fact, died two days before the news of his recovery reached Palermo.

Sicily learned of Charles II's demise only on December 4. Informed by a special messenger, the viceroy, Duke of Veragues, summoned Archbishop Ferdinando Bayan and all the nobles of the court to communicate the bad news. Five days later, the contents of the dead monarch's will were made public. Hearing that Duke Phillip of Anjou would be his successor, Palermitans once again exploded in jubilation. And the viceroy, "after dinner, dressed up in his finest and paraded through the city to show off his delight."

It took almost a week before Palermo would mourn for the dead king. Then on December 10, the funeral rites were performed. Three days later, the viceroy received the condolences of the authorities and the nobles. An ingenuous chronicler reported that on November 6, while Charles II was being buried in Madrid, Palermitans saw, "near the sun, a prodigiously splendid star through which the Heavens, perhaps, wanted to glorify our defunct king." This chronicler adds that, on the same day, the king's portrait hanging in the Senate Palace mysteriously fell to the floor as an unequivocable sign of the end he had met.

## 8. Europe in Flames Over the Spanish Succession

The desires Charles II expressed in his will were immediately respected in Sicily. On January 17, 1701—a little more than a month after Palermitans had heard the news of the Spanish sovereign's death—Phillip of Anjou was officially proclaimed Phillip V, King of Sicily. With exceptional rapidity, a white marble statue "placed on a noble and beautifully carved pedestal decorated with figures and inscriptions" was erected to him in Palermo at Customs Gate.

But while Palermo was so solicitous in recognizing the new sovereign, Paris, in view of certain reactions around Europe, was worried. To be cautious, Phillip V remained in Paris while Louis XIV sized up the European situation. Eventually, though, the French monarch acted decisively. First, he acknowledged his nephew's right to Charles II's throne. Then, opposing the dead king's stipulation in his will that the Spanish and French crowns never be united, Louis XIV declared his intention of making Phillip

**31. An engraving of King Phillip V.**

heir to his realm. Phillip V was ultimately proclaimed sovereign of Spain and lord of other territories, namely Italy and the Low Countries and Spanish Colonies.

Louis XIV took other imprudent initiatives that revealed his real objectives. First, he opened the frontier between France and Spain, intervening with a heavy hand in Spanish affairs. Then, the French king sent his merchants and navy to occupy key positions in the Hispanic-American trade route, installed French advisers in the Court of Madrid, and granted a monopoly in the slave-trade of Spanish colonies to a French company. As if those acts were not sufficient, Louis XIV established garrisons in Spanish outposts in Belgium and recognized the son of James II (who, exiled, had died in 1701 on French soil) as the legitimate heir to the English throne, thereby outraging the English monarchy in his support of a Stuart.

These openly provocative and imperialistic steps taken by the French monarch alarmed other European powers and drove them into opposing blocs. The first ruler to show his concern *in re* Louis's aggressive politics was Archduke Charles of Austria, son of Emperor Leopold I. To counteract Louis's move toward hegemony, the archduke united in a league with England, Holland, Denmark, Sweden, the Palatinate and Piedmont.

Throughout 1701, Europe witnessed troops constantly marching across its territories. Massive regiments were formed in Bavaria, and France was heavily mobilized. Then the War for the Spanish Succession erupted. Portugal and the Dukedom of Savoy, at first allies of France and Spain, joined the league, and a long and bitter conflict began.

The French went down to many a resounding defeat in 1704. But the crucial year of the war was 1709, when a famine struck. Louis XIV tried to negotiate a truce, then refused to yield after his adversaries demanded that he declare war on Phillip and send his nephew into exile.

Peace came only in 1713 with the Treaty of Utrecht. Herein, Phillip was recognized as Sovereign of Spain and the Indies. But Charles II's wish that Phillip be denied the right to the French crown was reaffirmed. Furthermore, Phillip had to cede (1) Gibraltar and Minorca to England and (2) Naples, Milan, Sardinia and the Low Countries to Austria. Sicily fell to Duke Vittorio Amedeo II of Savoy, who became its king. Once again, without knowing how or why, the Mediterranean island had a new ruler.

# Chapter X: Between Savoyards and "Alemanni"

## 1. European Powers Choose a King for Sicily

Thanks to England's clever political maneuvering on the international scene and the 1713 Peace of Utrecht, Duke Vittorio Amedeo II of Savoy became King of Sicily. The English did everything possible to keep this Mediterranean prize out of Bourbon and Habsburg reach. What England aimed to do was create a new power strong enough to confront and contain France and Austria but too weak to challenge English hegemony in the Mediterranean.

Actually, Vittorio Amedeo II had designs only on Milan; but he had to play England's game. Five years later, in 1718, via an international treaty, the Duke of Savoy would be given Sardinia in exchange for Sicily. (Although he retained the title of king of the latter, it would be in effect ruled by Emperor Charles VI.) In 1713, however, Vittorio Amedeo was forced to accept England's protection and manipulation. Thus on October 3, he and his queen, Anne of Orleans, and a host of Piedmontese nobles, were escorted from Nice to Sicily on a British ship commanded by Admiral Jennings.

Shortly before this voyage, the new king had received an official Sicilian delegation paying him homage. Now, arriving in Sicily on October 11, Vittorio Amedeo privately entered Palermo. On December 21, he made his grand appearance. Three days later, the Piedmontese king was crowned. During the ceremony, he swore to respect Sicily's ancient privileges and rights.

Sicilians took their new prospects to heart, hoping in a better future. Many of them believed that, in rising from mere Duke of Savoy to King of Sicily, Vittorio Amedeo would consider the island the prize of his dominions. But the islanders were deceiving themselves. The duke sojourned in Sicily for less than a year. Apparently, he was not lured to stay longer by the manifestations of euphoria that welcomed him upon his arrival. In spite of the Sicilian hospitality described by the Abbot Pietro Vitale, Secretary of Palermo Senate—"Sicilians rushed to embrace the Piedmontese warmly and clasp their hands just as their leader was uniting in fraternal warmth the two most remote and strong ends of Italy"—the northern Italian king seemed unimpressed.

The city of Palermo begrudged their sovereign nothing, heaping honors upon him. After all, it had been centuries since a real king had set foot on the island. Mongitore's chronicles and Di Blasi's more articulate accounts agree on one point: the sympathetic climate in which Vittorio Amedeo II was received in Palermo. Commemorative tablets were in-

**32. A 17th C. map of Sicily, showing Mount Etna erupting.**

scribed and medallions and coins were minted to apotheosize the king's triumphal procession into the city. As Mongitore reported in his *Diary*, on January 1, 1714, "the monarch dined outdoors so that all Palermitans could enjoy his presence and nobility."

Much against his will, Vittorio Amedeo II found himself involved in the age-old disputes between the Sicilian monarchy and the Church of Rome. The apple of discord in this instance was the so-called Apostolic Legation, i.e., the ancient privilege granted first to the King of Sicily by Pope Urban II in 1097 that made the island's ruler the pontiff's representative. This privilege, so sensitive an issue that historians and jurists had debated its validity for centuries, troubled popes so much that they sought any pretext to eliminate it.

The Papacy's chance came in 1711, during an incident on Lipari, the only diocese in Sicily whose bishop was chosen directly by Rome. The Lipari Controversy, most probably instigated by the Curia itself, gave birth to another long battle between Church and State. The immediate cause of the conflict was no more than "a handful of chickpeas." But, in the long run, it was inevitable that the delicate balance of power maintained under the Spanish would eventually be disturbed.

## 2. The Pope's War: No Masses in Sicily

The incident that ignited the Lipari Controversy occurred January 22, 1711 on that island. Two customs guards, as was their routine, went to a shop to collect the "display tax" levied on all foodstuffs merchants who exhibited their wares. This was a tax to be paid "in kind," and thus one "rotolo" (800 grams) of chickpeas was demanded. But, on this occasion, the Archbishop of Lipari objected, demanding immediate restitution of the chickpeas that, according to him, were part of *his* "table" (i.e., his revenue). On the spot, he excommunicated the two guards, quickly informing the Papacy of his measure.

Considering this excommunication invalid, the Sicilian Tribunal of the Monarchy absolved the guards. At that point, the rift between Rome and Palermo went from bad to worse. Bishop Monsignor Tedeschi, fearing his arrest was imminent, fled to Rome. Sicilian authorities subsequently arrested numerous prelates. As the conflict came to a head, Clement XI issued his interdiction against Sicily: on the island, masses would no longer be celebrated, no church bells could be rung, and the sacraments would not be administered.

This was the situation Vittorio Amedeo II had to confront in Sicily when he landed there toward the end of 1713. He attempted to make a conciliatory gesture to appease the pope by sending Clement news of his festive coronation. But the pope would accept neither his missive nor his investiture as King of Sicily.

Pressured to leave the island to attend to affairs of State, the Piedmontese monarch first decided to tour his new kingdom by land. Accompanied by the queen in her litter and a long train of trusted servants, Vittorio Amedeo II saw Sicily on horseback. After a brief stop in Catania, he spent considerable time in Messina, the city so ruthlessly punished by the Spanish for rebelling. To make restitutions, the king reinstated the prerogatives taken from the Messinese by the Count of Santo Stefano; and he promoted four local nobles to the rank of Gentleman of the Chambers.

As Di Blasi attests, Vittorio Amedeo II also restored public order by incarcerating "one of the most powerful knights protecting thieves and rogues." Moreover, the king found the time to donate a silver lamp worth 5,000 scudos to Saint Rosalie's chapel in Palermo Cathedral. This precious gift reached Palermo at the beginning of June. On the 14th of that month the lamp was on display in the cathedral.

The king spent that sultry August in Messina, where breezes from the Straits relieved him. Then he returned to Palermo by sea with a splendid fleet of English and Maltese ships and two imposing galleys.

Arriving in Palermo September 2, 1714, he met with Count Annibale Maffei, whom he had chosen as Viceroy of Sicily. Disappointed that they would not have their own king as a resident of the island, his subjects resigned themselves to having his representative close at hand. The king then spent his last days in Palermo in the cathedral, praying before the relics of Saint Rosalie, listening to mass and taking communion. Before sunset on June 5, he boarded ship for Genoa. The craft set sail with the first gusts of a favorable wind.

### 3. The Inquisition Fills the Gap Left by the King

Count Annibale Maffei, remaining in Sicily as Vittorio Amedeo II's viceroy, had a difficult time of it. Conflicts with the Papacy became more and more bitter, especially after the king's departure, and would only subside in 1718. In the four year interim, however, Clement XI, reviving the politics of his medieval predecessors, would continue to launch excommunication attacks. For example, on February 20, 1715, brooking no delays, he ordered that the Apostolic Legation granting the privileged status of Sicilian kings for centuries be abolished. This act, perceived by Sicilians as having grave consequences, spurred experts in jurisprudence to respond. Most noteworthy among the rejoinders to the Papacy were, in this case, two dissertations in favor of constitutional monarchy: the *Historical Discourse cum Apologla pro Monarchy in Sicily* by Giambattista Caruso, the "Sicilian Muratori," and the *Discourse on the Ancient Rights of Sicilian Sovereigns* by Marquis Girolamo Settimo of Giarratana.

Vittorio Amedeo II sought European court personages of authority to mediate between him and the pope. He even appealed to the Roman Curia and consulted with cardinals who disapproved of the pontiff's actions. But the king's efforts were in vain. Clement XI would not budge. Consequently, the sovereign lost his patience and ordered his military council, that he had formed to defend the monarchy in Sicily "against the aggression of the Roman Court," to take necessary measures against all those on the island conforming to the pontiff's wishes. The king then issued his own edict declaring all papal bulls, excommunications and epistles "null and void, unjust, out of order, violent and illegal." At the same time, he commanded that anyone possessing papal documents must hand them over to the crown. Failure to comply would mean exile and the confiscation of all properties for offenders. Of course, in such a confrontation, certain people were unjustly punished. Many prelates were driven from their sees and parishes, most notably Monsignor Giuseppe Gasch, Archbishop of Palermo, who had warmly welcomed Vittorio Amedeo II upon his arrival in Sicily and coronated him in the cathedral.

A conspicuous figure during this period was the particularly hard-nosed official, Matteo Lo Vecchio, after whom a Palermitan street in the Albergheria quarter where he lived is named. In his *Diary,* Mongitore provides us with some details *in re* the life and death of Lo Vecchio. Apparently, on the evening of June 21, 1719, the official "was dispatched with two shots of a carabine while he was strolling in the Cassero . . . This spy by profession was the temporal power's executor with the duty of forcing the clergy to give communion to the excommunicated. He was famous for his infinite abuses against ecclesiastical immunity." Naturally, in making this judgment, Mongitore himself was not impartial, for he was a canon of the Metropolitanate and an official of the Inquisition's Tribunal of Sicily.

The year before, that is, in 1718, Vittorio Amedeo II, willy-nilly, had taken possession of Sardinia, remaining King of Sicily only in name. The governance of the island had, in effect, fallen to Emperor Charles VI of Austria. Consequently, many intellectuals had fled to Piedmont. Among them were the jurist Nicola Pensabene and the Messinese architect Filippo Juvara. The latter would construct the Piedmontese Basilica of Superga.

Thus, Sicily's *ancien regime* was restored, and peace was made with the Church. Canon Mongitore could gloat when, in his *Diary,* he quoted an anonymous epigram in which Vittorio Amedeo was reputed to have "an avid heart": *Cor eius est avidus.* Prelates returned from exile to Sicily; and the pyres of the Inquisition burned once again.

### 4. A Three-way Scuffle with the Island as Prize

The transition from Savoyard to Austrian rule was not painless for Sicily, especially since Spain tried to re-establish its hegemony on the island it had held for so long. From 1718 to 1720, a three-way war raged on land and at sea, causing untold casualties in major Sicilian cities. Palermo would be the special target of numerous bombardments.

The morning of July 1, 1718, Palermo awoke to find its sea lanes blocked by the Spanish navy. Madrid, determined to regain its old posses-

**33. The Savoiards besieged by the Spaniards.**

sion, had launched a fleet of 432 ships carrying 22,000 men and 5,000 horses. Gianfranco of Bette, Marquis of Lede, was in command.

The city, taken by surprise, had to surrender. The Savoyard viceroy himself, Count Annibale Maffei, gave the order to give up—although he stalled long enough to send troops into the hinterland that might mount a counter-offensive. Torn by uncertainty, the Palermo Senate conveyed a message to the Spanish forces, requesting an explanation for this sudden intervention. The Marquis of Lede replied haughtily, "King Phillip V's Armada has come to liberate his most loyal subjects of Sicily from the Savoyard Pharaoh's tyranny."

International reactions were prompt. London took into serious consideration an appeal sent there by Vittorio Amedeo II in which he inveighed against Spain for having violated the Treaty of Utrecht by invading Sicily. King George I himself entreated Spain to withdraw from the island. But Madrid's reply expressed nothing but disdain for international opinion.

England, stung to the quick and anxious to assert its status as a great power, proceeded to come to an agreement with Germany, France, and Piedmont, thus founding the so-called "Quadruple Alliance" that would be fatal for Spain. This league stipulated that Sicily, once wrested from the Spanish, would be ceded to the Viennese son of the devout Leopold I, Emperor Charles VI, who at the time was 33.

The English acted rapidly to impose the alliance's decision. On August 11, 1718, the British armada attacked the Spanish off the shores of Pachino. While Spain's fleet was trounced in a resounding imperial victory, bloody battles still raged in Sicily. On May 29, 1719, the "Alemanni" landed near Patti with 14,700 men and about 4,000 horses to crush the Spanish troops amassed there. The Austrians then took Taormina by storm and besieged Messina. Under heavy bombardment and without food supplies, the latter city surrendered to the imperial forces.

In spite of the peace treaty signed at the Hague, the Spanish prolonged hostilities. Then on May 2, 1720, Madrid's orders to evacuate Sicily reached the Marquis of Lede. Finally, after a protracted struggle, Charles VI could take possession of the island.

At first, Charles invested his royal powers in Sicily in his lieutenant and man-of-arms Count Claude Fleurismonde of Mercy. The count did not hesitate to use these powers while he awaited the arrival of the Duke of Monteleone, the designated viceroy of the emperor, who had been detained at Messina. Displaying his iron hand, Fleurismonde promulgated two edicts that weighed on the Sicilian people: the first obligated all imperial subjects on the island to adopt Neapolitan coinage, the value of which was superior to the royal standard of Savoy; the second required that all Sicilians' fire-arms and swords be confiscated.

The new viceroy entered Palermo perfunctorily at the end of September. The infirmities of old ages impeded him from parading on horseback. Instead, the Duke of Monteleone had to accept a carriage ride.

### 5. The Madonna of the Heretical King

Palermo acclaimed Emperor Charles VI as King of Sicily with festivities, public illuminations throughout the city, and a *Te Deum* sung in the cathedral. The Senate had two silver medals coined and a commemorative tablet carved in his honor. Once the celebration had ended, however, Sicilians returned to reality. At the first parliamentary session convened by Viceroy Monteleone, they became fully aware of their new master's greed. The viceroy not only imposed the customary donations to the imperial crown; he also ordered that a special gift of 600,000 scudos be made via collection from subjects of all social classes. This sum, Monteleone explained, would be used to subsidize the sovereign's transportation and maintenance of troops and to repair the military fortifications damaged during the war.

The Senate took the occasion to ask for special privileges from the king, but he was far away, at his Prague court, and did not even respond until 1723. Then, via dispatch, Charles VI reconfirmed Sicily's ancient

**34. A Spanish representative hands Sicily to Charles VI.**

charters, prerogatives and privileges. He also granted Sicilians' request to have a representative at the Court of Vienna, on the conditions that he not be a "feudal baron" and that he be acceptable to the viceroy.

During the Austrian vice-regency, the age-old problems with the Papacy were solved and the resources of Messina were well-developed. The death of the pope (Clement XI) who had launched the interdiction against Sicily facilitated the reconciliation that the Savoyard King Vittorio Amedeo II had sought in vain. A concordat signed in 1729 by Charles VI and Pope Benedict XIII recognized Sicily as Tribunal of the Monarchy. This agreement, called the Benedictine Concord, was celebrated by Sicilians with jubilation.

Realizing Messina's importance for commercial and maritime traffic between East and West, the Austrians acted to develop the City of the Straits accordingly. Charles VI ordered Monteleone's successor, Viceroy Portocarrero, to reside in Messina, thereby reinstating an ancient privilege of which the city was so proud. A second Austrian viceroy, the Count of Sastago, put a royal decree into effect making Messina a free port. This provision, called for by so many of the Messinese, allowed their long-neglected commerce to take off once again.

The Messinese's first enterprise at this point was the revival of the silk industry in which they had previously led Europe. But Vienna denied Messina's request for a monopoly in silk production. The Messinese tried to skirt this obstacle by setting up a commercial society similar to that of Holland's, which was also under Austrian jurisdiction. The Emperor, however, continued to impose constraints on this Messinese initiative.

Coinage and currency still posed a serious problem in all of Sicily. The monies circulating at the time were not sufficient, so the metal needed for new coins was sought on the island itself. But this new project was unsuccessful, especially when the small silver mine in Ali, near Messina, could no longer be exploited.

In spite of the Benedictine Concord, Sicilians considered their Austrian rulers and their representatives heretics. To counteract public opinion, Emperor Charles VI had a marble column erected in honor of the Madonna in Palermo's Piazza of Saint Dominic. The construction of this column took two years (1724-26). Then, on November 9, 1726, the statue of the Blessed Virgin was hoisted onto this structure. The column rose 114 hands' breadth in height, six less that had been foreseen in the original plan (judged to be too ambitious).

## 6. Charles VI Loses Sicily

The erection of the statue of the Blessed Virgin in Palermo was not the Austrians' only political gesture via which they tried to deny Sicilians' charges that the "*Alemanni* were heretics." As Gioacchino Di Marzo observed, the Austrian Empire in Sicily "built many new churches and monasteries—as if the Spanish had not constructed enough! Amid all the pomp and circumstance of religious ceremony, the people were thus duped by this show of faith—so that the Austrians could milk them and suck their blood." The usually diplomatic diarist Antonino Mongitore was also emphatic *in re* Austrian extravagance: "The *Alemanni* had a burning thirst for Sicilians' money that could not be slaked in spite of the enormous sums they drained from the populace."

Sicily's Austrian masters, in fact, demanded ordinary and "emergency" donations of its inhabitants that came out to double the tribute exacted by the Piedmontese. To overflow his coffers, the viceroy asked Sicily to subsidize 18,000 imperial soldiers (when, in fact, the real number on Sicilian soil was half of that total). Furthermore, he sold titles of nobility to the first buyers and took bribes for exemption from the military service he himself had made obligatory. Under the Austrians, the tax on the milling of grain was also introduced. After five years, this hated tax was doubled.

Inquisition tribunals continued to flourish in this period. *Autos da fé* were held in Palermo in 1724, 1731 and 1733. Perhaps the most famous trial is that of April 6, 1724, described in minute detail by Antonino Mongitore. During this tribunal, two Caltanissettans, the nun Geltruda Maria Cordovana and the mendicant friar Romualdo of Sant'Agostino were condemned as "errant and formal heretics, not to speak of obstinate impenitents," handed over to the secular authorities, and "burned alive" on Palermo's Saint Erasmus Square where Villa Giulia was later erected.

The inquisitorial tribunal of October 2, 1731, is also worth recalling. In the absence of the accused, the Capuchin Michele Rappino from Spaccaforno (known as Friar Illuminato), a statue of him, previously declared unholy, was put on trial and condemned to burn at the stake. The Capuchin himself had managed to escape from the Holy Office's dungeon in Palermo. He was perhaps the only person to do so in the history of the Inquisition in Sicily.

During the Austrian vice-regency, earthquakes struck Sicily in the provinces of Trapani, Messina and Palermo. The worst of these quakes, described methodically by Mongitore, hit Palermo on September 1, 1726. Houses collapsed by the hundreds in Piazza Marina, in the Papireto District and along the Old Cassaro. Two hundred and fifty people were killed and about 150 were injured.

Sicily's worst seismic shock of all, however, turned out to be the political turmoil that resulted in Emperor Charles VI's loss of the island. The November 9, 1729 accord endorsed in Seville by Spain, France and England (and shortly thereafter supported by Holland) demanded the expulsion of Austria from Sicily. Charles VI attempted to stall for time by courting the favor of the great European powers. But by 1733, when another war of succession broke out in Poland, he could not stem the tides of opposition to his control of the island. The Austrians' inability to defend their outposts and garrisons in southern Italy opened the floodgates through which the Bourbons rushed to take possession of Sicily. As one chronicle narrated, "However great the confusion of the imperial *Alemanni* was, the Palermitans' jubilation was all the more immense, for they saw the day of reckoning at hand when they would be liberated from the Pharaoh's tyranny."

# Chapter XI: Madrid's Revindication

## 1. The Spanish Return

Toward the end of 1733, bad news arrived from the North for the *Alemanni* occupying Sicily. Austrian officials returning to Palermo after their leaves reported that the French and the Savoyards had formed an alliance and conquered Milan. In retaliation, the viceroy had two French ships docked in the port seized. Still in dismay, however, the viceroy consulted with his equally confused general-at-arms to mount an adequate defense of the capital. The only solution they could devise at first was to have trees cut down along the roads of Saint Francis of Paola and Monreale and used as timber fortifications for the viceroy's castle.

In this emergency, the Count of Sastago resorted to his normal fiscal policies. By decree, he imposed military service on barons and large land-owners and asked all his subjects to "bite the bullet" of new taxes. When the viceroy eyed the artisans of the city as a possible source of funds, however, the mayor intervened, explaining that these craftsmen were already reduced to virtual pauperism. As an alternative, a poll-tax was collected from all the French, Savoyards and Piedmontese still living on the island. Thus the forts of Palermo, Messina and Trapani could be refurbished with munitions.

All these precautions and measures were taken in vain. The second son of King Phillip, Infante Charles of Bourbon (soon to be Charles III) had already set sail from La Spezia with an imposing fleet and army and was on his way to take possession of the Kingdom of Naples. Consequently, in April of 1734, the viceroy sent a contingent of troops from Palermo to Messina and Manfredonia (Apulia). On April 30, after being notified that the Spaniards had reached Naples, the viceroy himself headed for the City of the Straits.

Naples surrendered on May 10, and Charles of Bourbon made a triumphal entrance into the city where he was greeted wildly by the people. Five days later a courier from Madrid brought Charles the royal parchment in which his father Phillip V declared him King of the Two Sicilies. As the *Alemanni* were hastening to retreat from Sicilian cities and fortresses, the Spanish swept in to take possession of the island.

One evening toward the end of August, 1734, a grand Spanish armada consisting of 300 tartans, five galleys and five ships of the line entered Palermo's waters. This 28th of August was the birthday of Elisabeth Christine of Brunswick, the wife of Charles VI of Austria. To celebrate this festive occasion, the nobles were parading in their carriages around the port.

**35. An engraving by A. Bova of the Quattro canti (Four Corners) in Palermo. Porta Nuova is visible on the left, Porta Macqueda on the right.**

Accompanying them was General Roma, who had been left in charge of Sicily when the Austrian viceroy departed. Suddenly, as the sound of merry motets filled the air in honor of the empress, the general descended from the Prince of Cattolica's carriage and rushed from the port with the other horse-drawn vehicles. He had been informed that Spanish ships were blocking Palermo's sea lanes and, therefore, he considered it prudent to pack his bags and head for Syracuse.

The Spanish actually landed the afternoon of August 29, at Solanto. Antonino Mongitore reported at that moment: "Palermitans were joyful in the extreme. As the Spanish fleet skirted the bay, citizens of all classes flocked to the port and climbed atop houses, palaces, convents and monasteries just to get a glimpse of the ships. After dinner, most of the nobles made their way to Solanto to pay homage to the Spaniards' general, Count of Montemar, and his commandants, greeting them as if they were old, long-awaited friends."

It appeared that Sicilians were anxious to bow once again under what Di Blasi called "the sweet yoke of the Spanish." The islanders had always longed for their very own king. Now, they thought, their dream would be realized. Disillusionment, however, was near at hand.

## 2. Charles III Reaches the Island

That 31st of August in 1734, when Spain entered Palermo, Sicilians proceeded in the customary ways seen in the past. Two envoys sent by the

Palermo Senate to Viceroy Designate and General, Count of Montemar, announced that the city was ready to receive the Spanish armada and asked only that it enter respecting those conditions established by Phillip V in 1718 under similar circumstances.

That same day, the first companies of Spanish soldiers landed, and marched to the Royal Palace to occupy it. The bulk of the army arrived later wielding banners and beating drums. Another 8,000 men, who had disembarked at Solanto, crossed Saint Erasmus Plain and reached the city via Saint Antonino Way. The troops then set up camp in the Malaspina District. General Montemar was hosted by the Duke of Sperlinga in his sumptuous country villa.

The Spanish were careful to stay out of cannon-range of the Castle-by-the-Sea where the Austrians were still barricaded. The imperial forces did unleash a steady artillery attack, but their cannon-balls did no damage to the opposing forces or to the population. Only the nuns of the nearby Monastery of Valverde thought it best to evacuate. These bombardments continued until September 12, the day the Austrians surrendered unconditionally.

On September 7, Messina had already fallen to the Spaniards, and the Count of Montemar had gone there himself to size up the situation. The next year, Charles III, on his triumphal march across Sicily, destination Palermo, would stop in the City of the Straits on the first leg of his journey.

Leaving Naples toward the end of February, 1735, Charles III reached Messina on March 9. For reasons of security, he lodged outside the city in the Monastery of the Most Holy Savior. This monastery, run by Basilian Fathers, was a good distance from the citadel where the Austrians, having capitulated, still were armed. Even in defeat, the imperial troops, leaving the fortress they had tenaciously defended, would march proudly with their unfurled banners, rattling drums, cannons and mortars down to the port where they embarked.

Once the Austrian forces had set sail, Charles III decided to visit the citadel. What he found was a veritable mine of munitions. One hundred and nine cannons were lined up along the walls, and there were enough cannon-balls for the longest of sieges.

The monarch spent most of March and April at Messina, receiving nobles, holding meetings with the authorities and bestowing honors. Then, in May, he decided to head for Palermo, where glorious festivities were being prepared to welcome the king. His first act, upon arrival in the capital, was to order that his rooms and halls in the Royal Palace be redecorated. The Royal Gallery was then reorganized, of course with paintings of the king put in the most prominent places. He also had the courtyard extended

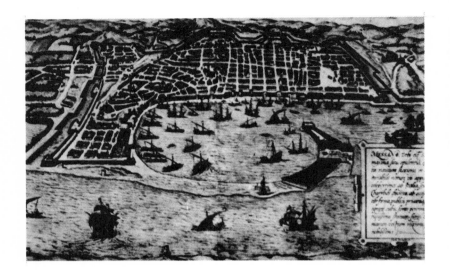

**36. A 17th Century map of Messina.**

so that he could climb to his own apartments directly upon descending from his carriage. Finally, the piazza in front of the palace was redone in the grand style befitting a monarch.

May 16, the day of his departure from Messina in the company of two galleys, Charles III had been detained by unfavorable winds. Therefore, he spent the night at the lighthouse. The next day, he set out again and reached Palermo in 23 hours. Landing toward evening, the king was met by the mayor in his carriage and escorted to the Jesuits' Quinta Casa where he slept. On May 18, he made his private entrance into Palermo.

### 3. The Coronation in Palermo

Charles III entered Palermo May 19, 1735, and was coronated in the cathedral on July 3. The month and a half preceding the ceremony were lived by the Palermitans as an extraordinary collective euphoria. Sicilians saw the arrival of the sovereign as a real turning point after which they would finally have their own king. As Niccolò Palmeri wrote in his *Summary of the History of Sicily,* "Sicilian monarchy seemed to be resurrected in the substance and contours of Roger I."

Antonino Mongitore, in his meticulous fashion, described the "advent" of Charles III from his arrival in Sicily to his coronation. I quote from the 40 page paean to the king that is contained in Mongitore's *Diary:* "Great was the jubilation of the whole island over the good fortune of having happened upon such a lovable king; but greater still was the joy of Palermitans for the pleasure of seeing him receive the Royal Crown within their own walls. The Austrian yoke had, in truth, been unbearable, not due to the August Charles VI, a pious and clement prince resplendent with virtues, but because of his ministers who drove the kingdom to the brink of perdition."

Landing at the Garita, where "a splendid bridge" had been constructed in his honor, Charles III proceeded in a stately carriage, followed by those of the authorities and the nobles. "He then proceeded up the Cassero where hosts of artisans and the populace hailed him." It was there that he heard the initial acclamations of "Long Live King Charles III." His first stop was the city jail of the Vicaria, where he was presented with the keys of the prison on a silver platter. The king immediately entrusted these keys to his captain and granted pardon to 24 prisoners, who joined the procession.

Once he had reached the threshold of the cathedral, the sovereign was received by the archbishop, who solemnly kissed his hand. Then hearing the *Te Deum*, Charles ascended to the throne erected for the occasion—only to fall to his knees in prayer. After praying, he tarried with authorities and dignitaries in Saint Rosalie's Chapel before returning to the Royal Palace.

In front of the palace he was to find the working classes "lined up in well-formed ranks" as if they were an army. In the absence of the Spanish troops that were still besieging the last of the Austrians in Syracuse, Charles had consented to this formation symbolic of the army's substitution by the populace. Such a gesture of trust was deeply appreciated by all the Sicilian people.

Charles III passed the next few weeks hunting on the Duke of Oneto's estate, giving audiences, accepting homages and visiting monasteries. The Monastery of the Immaculate Conception gave him "a carriage decorated in silver filigree with numerous ivory statuettes and coral ornaments," which the king sent post-haste to his mother in Madrid. In the Monastery of the Pietà, Charles tarried with the abbess and "even longer with the nuns who had written to him when he was in Naples, offering to form a regiment of cuirassiers in his service."

On June 11, the statue of Charles's father Phillip V, that had been removed by the Austrians, was re-erected at Customs Gate. At the same time, the statues of Charles VI and his empress were taken down from the column of the Blessed Virgin in Piazza Saint Dominic.

Charles made a ceremonious return to Palermo on June 30, swearing to respect the charters and privileges of the kingdom. Then, on July 3, he was coronated officially in the cathedral. In the offertory, Charles III kneeled before the archbishop and made a donation of gold coins stamped with his effigy. Such was the happy beginning of what turned out to be another disillusioning vice-regency for Sicily when, like other sovereigns before him, Charles III would leave the island's governance to one of his representatives and reside elsewhere, in this case, Naples.

### 4. Jubilation Over the New King

A marble sculpture still extant in front of Palermo Cathedral commemorates Charles III's July 3, 1735 coronation. Born in Madrid on January 20, 1716, Charles III of Bourbon was only 19 at the time. According to Harold Acton's description, Charles was slight, even lean, and stooped, but he was attractive and charming for the open and courteous manner he had with his subjects.

Actually, Charles spent only five days in Sicily as its king-in-residence before moving permanently to Naples, where he had decided to set up his court. During that short sojourn, however, he did make many public appearances and return to the cathedral to pay homage to St. Rosalie and donate to Palermo's patron saint a jewel worth 4,000 scudos. He also received the Maltese Ambassador, who brought Charles a falcon as the traditional tribute the Knights of Malta owed to the Kingdom of Sicily.

**37. Amphitheater built in celebration of a royal wedding. The "games" pitted a lion against a horse.**

Charles left Palermo on July 8, one day later than he had planned, because of unfavorable winds. Since his royal coaches were already on board his fleet, he rode to the port in the Prince of Cattolica's six-horse carriage. As he set foot on the ship that was to take him to Naples, cannons roared from the castle and the bulwarks in a grand salute. As Giovanni Evangelista wrote, "this was a day of mourning for Palermitans. All our citizens regretted the loss of their adorable prince, who had stayed within the walls of their country for about 50 days, endeared himself to each and every one for his tenderness, and demonstrated a particular affection for these subjects of his. Sicilians, overflowing with his infinite beneficence, were, therefore, in agony for being unable to convince him to stay forever and for returning once again to the unhappy state of a province."

Leaving Sicily to its grief, Charles, four days after arriving at his new court, enflamed Naples with immense joy. In the *Description of the Festivities Held by the Most Loyal City of Naples for the Glorious Return of his Holy Majesty Charles of Bourbon from his Sicilian Enterprise* published in November of 1735, the anonymous author bears witness to Neapolitans' trepidation in the face of Charles's journey to Sicily: "Oh, how we were afflicted by the rumors that our king would stay away all autumn and take up his fixed abode in the truly happy city of Palermo." But, by returning definitively to Naples, Charles dispelled its citizens' doubts.

Thus, to Sicily, even though it was a kingdom in and of itself, the role of province befell. Palermo was once again the seat of a viceroy.

The island, however, did reap some benefits from Bourbon rule. Learning from the experience of the Councils of Italy instituted by Phillip II to govern his distant territories more effectively, Charles III set up the Council of Sicily. Under Viceroy Bartolomeo Corsini—a member of the noble Florentine family to which the pope (Clement XII) elected in 1730 belonged—the barons of the Sicilian Parliament were, in consequence, able to elect their own President of the Council. Their choice was the Marquis of Geraci, Giovanni Ventimiglia.

The beginning of Viceroy Corsini's term, one characterized by Charles III's enlightened way of governing, coincided with the news of the king's marriage to the 15 year old daughter of Frederick August III of Poland and Saxony, Amalia of Walpurgis. In Palermitan Chancellor Don Pietro La Placa's magnificent *Account of the Ceremonies,* the city's celebration of this wedding-in-absentia is described in all its splendor. For the occasion, Palermo erected a majestic amphitheater in the Piazza of the Royal Palace for a battle between a lioness and a knight on horseback. When the lioness failed to fight with proper ferocity, both she and her opponent were substituted by bulls and matadors. The bullfights lasted well into the night.

## 5. Closer to Sicilians

Charles III had the extraordinary fortune to be sovereign of Sicily and Naples for 24 years, from 1734 till 1759, and to become King of Spain thereafter. Furthermore, he was able to rule Spain until his death in December of 1788, at the age of 72. All in all, his reign was a long one—more than half a century counting his time in Naples and Madrid.

A comment Charles made when he once exonerated Sicilians from paying an unjust tribute is indicative of his approach to them: "I want this realm to flourish again ... Besides, I want to save my soul and, at any cost, go to Heaven." Charles III did, in fact, treat Sicilians with magnanimity. For instance, unscrupulous courtiers suggested that the king have brought to Naples the two splendid Greek rams housed in Palermo's Royal Palace. But when these precious bronzes arrived at his court, the king ordered that they be returned to Palermo because, as he explained, he had not gone to Sicily "to despoil it of its beauties, but to allow it to make the most of its prizes and merits."

This son of Phillip V and Elisabeth Farnese clearly displayed in Naples his fine sense of royal dignity. Charles had beautification and reconstruction works completed throughout his realm. Notably, in Naples itself, he commissioned the San Carlo Opera House, one of the grandest in Europe. He also had royal palaces built in Portici, Capodimonte and Caserta, initiated the excavations at Pompei, oversaw the construction of Capodimonte's majolica factory, and committed himself to the enormous project of urban renewal realized along the Bay of Naples as far as Margellina.

Charles III's one great public works design completed in Palermo was the Hostel of the Poor. Started in 1746, this edifice was modelled after Naples's immense Royal Hostel of the Poor commissioned by Charles to the architect Fuga. The works for the hostel in Palermo, a large building with two courtyards that is still found on Calatafimi Boulevard, were financed via appropriations from the revenues of the See of Monreale. The Hostel was finished only in 1772, when Charles had already been in Madrid for thirteen years. In spite of the delays in construction, the building was opened on August 8th to the city's poor immediately upon its completion. The dedication of this public service structure was so grand that it earned mention in Prince Gabriele Lancillotto of Torremuzza's *Account.*

More important than his monuments left in Sicily, Charles's actions spoke to Sicilians. Via the Council of Sicily, presided over by a Sicilian with two jurists from Sicily and two from Naples as standing members, Charles, from his court, was able to consult with representatives of the island and often act in its interests. For instance, in 1741, the Sicilian Parliament was able to change its official language from Spanish to Italian. Two years later, during a plague epidemic in Messina, the king, heeding the Council, oversaw the sanitation campaign to control the dread disease with such efficiency and foresight that he earned the praises of L. A. Muratori.

During Charles III's reign, other achievements were outstanding: the serious reduction of brigandage, a thorough census, the selection of Sicilians as abbots and bishops, the limitations imposed on the Inquisition, and a "delegation" to shelter and assist abandoned children. Furthermore, many of Charles's reforms were applied equally in the Two Sicilies with the intention of developing a coherent policy to govern the two realms fairly.

## 6. Charles III Returns to Spain

In the 24 years he spent in Italy, Charles III governed Naples and Sicily with the added advantage of international recognition that not only granted stability to his realm but also spurred him on as an enlightened and dynamic monarch. The first endorsement of Charles as ruler of the Two Sicilies came on November 18, 1738, with the Treaty of Vienna. The second was the Peace of Aquisgrana signed on October 18, 1748, after the Austrian War of Succession (1740-48) following the death of Emperor Charles VI—an international pact which fully respected the Bourbon king's frontiers.

It is interesting to look at Charles's economic policies as well, especially as they related to the control of currency and ecclesiastical and foreign policy. Charles's most important economic reforms are embodied in his institution of the Supreme Magistrate of Commerce, the Grain Council, and the Council Against Contraband. Via appropriate judicial bodies, these organisms were committed to promoting commerce and the production of special crops like olives and mulberries, to combatting corruption in the grain industry, and to eliminating contraband (especially that of tobacco, the one most common in Sicily).

Precisely to encourage commerce in his realm, Charles III tried to attract Jewish merchants. The Jews, however, once driven out of Sicily in 1492 on the orders of Ferdinand the Catholic, were not drawn back in large numbers—in spite of Charles's concerted efforts in 1740 to welcome them in both Naples and Sicily. Besides, those few Jews that did come to Sicily and the slightly higher number that came to Naples were targeted and harassed by merchants and clergymen. These Christians were especially indignant that Charles had granted Jews free circulation without requiring them to display any identifying emblems or marks. Pressured by business and religious interests, Charles yielded in 1746, revoking the special measures that had opened his kingdom to Jews.

Charles was able to enforce his protectionist economic policies in Sicily, above all *in re* Messina's ancient pride, the silk industry. The king also imposed a ban on the export of gold and silver in the form of coins or ingots, succeeded in regularizing the circulation of currency with rigorous standards regarding the quality of the alloys, and established the equal value of Naples's and Sicily's coinage.

Meek in spirit and desirous of living in peace with the Church, Charles III adopted a policy toward the Holy See that was a veritable "waving of the olive branch." The king requested and obtained papal investiture for his reign, submitted to the custom of kneeling before the pope, and reaffirmed the Benedictine Concord dictating the nature of the relationship between the Papacy and the Bourbon Court.

Charles did not make any autonomous decisions *in re* foreign policy until his father Phillip V died in 1746. He did succeed before that date, however, in signing commercial treaties favorable to Spain with Port Ottoman in 1740 and with Tripoli in 1741.

When his brother Ferdinand VI died in 1759, Charles was summoned to Madrid and ascended the throne of Spain. Given new hostilities breaking out in Europe, he was forced to entrust his Kingdom of the Two Sicilies to his third son Ferdinand, only eight at the time. The latter became Ferdinand IV of Naples and Ferdinand III of Sicily.

# Chapter XII: The Viceroys and the People

## 1. The Revolt of Palermo

When Charles III ascended the throne of Spain in 1759, leaving the Kingdom of the Two Sicilies to his son Ferdinand, the Marquis Giovanni Fogliani of Aragon, who had served as Charles's Prime Minister in Naples, was already the Viceroy of Sicily. Respecting his father's wishes, Ferdinand reconfirmed Fogliani as head of the vice-regency. But, while the marquis was able to charm many Sicilians, his charisma did not suffice to root out a broad-based discontent in the populace. Thus, in the popular uprising of 1773, Fogliani was expelled from Palermo.

It was the Marquis Fogliani who promoted the foundation of a public library in Palermo by convincing the patricians to donate parts of their private collections. Once the Jesuits had been invited to leave Sicily in 1776—as they had been in Naples and Spain—buildings previously occupied by them in Casaprofessa were assigned for the senatorial library. The viceroy also repopulated Ustica, that had for so long been only a pirates' cove. The island, however, unprotected and unfortified, once again fell prey to Algerian pirates, who captured and enslaved 42 people.

In spite of being courted and backed by the aristocracy, Fogliani lost their support when he was forced to raise taxes on luxury and staple consumer items in order to compensate for "inflation" and grain shortages. But after the good harvest of 1765, social tensions were relieved, and Fogliani resumed "making Palermitans rejoice by allowing Carnival celebrations with his subjects all decked out in traditional masks." Fogliani brought this festive climate to its peak when, in 1768, he organized grand fêtes in honor of the marriage of Ferdinand and Maria Carolina. For this occasion, in the Piazza of the Royal Palace, "a giant and sumptuous cornucopia in the Neapolitan style" was arranged, out of which poured food for the taking of the first comers and even live animals like wethers, goats and sheep. To add to such public entertainment, the viceroy also organized bullfights in Piazza Saint Honofrius and a raffle in Piazza Bologna.

But the bad harvest of 1773 led to widespread disturbances. Rich and poor started to scapegoat each other, and the atmosphere was charged with mystical furor. "Penitents" held processions in the streets, wearing crowns of thorns and flagellating themselves. Anxiety and hardship were united in the populace. To make matters worse for the viceroy, he was unjustly blamed for a regrettable incident. When a Palermitan noble fell ill, suffering from kidney stones, Fogliani advised him to be operated upon by a famous surgeon who had just arrived from France. Unfortunately, this operation turned out to be fatal for the patient.

Consequently, Palermo witnessed a crisis. A young man by the name of Francesco Maurigi took to the streets, dashing up the Cassero with a loaf of bread hoisted on a canestalk and shouting "People of Palermo, rise up now! We want bread, real white bread!" As he proceeded, a crowd joined him and headed for the Royal Palace. Disarming a palace guard, the throng raised their "standard" on a rifle. Things quickly went from bad to worse. Allegedly, the riots were further instigated by conspirators. Whatever the case, a group of insurgents went on a rampage, breaking into prisons and burning police records. From his horse, one Giuseppe Pozzo, nicknamed Nasca, began to chant, "Down with Fogliani! Long live the king!" Then another angry mob streamed toward the Royal Palace. Taking possession of some cannons, the crowd aimed them at the viceroy's residence.

## 2. Fogliani Driven Out

The expulsion of Viceroy Giovanni Fogliani from Palermo on September 20, 1773, was the result of a rapid succession of dramatic events. The rebels, armed with rifles and cannons, easily reached the Royal Palace where the viceroy was residing. Guarding the gates, halberdiers, backed by two regiments, were able to hold off the mob. But, from within the palace, no resistance was mustered. In fact, the viceroy's officials and soldiers opened the doors of the palace and allowed themselves to be disarmed. Allegedly, they were acting on the orders of Fogliani, who wanted to avoid any conflict.

The insurgents, thus, had free access to the palace. Flushing out Fogliani, who had withdrawn to the chapel to seek comfort from his confessor, they gave him an alternative: pay with his life for any resistance or leave the city immediately. Post-haste, Fogliani chose the former solution and had his carriage prepared. The people then summoned a man they trusted, the Archbishop Monsignor Serafino Filangeri, to escort the viceroy. Fogliani, before departing, turned to the crowd and said, "here I am, at your service. What have I ever done to you?" The rebels responded by virtually pushing him down the stairs and out the door.

Once the coachman had pulled out of the palace with Fogliani and the archbishop on board, the carriage was blocked by a mob at New Gate, preventing it from using that road to the port and insisting that the viceroy proceed on the Cassero route, as he had done for 18 years. Up and down this boulevard where he had always been greeted with deference, the marquis was mocked and insulted. When the carriage reached Felice Gate, the horses were untied. Walking the rest of the way to the harbor, the viceroy had to be content with a dingy that took him out to "a small Catalan ship flying a French flag." Without provisions, the captain decided to set sail notwithstanding to save Giovanni Fogliani from further outrages.

The tumultuous crowd then escorted Archbishop Filangeri back to his palace. But the people would not let him retire after this trying day, for they demanded that the prelate take Fogliani's place. On the spot, in fact, the mob started to pull the carriage toward the Royal Palace. Only when the archbishop clambered down and pushed his way through the crowd into one of the rooms of the palace was he able to free himself.

The riots continued through the night. Fogliani's friends were flushed out and punished. The house of Baron Lo Guasto was looted, and all his household effects went up in a bonfire in Piazza Ballarò. As the rebels were about to enter Prince Comitini's palace, he used all his wits to divert them. Inventing the story that Fogliani had snuck back into Palermo and was hiding in the Quinta Casa (once of the Jesuits), the prince managed to dispatch his would-be aggressors toward the dock.

Disturbances broke out in Palermo province as well. Emulating the Palermitans, the Monrealese drove out their governor, the Prince of San Vincenzo. Uprisings ensued in Montelepre, Giardinello, Partinico, Palazzo Adriano, Carini and Parco. The capital itself feared new riots. Rumor had it that "when a rocket went off in Piazza Vigliena, it would be the signal for the common people to revolt," that the Public Bank and Monte della Pietà would be robbed, and that ministers and nobles would face the firing squad.

The authorities finally responded decisively. The reputed instigators of the riot—two youths of 17 and 24 and an elderly man of 70—were tried summarily, condemned to death, then strangled and mutilated in jail. The pieces were displayed at the Four Corners. Although there was no evidence to convict them, these men were used, as so many others had been in the past, as terrifying examples of what happened to rebels.

### 3. The Worker Classes' "Coup"

After the expulsion of Fogliani from Palermo, the reins of government were seized rapidly by the authorities. But, pending orders from the Court of Naples, the state of affairs was uncertain.

Provisionally, awaiting directives from Ferdinando IV's Minister Bernardo Tanucci, Archbishop Serafino Filangeri—"the people's choice" during the revolt—exercised the powers usually vested in the viceroy. Later, Tanucci, conveying the king's disapproval of Fogliani's conduct as viceroy, brought orders from the sovereign that "the uncalled-for interruption of the governance of the population be remedied." Herein, it was not clear if the court of Naples planned to replace the governing officials of the capital or those of all of Sicily, or if the king was admonishing Palermitans or each and every Sicilian. To confuse matters even more, Ferdinand's response had arrived four days after Fogliani had received a warm welcome in Messina (on September 30)—in a reception to be expected given the ancient rivalry between Palermo and Messina.

Before following this narrative thread, however, we would do well to understand more fully the reasons for the expulsion of Fogliani from Palermo. In apparent conflict with popular feeling, chroniclers of the times did not tire of writing of the viceroy's generous soul and the insane behavior of the mob. The usually moderate Di Blasi had this to say of the common people who drove out the viceroy: "the lower born is an animal who becomes, the more you pet it, all the more audacious and insolent." The only fault Di Blasi found with Fogliani was that the viceroy trusted too much in his confidants and advisors and did not listen to "those honest citizens who were telling him the truth."

Another chronicler, the Marquis of Villabianca, extolled the virtues of Fogliani for his generous treatment of the poor. The marquis's one reservation regarding Fogliani was that "the viceroy tried to be mayor, senator, rector and deputy all at once." Such a desire to concentrate all powers of the realm in his person alone, according to Villabianca, led Fogliani to surround himself with flatterers, "greedy, ambitious, overweaningly proud, unjust individuals striving to exploit him in their own interests and showing unadulterated indifference to accusations and complaints and rumblings against their abuses of power." In the long run, however, Villabianca had nothing but pity and compassion for the viceroy, "expelled by the most cowardly, miserable and iniquitous rabble of this metropolis."

The chroniclers' heated apologies, unfortunately, do not tell us much. Today, historians prefer to explain the September 20, 1773 rebellion against the viceroy as a sign of the evolution of Sicilian society. While Sicilians, according to contemporary interpretations, were still suspended between the old and the new, their major tendency was toward reform. Furthermore, the growing intolerance of bad government, incarnate in the viceroy in charge, was a barometer of the progressive mood of the times. The above is the thesis of Salvatore Francesco Romano, who, taking into account an eighteenth century chronicler's estimate that 30,000 armed men participated in the revolt driving Fogliani from the Royal Palace to the port, adds that the "mob" could not have consisted of many "human dregs." Romano notes further that, among those thousands of people were the honest working masses, the real protagonists of the insurrection.

The worker classes, in fact, represented a major force in the 1700s vis-à-vis their organization of various popular demonstrations and religious processions to stake their claims. In all likelihood it was their organized strength that gave impetus to the expulsion of the viceroy and to the action of the crowd rushing toward the Royal Palace. It has been verified that these artisans and workers also quieted the mob in the aftermath of the revolt.

This restoring of social order was achieved after Archbishop Filangeri issued a pardon for the rebels. When Filangeri assumed the responsibilities-in-absentia of the viceroy, the worker classes served as Royal Palace guards in still troubled times. Their role, both reformist and peace-making, is evident in every step they took.

## 4. The New Colonna Lampooned

The scroll beneath Fogliani's portrait in the Hall of the Viceroys in the Royal Palace—today the seat of the Regional Sicilian Assembly—indicates that the marquis's term came to an end in 1774, the year after he was expelled from Palermo. Entering Messina triumphantly, Fogliani did in fact remain there as Viceroy of Sicily till his term expired. At the beginning of 1774 he was even hatching plans to return to Palermo. But the Court of Naples and Minister Tanucci himself, not a great admirer of Fogliani's, thwarted such a design.

Madrid had charged Fogliani to convene an ordinary session of the Parliament in that year. The king's ambiguous orders, however, stipulated that its three branches meet neither in Palermo nor in Messina, but in Cefalù "so that the competition between our two greatest sister cities be diminished." Once Fogliani had discharged his duty, at the end of the session, a letter from Minister Tanucci was handed to him. The missive said briefly that "the sovereign, to unburden his loyal servant, had decided to select a new viceroy." In effect, Fogliani was fired!

This man who had governed Sicily for 18 years then presented himself at the Court of Naples. But he was *persona non grata* there, so he proceeded to Spain. Charles III, however, received him coldly. Discouraged, he returned to his castle in Valdemozzola, near Parma, to live out his life in oblivion.

In the interim between two vice-regencies, Archbishop Filangeri was elected Presider over the Realm. He held this position until the new viceroy, Marco Antonio Colonna Stigliano, namesake of one of the viceroys of the sixteenth century, arrived. The archbishop had neither time nor authority to have much influence in the affairs of state. He did promulgate one decree to "validate the sanctification of festivals" and another to prohibit the "scandalous proceedings" on the Day of the Dead when, traditionally, Palermitans had celebrated by "selling sugar and flour shapes of skeletons, bones, skulls, corpses and other outrageous blasphemies."

The new viceroy reached Palermo on October 24, 1774. He was 55 years of age and was married with three children. Slightly more than one year after they had ousted Giovanni Fogliani, the Palermitans jubilantly welcomed the king's representative. Since the cathedral was under a reconstruction to be completed only at the beginning of the nineteenth century, the traditional religious ceremony of investiture took place in the Church of Saint Joseph. Military parades and festivities lasted for three days. Men of letters, with the usual wheedling and bombast, tried their hand at honoring the viceroy in verse and prose. Nine of these compositions are preserved in Villabianca's *Diary*. But a more popular version of Colonna's "advent" was an anonymous lampoon circulated all over Palermo in which the viceroy was portrayed as a "schmuck."

The year following Colonna's arrival, on February 13, 1775, the worker classes of Palermo sent a petition to Ferdinand requesting "that his majesty honor our city with his presence in conformity with the 1735 practice of the august Catholic king his father." To make this request more compelling, they promised to hand over all the cannons from the bulwarks and city forts to the king. A few days later, in preparation for the sovereign's visit, the viceroy issued a constraining order on the circulation of carriages along the major arteries of Palermo.

Marco Antonio Colonna served officially until 1781. His last three years, however, he did so in absentia because his own poor health and problems related to the death of his father forced him to move his family to Naples. When Colonna's term ended, Caracciolo took his place in Palermo.

### 5. A Diplomat From a Far Away Place

Domenico Caracciolo, Marquis of Villamaina and Capriglia, landed at Palermo the morning of October 15, 1781. Actually, in May of the previous year, this Sicilian noble from Sambuca, then Prime Minister at Naples, had been designated for the viceregency of his homeland by Ferdinand. Not pleased with his assignment, he had tried to contest it for one and a half years. An unwilling governor who served as viceroy for a relatively short time, Domenico Caracciolo nevertheless would win the only major political victory of his career on the island: the abolition of the Inquisition.

The royal dispatch announcing Caracciolo's selection as Viceroy of Sicily reached him while he was in Paris as Bourbon Ambassador to France. Born in Malpartida de la Serena, Spain, on October 2, 1715, this son of a lieutenant colonel in Phillip V's army was already advanced in years (almost 65 to be exact). Educated in Naples at a boarding-school bearing his family's name, Caracciolo had excelled in poetry, music and mathematics in his youth. After graduating, he served as Judge of the Vicariate.

Then, in 1752, at the age of 37, the marquis who, according to Benedetto Croce, "could not stand Neapolitan society," took up the career of diplomat. His first regular post was in Paris. Subsequently, he was a special envoy to Turin, where he stayed for ten years (1754-1764) before moving on to London. Enjoying the English court until 1771, he was then transferred back to Paris. While he was still there as Ambassador to France, Ferdinand, in 1780, nominated him as Viceroy of Sicily—a position he would hold until 1786. When he himself resigned in that year, a January 6 royal dispatch designated him as Prime Minister of the Kingdom of the Two Sicilies. Caracciolo performed this duty until his death at 74, on July 16, 1789.

Serving as a diplomat for 30 years, Caracciolo was not deeply involved in major political struggles. But as a keen observer and man of intelligence, he was able to leave an important testimony of his times, their prime movers and vicissitudes in an epistolary correspondence that he maintained with characteristic intensity and vitality during his entire life as a public servant. For instance, from Turin, Caracciolo sent detailed letters to Bernardo Tanucci, explaining how enlightened Piedmontese laws might work in Naples. From London—where he made the acquaintance of the great Italian dramatist Vittorio Alfieri—he described how commerce could function to the detriment of politics.

Paris, however, was Caracciolo's real passion for that city's intense pace of life and rich and refined emotional experiences. During those ten years spent in the French capital, he cultivated many friendships with major cultural figures and frequented the most important literary salons. Most notable among these centers of culture was the salon of Madame d'Epinay, where Caracciolo shone for his verve, knowledge and spirit. He also maintained correspondences with the Encyclopedists D'Alembert and Diderot. Thus one can imagine his vexation when he was assigned to Sicily, a land this anti-clerical marquis himself defined as the "last ditch of Christianity." Openly intolerant of that Neapolitan ambience he saw dominated "by the arts of ecclesiastical charlatans," Caracciolo made it clear that he bore ill-feeling toward Sicilians as well.

Before Caracciolo left Paris, Louis XVI tried to console him by assuring that he was on his way to "one of the most beautiful spots in Europe." The marquis replied, "Sire, the most beautiful spot in Europe is the one I am leaving. It is here, in Place Vendôme!" Caracciolo reached Naples on June 6, but tarried the entire summer before sailing for Palermo.

## 6. Caracciolo and the Inquisition

Arriving at Palermo inconspicuously on that Sunday evening of October 14, 1781, the new viceroy waited a day on his warship manned by

60 cannons before receiving the authorities there. On October 17, since the cathedral was undergoing reconstruction, the usual swearing-in ceremony took place in the Church of Casaprofessa. According to Caracciolo's wishes, the ritual proceedings were hasty and without pomp and circumstance because the viceroy was intent upon demonstrating from the outset that he would introduce innovations in the performance of his duty as the king's representative in Sicily.

Profoundly influenced by the spirit of the French Enlightenment, Caracciolo committed himself immediately to making significant changes on the island. As he said himself on one occasion, he meant "to liquidate the inheritance of a dismal past."

His first measures were taken in this innovative direction. On December 16, he ruled that communiquès destined for the king should be sent to his office in Palermo rather than to the Court of Naples. On January 7, 1782, he issued a decree forbidding that parish priests take special collections for funerals. And when, in response to his January 22 ban on exorbitant spending for the investing of novices, "defamatory manifestos" began to circulate, Caracciolo promulgated another decree, in February, offering a reward of 300 gold ounces to whomever denounced the authors of such pamphlets.

From that point on, Sicilians referred to Caracciolo as the "Philosopher"—a term they used in a pejorative sense. For here was this friend of French Enlightenment thinkers who, as unbeliever and radical reformer, was shaking Sicily's *ancien regime* at its very foundations.

Undaunted, Caracciolo set out to suppress the Inquisition. To do so, he won the support of Naples, first through its Ecclesiastical Ministry, then from the Ministries of Internal Affairs and Justice, the Secretary of State and even the Council of Sicily. But it was Caracciolo's own determination and Ferdinand's cooperation that turned the tide against the Holy Office. While the viceroy limited its power in Palermo by withdrawing its tribunal members' right to bear arms and by conducting an investigation within the inquisitors' palace—the Steri—the king, from Naples, took the giant step of abolishing the Inquisition in his realm. His royal proclamation to that effect, dated March 16, 1782, and expressed to his viceroy, reached Palermo ten days later. March 27, a Wednesday, the ceremony making this decree public was held with due solemnity. Caracciolo, dressed most austerely for the occasion, ordered that all the authorities of the kingdom attend him. Giuseppe Gargano, Secretary of the Realm, read the royal dispatch aloud. Immediately thereafter, the viceroy commanded that each and every "penitent" under the Inquisitor's custody be released. By that time only three old women accused of witchcraft were still in jail since, according to

Villabianca, the inquisitors "had the astuteness" to free their prisoners in advance. One of these women, however, asked if she could stay in the dungeon so that she would not have to roam the streets and starve to death.

By the time it was eliminated in Sicily, the Holy Office had actually lost some of its virulence and was serving mainly as stronghold where nobles could obtain and secure their privileges. As Francesco Brancato aptly notes in his essay on Caracciolo, "the viceroy struck at the barons who had taken advantage of inquisitorial power to further their own."

The viceroy proceeded to have the iron cages, many of them still containing skulls, removed from Steri Palace. He also had all the insignias of the hated tribunal destroyed. Unfortunately, Ferdinand, in response to the last Grand Inquisitor's request, ordered that compromising documents in the Holy Office Archives be burned to "annihilate them from history and for posterity."

### 7. Enlightened Reforms

The suppression of the Holy Office in Sicily was Caracciolo's first tangible achievement. The viceroy displayed his satisfaction with such a *coup* in a letter to his Parisian friend D'Alembert: "The day the terrible monster fell was one ever memorable on King Ferdinand IV's island." While Caracciolo wanted to have a *Te Deum* sung in thanks for the Inquisition's departure, he heeded the advice not to do so. But he did manage to divert the Holy Office's revenues so that they could be used by the Royal Academy of Studies (the old Collegium Massimum renamed in 1779) for the construction of botanical gardens, an observatory, a chemistry laboratory, an anatomy "theater," and a museum of natural sciences.

The enlightened viceroy then fully committed himself to carrying out further reforms. Determined to discount all opposition, especially that of the barons, he decided to emulate the most civilized countries in Europe by reforming the land-office and collecting tributes more equitably. His forward progress, however, was suspended on February 5, 1783, when a violent earthquake devastated Messina and several cities in Demone Valley. During this emergency, since the Bourbons could not meet immediate financial needs, the Sicilian Parliament, in a special session, proposed a tribute of 400,000 scudos to be paid in four annuities by each of its branches. Caracciolo, however, convinced that these fiscal burdens were unfairly distributed, insisted that the Branch of the Demesne be exonerated from contributing the same sum as the more privileged Ecclesiastical and Baronial Branches. Exhorting the latter two branches to cease exploiting the public domain "behind the veil of apparent equity," Caracciolo launched an attack against protocol that led to the definitive break between the viceroy and the Parliament and to the personalized struggle between the Marquis of Villamaina and the barons. The subsequent parliamentary appeal to the king resulted in victory for "the partisans of Sicily" and in the viceroy's humiliation. As the Court of Naples deemed, it was "irregular and capricious" of the Demesnial Branch to presume to have its tribute reduced.

Nothing stopped Domenico Caracciolo, however, from fighting to restore royal authority in Sicily or from improving and "rationalizing," civic life. Specifically, he attempted to control the issuing of permits to bear arms and to dissolve the guilds that were guilty of abuses in this area. Furthermore, Caracciolo's reformist zeal impelled him to reduce from five to three the number of days for Saint Rosalie's Festival and to propose that the money saved via such a reduction be utilized in works of charity.

Caracciolo's "Battle against Saint Rosalie" was long and hard, and destined to be lost. One day, on a wall near his royal apartments, the viceroy found the graffito "Either the festival or your funeral!" Parliament appealed once again to the king, protesting the viceroy's "savage treatment"; and Ferdinand pronounced his "judgment" from Naples: while he admired a certain "zeal inspiring innovation," the king decreed that "the festival would carry on this year without any changes." Thus, Saint Rosalie reigned in Palermo for five full days, much to the joy of Palermitans and in spite of Caracciolo, who was forced to swallow his pride and rage during all the ceremonies.

The viceroy was equally unsuccessful when he tried to eliminate the House of Villafranca's monopoly on the Sicilian Postal Service. As Caracciolo insisted, "it was easier to send a crate, a trunk, or a package from Palermo to Milan or Turin than from Palermo to Messina or Syracuse." But, in response to the viceroy's proposed changes in this service, Naples ordered him to await the king's decision regarding this matter. No decision was ever made.

Caracciolo's departure from Sicily, an event "sorely to be wished" by the Sicilian barons, occurred unexpectedly on January 18, 1786. Weary and disillusioned, the Marquis of Villamaina was summoned to the Court of Naples to serve as its Prime Minister, replacing the Marquis of Sambuca, who had been forced to resign.

### 8. A Second, More Cautious Diplomat

The sudden return of Domenico Caracciolo to Naples in January of 1786 was provoked by what one chronicler of the times called the "storm in the Court." This conflict arose, in fact, at the hub of Ferdinand's power when his queen, Carolina, conspired with an Austrian faction against the Spanish. At that crucial moment, the king himself wanted Caracciolo, rather than the Marquis of Sambuca, at his side to carry out the most prestigious duties of the Neapolitan State as Prime Minister and concomitant head of the Ministries of Foreign Affairs, the Royal House and the Postal Service. The monarch, it seems, was convinced that an open-minded man like Caracciolo was best suited to deal with international matters and, even more importantly, could improve the relations between Naples and Madrid that had deteriorated because of the intrigues of the Austrian Carolina and the weakness of her very own husband.

Caracciolo, at that time a 71 year old overweight bachelor suffering from rheumatism, failed to frame an accord between Charles III and his son Ferdinand. But he did make progress with his anti-clerical policies. In 1788, for instance, he managed to abolish the last vestiges of the Neapolitan crown's feudal submission to the Holy See, that is, the annual gift of a white saddle-horse and 7000 gold scudos. Unfortunately, Caracciolo could not proceed further with his reforms since he died the following year.

But let us return to Sicily. In 1786, Domenico Caracciolo himself had chosen his successor as Viceroy of Sicily. Disappointing a number of pretenders, notably General Pignatelli and Cardinal Spinelli, Caracciolo favored Prince Francesco D'Aquino of Caramanico, the man who had succeeded him as Neapolitan Ambassador to France.

Francesco D'Aquino, scion of a noble Neapolitan family, was, like Caracciolo, a diplomat and a man of great experience and enlightenment background and thinking. Furthermore, Caramanico had been the Neapolitan Kingdom's Grand Master of Freemasonry and member of the Council of State. According to the historian Pietro Colletta, he was also "grateful and perhaps dear to the queen." Caramanico's vice-regency was to endure from April 21, 1786, when he arrived in Palermo, to January 9, 1795, the day he died suddenly "due to a scandalous poisoning."

Prince Caramanico, a highly esteemed and well-connected personage in Neapolitan society, immediately displayed his abilities as an able and prudent governor in Sicily. First and foremost, he was bent on achieving carefully defined goals without the haste, severity, and intolerance characteristic of his predecessor. Significantly, he succeeded in winning over the nobles by openly demonstrating his respect for them and by being available to the representatives of the most illustrious houses. At the same time, Caramanico, sensitive as he was to the needs of the disinherited, did not neglect the lower classes. On the contrary, he offered them all his help and protection.

Taking advantage of the consensus of all social sectors, Prince Caramanico gained the trust of those Sicilians struggling for reforms. In a strong alliance with the Sicilian government and the educated classes, he was able to implement innovative policies without provoking the violent reactions so typical of Caracciolo's vice-regency.

It was Caracciolo himself, who, sending Caramanico to Sicily, wished the prince the utmost success in performing miracles more wonderful than those of Saint Anthony and in "reaping the fruits of a good planting." Caramanico, with slow but agile steps, won his first victory only a few months after his nomination to the post of viceroy. Under his auspices, the Parliament ratified a land reform law similar to the one that the stormy Caracciolo had failed to enact.

### 9. Reforms and Counter-Revolution

While Caramanico did have to make certain compromises with the Barons *in re* the land reform, the prince proudly took its passage as a sign that he could push for further anti-feudal changes in Sicily. In 1786 and 1787, according to directives initiated by Caracciolo and reaffirmed by his successor, numerous communes still administered in feudal fashion contested the local duties and excise and customs taxes they traditionally owed to the Barons. In spite of his successful courting of the nobles in the first months of his term, Caramanico, less impetuous than his predecessor, thus applied shock treatment to the *ancien regime* in his attack on hereditary privileges.

The Sicilian Barons were to be dealt another heavy blow in 1788. On November 14 of that year, the vice-regency sanctioned in Sicily—as it had done in Naples—the practice of transferring fiefdoms to the Treasury for public administration. It was also established that feudal land-owners without legitimate heirs could not determine the inheritance of their estates and that the extension of ranks of succession was not granted. These dispositions were made known a few days after the official dispatch of November 8 that cancelled the legitimacy of the Barons' privatistic feudal rights. These reforms set the stage for the viceroy's next action: the issuing on May 4, 1789, of an order in which Caramanico, anticipating French legislators, declared that, since all forms of feudal servitude had been abolished, every individual in the kingdom was granted the inalienable rights of personal freedom, juridical appeal and civil equality.

The precipitous turn of events in France in that same year put a damper on reformist zeal in Naples and Sicily. Appalled, the Court renounced its whole liberalizing, progressive approach, imposing most severe measures to maintain order and assure that Naples and Sicily would not be infiltrated by exporters of the French Revolution. Once the Bastille was stormed on July 14, Ferdinand's fears erupted in panic. And when the Sicilian town of Niscemi rioted in March of 1790, the hysteria of the moment led authorities to conclude that revolution was at hand.

Caramanico was therefore advised to be vigilant on his frontier and to control the entrance of any foreign travelers, most notably the Florentine Scipione Piattoli, who was believed to be a disseminator of revolutionary ideas. Both parties influenced by Rousseau's thinking—i.e., the Girondists and the Jacobins—were regarded with apprehension in the kingdom. But while the former were considered mere pragmatists who would leave monarchy intact, the latter were feared as fanatics and extremists bent on overthrowing all kings. As it evolved in Sicily, the term Jacobin referred to any subversive with whom no compromise or truce was possible.

The specter of Jacobinism, ironically, helped to ease the tension in Sicily between the viceroy, prime defender of the monarchy, and the barons. The execution of Louis XVI on January 21, 1793, induced Ferdinand to sign a defensive-offensive alliance pact with England, to assemble an army, and to declare war on France. Given the circumstances, in 1794, the Court of Naples requested of the Sicilian Parliament not only its usual tribute, but also a generous emergency subsidy for the duration of the war. The Parliament, nevertheless, agreed to pay less than Naples desired, deciding "of its own free and spontaneous will" to allocate one million ducats only a part of which would be donated "in cash." As Ernesto Pontieri asserted, this choice signified "an awakening of the Sicilian barons' constitutional spirit." It was, indeed, the beginning of the opposition to royal power that would reach its summit in the constitution of 1812.

## 10. The Island's Opening to Enlightenment Culture

The French Revolution and the Neapolitan Monarchy's consequent resistance to "reformist squalls" gave new life to the Sicilian barons. Courted again by Prince Caramanico and honored by King Ferdinand, the nobles saw themselves virtually restored to their old status. A great defender of the barons could proudly write toward the end of the century that the real bastion of the crown was not the populace but "the baronial class, which, on a whim, could summon the Foreigner to overthrow the king."

Caramanico was soon marching in step with the times. At the parliamentary session of 1790, the prince himself suggested to Minister Acton that, since the barons were committed to paying their usual tribute and to making special contributions to the Royal Treasury as well, the application of land reform laws "could be bypassed."

In other areas of his jurisdiction, however, the viceroy did not fail to move in liberalizing, progressive directions. During his term, in 1790 to be precise, Italian replaced Latin as the official language for all Supreme Tribunal proscriptions and decisions related to Sicily. At the moment, in

Naples, no one could imagine that the island, in the following half a century, would call for one Italy in the name of linguistic unity.

Caramanico also worked hard to spread education and culture across the island. To do so, he charged the pedagogue Giovanni Agostino De Cosmi, who had developed his expertise at Naples, to establish normal schools all over Sicily. To finance these schools, revenues from un-authorized cultural associations were allocated—in spite of the barons' vociferous protests.

The viceroy then turned his attention to higher education. Instituting reforms at the University of Catania and in licea throughout Sicily like the Cutelli of Catania and the Nautical School of Palermo "to give noble youth a proper upbringing," Caramanico attracted illustrious figures in their fields to fill important posts. The Abbot Paolo Balsamo, expert agronomist, took the Chair of Agronomy at the Academy of Palermo. This professor was subsequently dispatched on an extensive trip through Italy, France, England and Holland to learn of the methods of cultivation used in those advanced European countries so that he could apply them in Sicily. His colleague at the Academy of Palermo, the famous jurist, historian and Arabist Rosario Gregorio, occupied the Chair of Public Law at the same time.

Under Caramanico, the laying of the capital's Botanical Gardens, begun in 1782 by Caracciolo with funds transferred from the deceased Inquisition's revenue, was completed. The gardens, that, judging from the writings and drawings of the Marquis of Villabianca, were once again under construction by 1789, were inaugurated toward the end of 1795. The supervision of the Royal Gardens was entrusted to Giuseppe Tineo, a scholar trained in a Sicilian climate of great intellectual ferment in the field of botanical studies. The publications of other specialists like the Franciscan Father Bernardino of Ucria attest to such vitality and seriousness.

Caramanico's crowning achievement, finally, was the founding of the Observatory. Heading this center was the great astronomer Abbot Giuseppe Piazzi, who, on January 1, 1801, would discover, with the Observatory's instruments, the asteroid to be called Ferdinandean Ceres in honor of Sicily's sovereign. Piazzi, moreover, was sent to England and France to perfect his knowledge of astronomy and acquire skill in the use of highly sophisticated instruments. These tools of his trade can still be found in the Observatory of Palermo in the highest tower of what was once the Royal Palace.

As Rosario Romeo has emphasized, it seemed that, with Caramanico's vice-regency, "Sicily enjoyed the kind of alliance between the government and the educated classes that had borne so much fruit in Naples—even though, during that period, the healthiest elements of Sicilian culture were

38. Giuseppe Balsamo, known as Count Cagliostro.

oriented toward a liberal parliamentary system in direct antithesis to enlightened absolutism."

## 11. Great and Infamous Men, and Women, during the Age of Caramanico

Caramanico was Viceroy of Sicily when, in April of 1787, Wolfgang Goethe disembarked from the Tartaro, which had originated from Naples, and, under the false name of Johan Phillip Moeller, merchant from Leipzig, checked into a Palermitan hotel. A few days later, when he was discovered, two of Caramanico's envoys, dressed in regal garb, appeared at Goethe's lodging to invite the famous author of *The Sorrows of Young Werther* (but not his travelling companion the painter Kniep) to dine with the viceroy. Evidently, Caramanico, a Mason and once Grand Master in Naples, was eager to entertain this great German writer and advocate of freemasonry. In fact, the viceroy demanded that Goethe dine at his side, paying him an honor due only to personages of high rank.

During Francesco D'Aquino's vice-regency, the poisoner Giovanna Bonanno, nicknamed the *Vinegar Crone*, was apprehended and executed. Moreover, the period witnessed exploits of two infamous frauds and impostors, the Maltese Giuseppe Vella, active in the Sicilian capital, and the Palermitan Giuseppe Balsamo, self-baptized as Count Alessandro Cagliostro, whose theater of operations extended throughout Europe. Finally, during the Caramanico years, Vincenzo Lunardi, a man from Lucca, launched his hot-air balloon under Palermo's skies.

Giovanna Bonanno was caught in one of her acts toward the end of August or at the beginning of September, 1788. But this "hag" had been

39. "La vecchia dell'aceto" (The Vinegar Crone). Engraving

operating for years, selling, for six "tarì" (ancient coin introduced by the Arabs), an arsenic-based powder (prepared by an apothecary from Papireto to kill lice) to any "crony" interested in freeing herself from her husband. Arrested, tortured, and tried, the elderly Bonanno was sentenced by the captainate of the Royal Court to hang on April 13, 1789. The sentence was actually carried out the morning of July 30, 1789. For the occasion, in Piazza Vigliena, a scaffold was erected higher than usual in observance of the custom of punishing the gravest of crimes via the utmost dramatic effects.

The case of Abbot Vella is notorious. What has come down in history as "the Arabian imposture, the Saracen lie" was, in effect, a scandal involving not only Sicily but the whole literary world of eighteenth century Europe. At the center of this incredible hoax was the Maltese Chaplain Giuseppe Vella, who bold-facedly claimed that he had discovered, in the Cassinese Fathers' Library of San Martino delle Scale, a "record of the Arabs' chancellery during their occupation of Sicily." Although it was revealed later that he knew no Arabic, Vella also promised to translate this document into Italian. Contriving this *Diplomatic Code of Sicily under Arab Rule,* Vella then had it published in six volumes (1789-92) by the Royal Printing House, through the patronage of Viceroy Caramanico and Archbishop Alfonso Airoldi! Eventually exposed by real Arabist scholars, the Abbot was sentenced to fifteen years in jail on August 29, 1796. Shortly thereafter, however, Vella's sentence was commuted and he was allowed to retire to his Mezzomonreale villa, where he died in 1814, at 65.

Giuseppe Balsamo, alias Count Cagliostro, was condemned to death by the Inquisition in Rome. But on April 7, 1791, Pius VI intervened and had him imprisoned for life. In no time, an edition of his *Compendium* was issued in Palermo, complete with a portrait of the impostor as a young man. This work was probably done by an engraver who had met the adventurer upon the latter's return to Palermo in 1773 (when he was 30). Cagliostro died in San Leo on August 26, 1795—the same year of Caramanico's death.

Finally, we should speak here of Vincenzo Lunardi's flight. The intrepid Lucchese arrived in Palermo in October of 1789 after having launched his mongolfiere over Naples to the amazement and delight of Ferdinand and Carolina. After a number of unsuccessful attempts before Palermitan spectators, Lunardi managed to fly again on July 31, 1790. Taking off from Piazza Saint Francis of Paola, he soared across the capital's firmament for an hour and 45 minutes—before he plunged into the sea off Cape Zafferano. Fished out, he was received by Viceroy Caramanico in the Royal Palace.

## 12. Jacobins Everywhere

The last years of Francesco D'Aquino's life were bitter due to his ill health, but more so because of the deep impression left by the French Revolution in Naples and in Sicily. While the sad end of Louis XVI and his consort Marie Antoinette (Maria Carolina's sister) convulsed the Bourbon sovereigns, Jacobin infiltration of the Kingdom of Naples created an atmosphere of hysteria most difficult to control. Given the fear of similar infiltration in Sicily that might lead to a revolutionary coup d'etat, in August of 1794, Ferdinand urged the viceroy to guard closely against any potential threat to the monarchy and not to hesitate in apprehending suspects. At the same time, the king requested that the Barons organize a militia, permanently armed and prepared to defend the kingdom against subversives. Moreover, all bishops were mobilized to warn the faithful from the pulpit of the dangers posed by the enemy, "despiser of the true faith."

At this point, Caramanico went to Naples to convalesce after a serious illness. But he met with hostility throughout the court. Most obdurate of all was the Prime Minister, the Englishman Acton, who enjoyed the favor of the queen and was fearful that his old rival could win back her heart. Rumor spread that Caramanico, ex-ambassador in Paris and friend of many important Frenchmen, might try to win sympathy for Neapolitan Jacobins or even conspire against the king. Whatever the case, the viceroy, after sixteen days spent in Naples, returned to Palermo. There, on January 9, 1795, as reported in the Marquis of Villabianca's *Diaries*, Caramanico was "struck down by a sudden malaise" and died before last rites could be administered.

All over the Kingdom of the Two Sicilies, news of his sudden death spurred disconcerting rumors. It was said that the viceroy had taken his own life to hide the fact of his participation in a Jacobin conspiracy to seize

Naples. Another version of his death implicated old rival John Francis Edward Acton as his poisoner. According to a recent theory, however, the viceroy was eliminated by Francesco Carelli, Secretary of the Government of Sicily who had been involved in the Vella Scandal. Perhaps the truth regarding Caramanico's demise will never be known, although Ernesto Pontieri has recently discovered in the Archives of the State of Naples a number of letters written by Caramanico's attending physician in which there are explicit references to "the gravity of the viceroy's liver disease." Such details, while they do not totally disprove the hypothesis of poisoning, do make it a less probable cause of Caramanico's death.

After the passing of Caramanico, the governance of Sicily was entrusted to Archbishop of Palermo, Monsignor Felipe Lopez y Royo of the Dukedom of Taurisani. At this delicate moment when the Neapolitan monarchy was threatened from without by the French and from within by Jacobin conspirators, the Archbishop assumed the positions of Viceroy, Presider of the Realm and Captain General. Lopez y Royo, a weak man by nature, surrounded himself with spies who were to detect any traces of intrigue and eradicate its perpetrators that, according to Naples, were infiltrating Sicily.

Meanwhile, to ingratiate himself with the populace, the archbishop permitted bullfighting in the square in front of his palace and strove to limit the damages caused by scudo "shavers." But none of his measures could alleviate the gravity of the times. While heavy tributes of gold and silver were being exacted in Sicily, even from monasteries, so that the whole kingdom could be armed and defended, the Jacobin conspiracy organized by Francesco Paolo Di Blasi erupted in Palermo.

# Chapter XIII: The Specter of Revolution

## 1. Di Blasi's Conspiracy

Francesco Paolo Di Blasi, one of the most outstanding enlightenment thinkers of the late 1700s in Sicily, was the first illustrious victim of Bourbon reaction. Inspired by Rousseau, Di Blasi paid for his idealist faith in liberty with his life. Born in Palermo in 1753, this scion of a noble family distinguished himself from adolescence for his acute intelligence and dynamism.

Man of letters and jurist, he was scarcely 25 when he published the 1778 *Dissertation on Equality and Inequality Among Men as Related to Their Happiness,* a work rooted in the social philosophy of Rousseau and informed by a vision of liberal reforms within the institutions of the Kingdom of the Two Sicilies. In his next essay, *On Legislation in Sicily* (1779), Di Blasi argued for the abolition of the death penalty. Eight years later, upon the urging of King Ferdinand and Viceroy Caramanico, he assembled the collection called *The Praxes of the Kingdom of Sicily,* a two volume compendium issued in 1791 and 1793 to which he dedicated all his energy and talent. The king himself, hoping to strengthen his authority in the confrontation with Barons and land-owners via this research on ancient

**40. Francesco Paolo Di Blasi. Engraving.**

institutions, did not fail to show his gratitude to Di Blasi by offering him "togas cut according to his merit and capability"—rewards which the young scholar never solicited.

Such is the context in which the rest of Di Blasi's life can be best understood. Furthermore, by 1795, the political climate in Naples and Sicily had become feverish, if not violent. The Bourbon Court was in the process of asking emergency tributes and unreasonable sacrifices of its populace and, simultaneously, reciprocating with nothing but repression as its fear of a French invasion spread. In reaction, discontent was rampant throughout Sicily's urban centers large and small, where it assumed local forms of Jacobinism. And the Bourbons' only response was police action that, increasing in severity every day, became the instrument of absolutism.

Given this tense situation, certain groups deemed it possible to make radical political changes. Rooted in such a consciousness, a conspiracy was organized involving certain urban worker classes and rural peasant nobility. Their plan was to rise up on Good Friday, April 3, 1795, to the cry of "Long Live the Republic!" They aimed at nothing less than taking Archbishop Lopez y Royo prisoner, breaking into his castle and, with the aid of turncoat military officers, disarming the viceroy's forces. Their ultimate purpose was to declare an end to absolutist rule on the island.

Many of the meetings to put the finishing touches on this plot took place in Di Blasi's home. Francesco Paolo himself had recently expressed his own intolerance of Naples's authoritarianism by educating people in the countryside as to the meaning of the French Revolution. Evidently Di Blasi and his fellow-conspirators thought they could count on outside help to launch their revolutionary ideas. But their fragile scaffolding collapsed resoundingly on Monday, March 30, when one of the conspirators, the goldsmith Giovanni Teriaca, informed the parish priest Pizzi of the insurrection in the wings.

Teriaca revealed to the priest that two silversmiths had invited him to a meeting to finalize plans for an attack on a usurer's house. The money taken there, Teriaca added, would be used to finance the revolt. Further evidence used against Di Blasi was provided when a foreign corporal implicated him as chief conspirator. On March 31, Di Blasi was apprehended and imprisoned in the fort of Castellammare. Contrary to the wishes of the Revenue Attorney, Di Blasi was not put on the rack, but he was tortured seven times "by fire." Nevertheless, he did not "talk." Nor did he name any names. Weak links in his chain were revealed, however: some of his comrades, in search of amnesty, turned informers; other conspirators, trying to flee, were arrested; and the stolen key with which the insurgents planned to enter Lopez y Royo's castle was found by the police.

Di Blasi was tortured again to exact a confession. Still, he was silent, implicating no one. On May 18, he was sentenced to death by decapitation—as was befitting a noble. Three of his fellow-conspirators—Giulio Tinaglia, Benedetto La Villa and Bernardo Palumbo—were destined for the gallows. Suspects were sent into exile on islands off the coast of Sicily.

Two days later, May 20, 1795, Di Blasi made a Christian confession and was escorted to Piazza Santa Teresa where a scaffold had been erected. Without complaint, he ascended the stairs and put his head on the block. The executioner did the rest with his axe. Di Blasi's body still lies in the Church of Santa Teresa on the square.

## 2. Ferdinand Between War and Peace

The deaths of Francesco Paolo Di Blasi and his three fellow-conspirators, rather than easing tensions, aggravated them. All over the kingdom, in Naples and in Palermo, every foreigner was considered a subversive or an agent of the French enemy. What was defined in an official Bourbon document as "the Jacobin mania" drove Ferdinand to forbid entry into the realm not only of persons suspected of revolutionary tendencies but also of politically dangerous books. The climate of fear worsened to the point where the inhabitants of the mountain town of Gioiosa Guardia were branded as Jacobins simply for wanting to relocate on the coast near Palermo "in order to be on watch for enemy ships."

On May 17, 1796, Naples sent a dispatch throughout the kingdom calling for the formation of volunteer militias "to defend Religion, Throne and Country." Moreover, the crown demanded of churches and monasteries all the gold and silver in their treasures. At this moment, any one accused of Jacobin sympathies who could afford to leave Sicily did so. Judging from the May 1796 outlawing of emigration for Sicilian subjects, the exodus must have been virtually massive.

Meanwhile, Napoleon's lightning strike at Lombardy, Piedmont and the dukedoms of the North had confirmed the worst of Ferdinand's fears. Unable to organize any resistance to the French invasion, the Bourbon monarch proposed a truce. Thus in June of 1796, a pact was signed establishing "peace, friendship and a common mind between His Majesty the King of the Two Sicilies and the French Republic."

Temporarily at least, Naples and Palermo could breathe easy. Their monarch, once again able to rest on his royal laurels, congratulated his "loyal Sicilian subjects" who in one year alone had poured into his treasury 3,700,000 ducats. In the relaxed atmosphere of Palermo, Archbishop Lopez y Royo organized a special clean-up and beautification campaign; and a distinguished patrician, Asmundo Paternò Sessa, donated the funds for the construction of two pavilions within Villa Giulia and two ponds in the Botanical Gardens.

That same year (1796), a bad harvest caused a general state of alarm, and 12,000 tons of grain had to be transported from Apulia to solve the problem of food shortages. To make matters worse, piracy increased. Prince Luigi Moncada of Paternò, aboard a Greek ship bound for Naples, was seized by pirates and released only after paying a 170,000 scudo ransom, part in currency and part in jewels. The Turks, however, refused to accept one of the prince's precious objects as ransom: a diamond-studded cross that they considered "profane."

As the raids of Barbary pirates extended to the tuna fishery of Mondello and the gates of Palermo, bad news arrived from Naples: the French and Ferdinand had resumed hostilities. Thus French hunting season began once again and reached its peak on August 30, 1797 in Palermo when all French articles stamped with the image of Napoleon Bonaparte were withdrawn from the markets.

Less than a year later, on July 22, 1798, the new viceroy, Prince Tommaso Firrao of Luzzi and Sant'Agata, arrived in Palermo. He was bringing very clear instructions from Naples: enlist fresh troops to defend the kingdom and impose new sacrifices on its citizens to finance a war rapidly spreading toward the South. Trying to relieve the pressure of these policies, Firrao had several persons accused of Jacobinism released from prison. Nevertheless, he maintained the network of spies created by the Presider over the Kingdom.

### 3. The Rapid Flight of the King

Two months after his September 29, 1798 arrival in Palermo, Prince Luzzi, the last viceroy of the eighteenth century, addressed a newly convened Parliament regarding the Kingdom's urgent need of human and financial resources. His arguments were not novel, but his tone was strikingly resolute. The viceroy was asking of all branches of the Parliament not only an outright gift of two million ducats but also, for the war's duration, a monthly contribution to the Court of sixty-thousand scudos.

These sums seemed exorbitant to the members of the Parliament, and they reminded the viceroy that they did not have the power to deliberate as to subsidies for the Court. A lively debate ensued, and trade-offs were proposed; but, in the end, the heavy tax-expenditure was approved. At the same time, Palermo prepared for war. Its fortifications and batteries were repaired; and measures were taken to stop, or at least curtail, the phenomenon of military desertion.

These preparations were a specific response at a key juncture. King

Ferdinand, mindful of the two factors of the emotional reaction to the French invasion of Malta and the fear of a similar invasion of Sicily, had suddenly decided to march on Rome. Moreover, he was being backed by the inept Austrian general, Karl von Marck, who had reached Naples to fulfill a secret alliance pact made with Vienna.

After emanating a November 21 decree in which he proclaimed himself defender of the faith and liberty, Ferdinand issued an order to von Marck, stipulating that the general, at dawn the next day, set out for Rome with the army. Accompanied by Acton, the king followed in his carriage. In spite of some initial mishaps (for instance, the arduous fording of the Mella River), the march turned into a pleasant outing for Ferdinand since the French troops of General Championnet, seeing that the matter at hand was a mere violation of a treaty rather than a state of war, withdrew without firing a single shot at the Neapolitans. Thus, on November 29, Ferdinand cavalcaded victoriously into Rome, establishing himself in Farnese Palace, where he received high-ranking prelates and Roman nobles. His triumph, however, was short-lived. On December 7, General Championnet ordered his forces to attack the Neapolitans; and the Bourbon monarch, to avoid being taken prisoner, fled Rome post-haste in civilian clothes and found refuge in Caserta.

By now, the die was cast. In fact, before leaving Rome, on December 4, Ferdinand, strengthened by new alliances with Russia and England, had declared war on France. Furthermore, the infelicitous Neapolitan incursion to Rome gave the French the "providential" pretext to attack Naples. With such a threat looming, Ferdinand heeded von Marck's advice and feverishly readied himself to depart from his Neapolitan territory. On December 21, the royal family, escorted by Admiral Nelson (recently returned from his victorious battle at Abukir), slipped through a secret passageway under the palace and hied it to Naples Harbor. There, the English ship Vanguard had already been laden with the treasures, jewels and monies of the Neapolitan crown (amounting to the estimated equivalent of one million, five-hundred-thousand pounds).

The ship set sail December 23. On board with the royal family and its entourage were Sir William Hamilton, English Ambassador to Naples, and his lovely wife, Lady Emma, who was of course romantically prone to Horatio Nelson. The Vanguard with its precious human cargo was escorted by two Neapolitan ships, the Archimedes and the Sannite, commanded by Francesco Caracciolo.

The voyage was a horror due to heavy storms at sea. The king's six year old son, Prince Carlo Alberto, suffered convulsions and died in the arms of Lady Hamilton, who, on this occasion, shone for her courage. The distinguished passengers were forced to spend Christmas Day aboard ship. Only the livid morning of December 26, 1798, was the royal family able to land in Palermo's port.

### 4. Horrors in Naples, Pleasures in Palermo

As soon as his ship, the Vanguard, docked at Palermo, Ferdinand gave the impression that he had forgotten about his loss of Naples and about his six year old son's corpse, which was still aboard the Vanguard. Instead, he seemed more concerned with the dogs he had brought along so that he could abandon himself to the pleasures of hunting in Sicily. After eating a large breakfast, Ferdinand disembarked, decked in regal garb with insignias and frills. He was received by Viceroy Luzzi, who ceremonially transferred his power to the king. With no further ado, Ferdinand climbed into a royal six-horse carriage which was escorted to the cathedral by cavalrymen wielding unsheathed sabres. Before the relics of Saint Rosalie, the partly deposed monarch kneeled in prayer. Finally, he processed to the Royal Palace.

Queen Maria Carolina, anguished for the death of her son and totally exhausted, immediately fell ill. Nelson, also indisposed, decided to lodge at the home of Sir William Hamilton and his wife Emma—where they set

**41. Giovanni Meli (1740-1815), the most celebrated poet of the 18th century who chose to express himself in Sicilian.**

*182-Chapter XIII*

42. Admiral Nelson who escorted the fleeing royal family to Palermo. For his service Nelson was made Duke of Bronte.

up the kind of *mènage à trois* customarily tolerated by the elderly English ambassador and the Court itself.

Once General Championnet declared Naples a French-style republic on January 23, 1799, the hysterical assault on Jacobins, called "scoundrels and assassins" by the diarist Villabianca, recommenced in Palermo. Ferdinand, apropos of this mood, constituted a special State Council "to tend to the security of all loyal subjects, hunt down evil-doers, and expose all riotous plottings." This struggle assumed grotesque proportions when the French styles of wearing long pants and growing beards and long sideburns were abolished. The king went so far as to have a Palermitan noblewoman, Donna Giovanna del Bosco, arrested for not heeding his public ban on wearing Parisian-style wigs.

At the same time, fearing a French invasion of Sicily, the king exhorted the barons to form a corps of 9,000 soldiers and ordered the arming of the island's major fortresses and the building of eight warships equipped with cannons. In this witch-hunt environment, thousands of volunteers were enlisted in a militia designed to maintain royal power.

These militiamen, feeling they were above the law and exempt from paying taxes, provoked, via their arrogance, serious riots all over Sicily: in Biancavilla, Cefalù, Agrigento, Butera, Termini, and Trapani, for example. With the pretext of persecuting Jacobins, the militiamen, shouting "Long Live the King and the Holy Faith," intimidated and infuriated peaceful people around the island. During this period, with the French still in Naples, the *Neapolitan Monitor* published an article stating that, in Caltagirone, its citizens had hoisted the "tree of liberty," and that, in Agrigento, an effigy of the king had been burned. Without sufficient evidence, many arrests were made, and a considerable number of the detained were condemned to death.

When the ephemeral Neapolitan Republic fell in June, the repression ordered by Ferdinand drew blood in the extreme. After Cardinal Ruffo marched his troops through southern Italy and reclaimed Naples for the Bourbons, scores of men and women from noble families and of great social prestige lost their lives. Admiral Caracciolo, who had sided with the Neapolitan Republicans, was hanged from the mast of his ship.

Looking on the carnage from Palermo, Ferdinand apparently felt serene. A prey to his hunting passion, he spent more and more time in the hills outside the city. Lodging in the Chinese log-villa belonging to the Marquises Lombardo of Scala, he reconnoitred through their game-rich green bosks and glades. Finally, Ferdinand decided to purchase the miniature palace and have the area around it walled in and further graced by the now famous Chinese Palace originally designed by the architect Venanzio Marvuglia. It was here that the king established his Palermitan residence.

## 5. A Culture Receptive to Europe

Ferdinand's vicissitudes, most notably his temporary withdrawal under French pressure to Palermo, coincide with the end of the eighteenth century. At this juncture, then, it is appropriate to look back at Sicilian culture in the 1700s and at the heated debates in modern historiography regarding this topic. As a point of departure in evaluating the depth, breadth and substance of Sicilian culture in the eighteenth century, let us consider Giovanni Gentile's famous essay, *The Decline of Sicilian Culture,* which this philosopher from Castelvetrano published in 1917. Therein, Gentile maintains that, in the 1700s, Sicily was "sequestered," i.e., cut off from the major currents of European thought. To strengthen his argument, Gentile refers to the objective conditions on the island as documented by its most prominent foreign visitors, namely the Scotsman Patrick Brydone, who travelled through Sicily in 1770, and the German Wolfgang Goethe, who landed in Palermo 17 years later. Certainly, given the hazards of the voyage from Naples to Palermo, the frequent pirate incursions, the lack of roads and lodgings on the island, and its plethora of bandits, it took courage and initiative to make such journeys.

Yet, especially in the second half of the eighteenth century, Sicily seemed to be in the upheaval of a great awakening. Perhaps this new consciousness was rooted only in the privileged classes, while the poor were barely surviving in their exploited state of a subculture. But Brydone witnesses a true intellectual ferment when he notes with amazement how young Palermitan noblemen address him in English and how Palermo's bookstores are full of English versions of Milton, Shakespeare and Bolingbroke.

I do not mean to tarry, refuting Gentile's thesis of intellectual decline. It is more interesting, simply, to enumerate the works of serious scholars of the period: Antonino Mongitore's *Sicilian Library,* a genuine encyclopedia of island knowledge; Giovambattista Caruso's *Historical Library of the Kingdom of Sicily*; Vito Amico's *Sicilian Lexicon,* a six volume history; the detailed *Chronicles* of Giovanni Evangelista di Blasi; the *Diaries* of the Marquis of Villabianca, perceptive observer of a good part of the century's major events. Simultaneously, we should stress how Sicilians' social consciousness matured in the authentic movements to reform the monarchy and in a bona fide cultural, political and social renascence very much in tune with the most enlightened developments on the continent.

The intellectuals and artists who best plumbed the depths of the island's culture and flowed in the major currents of European thought and creativity were the following: Francesco Paolo Di Blasi, who paid for his quest for liberty with his life; Tommaso Natale, who articulated the philosophy of Leibniz in Tuscan verses; and Michelangelo Fardella, the mathematician and philosopher who introduced Italy to Cartesian logic. Among the other distinguished Sicilians who illuminated eighteenth century culture, we should finally mention the historian Rosario Gregorio, the scientist and man-of-letters Domenico Scinà, the reformist pedagogue Agostino De Cosmi, the architect Filippo Juvara, the scientists Francesco Ferrara and Giuseppe Gioieni, the painter Giuseppe Velasquez, and the sculptor Ignazio Marabitti.

As a synthesis and culmination of the ferment of the 1700s and as a precursor of a new spirituality, the works of the poet Giovanni Meli occupy a prime position. In the Sicily deeply imprinted with the reforms of Caracciolo and Caramanico, Meli's often melodic, deeply ironic and enlightened, and even provocatory verses expressed the awakened consciousness and new knowledge of an island receptive to the outside world and to the free exchange of ideas via its numerous academies. Furthermore, this revival was possible in a transitional context of raging conflicts between conservative forces in their backlash against the rapid changes occurring beyond the Alps and the explosive ideals of a free culture and an emergent political and social dignity.

## 6. The End of "A Perverse Association"

While, in Naples, Bourbon repression was transformed into an indiscriminate massacre of men and women who believed in Neapolitan republican ideals, Ferdinand and Maria Carolina lived a life of luxury and idle pleasure in Palermo. The queen could never part from Lady Emma Hamilton, the wife of England's Ambassador to Naples who had become

Carolina's trusted advisor. Nelson was also seen in public, constantly doting on the beautiful Emma. In recognition of Nelson's intervention whereby he had given the royal couple safe conduct from Naples to Palermo, Ferdinand had made the British admiral an honorary citizen of his new capital and had granted him Bronte, at the foot of Mt. Etna, a dukedom that brought Nelson an annual revenue of 6,000 gold ounces. Insensitive to the trials and tribulations of Naples, Ferdinand, Maria Carolina, Lady Hamilton and Lord Nelson showed themselves off in Palermo during official ceremonies and went to the theater in masks as if it were carnival time.

The first year of the new century, however, would mark the end of "the perverse association" between the Bourbon sovereigns and the two lovers. After 36 years of service at the court of Naples, Sir William Hamilton was recalled to London, and his wife was forced to accompany him. Nelson himself, with his term as Chief Commander in the Mediterranean expired, also had to return to England. Meanwhile, the queen journeyed from Palermo to Vienna in search of new political alliances, bringing with her the more than modest sum of half a million ducats.

In Palermo, the political climate became less tense, to the point where the State Council decided it could ease up on the persecution of Jacobins. King Ferdinand himself declared a general amnesty "in order to silence the dirge of past vicissitudes." This atmosphere of reconciliation was further improved by the signing of a March, 1801 peace treaty between the French and the Bourbons in Florence. By all appearances, the Jacobins no longer instilled fear in their adversaries. Even when, in Vizzini, a dozen contrabanded handkerchiefs were seized that were embroidered with that phrase so terrible to Ferdinand's ears—*Liberté, Egalité, Fraternité*—no measures were taken against those merchants trying to sell such dangerous articles in Sicily.

In spite of the political amnesty, however, liberals continued to be persecuted and imprisoned. In reaction to the king's sham of a general pardon, a new anti-monarchic conspiracy was organized in Catania by the merchant Antonio Piraino. His aim was to incite a popular uprising, loot the homes of the rich to fund the revolt, take possession of the castle, and overthrow the government. But, as it had happened so often in the recent and distant past, an informer undermined one more revolutionary design. On December 12, 1801, Piraino was condemned to death. Some of his co-conspirators received less severe sentences.

On March 24 of the following year, during a parliamentary session attended by the king, the representatives, after approving their customary tribute, appropriated the special sum of 150,000 gold ounces so that Ferdinand could maintain a permanent royal court in Palermo. But this allocation never materialized because the sovereign returned to Naples on June 3, 1802, leaving behind as his viceroy the 80 year old Archbishop Domenico Pignatelli. Shortly thereafter, Pignatelli became cardinal, Presider of the Kingdom and Captain General. Nonetheless, he made few friends among his subjects because he set up a spy ring that infiltrated social clubs, both public and private. The main reason for no organized protest or revolt during his term was that the king's representative died a few months later, in February of 1803.

### 7. Experts in Fleeing Still in Flight

After leaving Palermo in June of 1802, Ferdinand returned less than four years later (January of 1806), driven from Naples by the onslaught of Napoleon's troops. Already Emperor of France and King of Italy, Napoleon had overcome the stunning defeat of his French fleet at Trafalgar and decided to challenge English hegemony once again, this time by occupying the Kingdom of Naples. First installing his brother Joseph there as king, Napoleon changed his mind two years later in favor of his brother-in-law, Joachim Murat.

At this point, Sicilians had to play a waiting game. After Pignatelli's death, Alessandro Filangeri, Prince of Cutò and Duke of Misilindino, was nominated Lieutenant and Captain General of the Realm on February 16, 1803. He served until January of 1806, when the king returned to Sicily and, according to custom, Filangeri stepped down in deference to his monarch.

During his term, however, Filangeri was plagued by another grain

**42. Ferdinand I, jokingly called "Big Nose" by the people.**

shortage resulting from a poor harvest and by a resurgence of piracy. Barbary ships based in Tunis continued to ravage the coast around Sciacca and Agrigento and even reached Sferracavallo, not far from Palermo.

In 1805, the Jesuits, expelled in 1767, returned to the island. Thirty-eight years after their clamorous departure, many of their possessions had been transferred to other parties. Thus, the Jesuits had to establish themselves in the only properties still belonging to them: the Collegio Nuovo and the Casaprofessa.

In the meantime, the European stage of battle lit up again. Ferdinand, upon Carolina's insistence, had tried to court Napoleon by giving him precious objects from the excavations of Pompei and Herculaneum. Placated, the Emperor, on September 21, 1805, was happy to sign a pact of neutrality between himself and the Bourbons stipulating that the latter would not allow the ships of France's enemies to land in their harbors. Bonaparte's side of the bargain was the promise to withdraw his troops from the Kingdom of Naples within 30 days. Queen Carolina, however, convinced by recent advances of Austria and the Anglo-Russian League, subscribed to a secret accord opening the port of Naples to a fleet of this coalition. Such a maneuver naturally alarmed the French Consulate there.

At first Ferdinand tried to bluff, insisting that the presence of these ships did not constitute a breaking of the neutrality pact. But subsequently he had to join the opposition to Napoleon. Bonaparte, in turn, spurred on by his victories at Hulme and Austerlitz, declared that Queen Carolina's perfidy had put an end to the Bourbon dynasty in Naples. As a consequence, Ferdinand was forced to flee to Sicily a second time.

Led by Joseph Bonaparte, General Massena's troops entered Naples on February 14, 1806. The Bourbon forces offered no resistance and retreated haphazardly into Calabria. Ferdinand's only consolation prizes were the Isle of Capri, held by his English allies, and the island of Ponza, garrisoned by Sicilian troops under the command of the Prince of Canosa.

The French proceeded to invade Calabria; and the English general Stuart prepared to meet them with his 6,000 soldiers. Landing in the Gulf of Saint Eufemia on July 2, Napoleon's forces were defeated. The British, however, failed to sustain their offensive, and General Massena's troops eventually succeeded in occupying all of Calabria.

The Parliament reconvened in Palermo on July 10. Although sympathies for the king had diminished, the three branches of the Sicilian government not only "rubber-stamped" their usual tributes but also graciously on this special occasion donated 100,000 ducats to Queen Maria Carolina so that she could "at least in part satisfy the generous longings that spring from her heart."

# Chapter XIV: The Intervention of London

## *1. The English Arrive in Sicily*

The year of 1806 was one of great uncertainty for Sicily. While Murat, installed as King of Naples, was marching his troops through Calabria and directly threatening the island, the English exploited Sicilians' fear of a French invasion. Winning the Bourbons' consensus, the British stationed an army of 8,000 men along the coast between Messina and Syracuse and a powerful fleet in Sicilian waters. At the same time, an emergency defense council composed of the Princes of Trabia, Cassaro and Belmonte was charged with the duty of raising an army of 30,000 volunteers.

In this instance, young men rushed to enlist because they were called upon to defend their homeland, not some remote country. Within a few months, these new militia (36,000 strong) were ready, thanks also to the barons' financial support and British weapons. To honor these fresh troops, Queen Maria Carolina was effusive with praise and the royal princesses presented them with hand-sewn banners.

The militia's enthusiasm, however, was short-lived. Jealous of this all-Sicilian army, Neapolitan refugees who had followed Ferdinand and his

43. Lord W. C. Bentinck, Supreme Commander of British forces in Sicily. From a printing by Sir T. Lawrence, 1816. (Palisi Collection)

Court back to Palermo schemed so successfully with the voluble queen that she persuaded the barons not to command the Sicilian battalions. In consequence, the militiamen disbanded after being disarmed.

In the midst of this crisis, the English Cabinet pressed Palermo to renew old treaties and recognize British supremacy on the island. Russia, using the French occupation of Dalmatia as a pretext, tried to land troops on the island in garrisons not held by the British. But their proposal was rejected by Acton and by the king himself.

Finally, on March 30, 1808, the Courts of London and Palermo signed an alliance pact. The treaty granted to England's troops and fleet all manner of safeguards and privileges in Sicily. In exchange, the British were to maintain on the island an expeditionary force of 10,000 men and to pay a subsidy to the king of 300,000 pounds. While a May 13, 1809 amendment to the pact raised the sum to 400,000 pounds, England paid only 100,000 that year.

At the same time that Ferdinand and Maria Carolina were supporting England's political approach to Sicily, they had their own designs, especially dear to the queen: the reconquest of Naples via secret, and very costly, diplomacy. For these intrigues and the life style to which they were accustomed, the Court of Ferdinand and Maria Carolina was always in need of extravagant funding. In response, at the general parliamentary session of February 15, 1810, the three branches granted the sovereigns the usual and supplementary tributes and a special allocation amounting to the enormous sum of 793,510 gold ounces. Furthermore, for the second time, the queen received "a personal gift" of 100,000 ducats. As if this money did not suffice, a royal edict of February 14, 1811, imposed a one percent tax on payments of every sort. A final decree during this period effected the transfer of all patrimonial lands of the Communes to the State.

The barons mounted a protest at this point, presenting a petition to the sovereigns that called for the repeal of the one percent tax. In answer to their request, Maria Carolina used her heavy hand and ordered the arrest of five of the major protesters, the Princes of Belmonte, Castelnuovo, Villa Franca and Aci and the Duke of Anjou. Apprehended on July 19, they were subsequently deported to Sicily's peripheral islands. With Ferdinand more and more isolated from the affairs of State and absorbed in his hunting trips, the queen, acting with naked might on her own initiative, merely precipitated her own final undoing.

## 2. The "Medicine" of Lord Bentinck

The five Sicilian barons, "riotous disturbers of the public peace," had hardly embarked on the Bourbon ship Tartaro for Ustica, Favignana,

Marettimo and Pantelleria when they allegedly sighted the English schooner bringing Lord William Cavendish Bentinck to Sicily. Lord Bentinck had been charged by London with two precise duties: Plenipotentiary Minister at the Court of Palermo and Commander-in-Chief of the British forces in the Mediterranean (excluding the standing garrisons on Malta). This sighting on the high seas was a major topic of conversation at the time—although it is doubtful that it ever occurred. But the fact that people attributed so much importance to a reputed episode gives us a sense of the drama of England's intervention in Sicily, a timely move in sharp contrast to the heavy handedness of the Palermitan Court and a classic example of how London maneuvered on the island in tune with its whole European strategy.

Actually, two months before, the English had decided to take a firmer stand regarding its relations with Sicily and the worsening of the island's political and economic crises. London had two major concerns in this context. First, the marriage of Maria Carolina's niece, Maria Luisa of Austria, and Napoleon I now gave the queen the previously undreamt of chance to form a new alliance with Bonaparte and to "trade" with the French, giving up Sicily in exchange for Naples. Secondly, England had wind of Maria Carolina's attempts to make secret pacts with its implacable enemy, France.

Lord Bentinck landed in Palermo on July 23, 1811, determined to rise to the occasion of these crises. He was a man of liberal ideas, a decisive and energetic soldier/diplomat; and he was fully aware of the delicate and weighty mission entrusted to him. At the time he was 37. Born in 1774 to the third Duke of Portland, Bentinck had distinguished himself in numerous military campaigns all over Europe and had quickly risen to the rank of lieutenant general. He had also served as Governor of the Indies.

From London, Bentinck brought a whole portfolio of proposals to Ferdinand, hoping to win the concessions his government wanted with the weapon of persuasion. Therefore Bentinck got to the point during his very first meeting with Ferdinand. London was requesting (1) Sicily's cooperation in resolving the crises "in total conformity to the principles of sincere friendship and allegiance"; (2) the Palermitan Court's acceptance of Britain's supreme command of all troops on Sicilian soil; (3) the formation of a new government on the island; (4) the eschewing of authoritarian measures (like the deportation of the five barons).

The king and queen, outraged, lashed out at Bentinck, who then was forced to abandon his diplomatic approach. The lord and the queen virtually locked horns. When he accused her of making secret deals with the enemy French, she scoffed and reminded him that she was Mistress of the Kingdom and he was just "a petty officer sent to pay homage and bow."

After this stormy session, Bentinck deemed it opportune to return to England for further instructions. Leaving Palermo on August 28, he was back by December 7, this time with more authority bestowed upon him by London. His Sicilian agenda was the following: (1) to accept the resignation of the government; (2) to form a new cabinet with ministers acceptable to the English; (3) to assume the command of all troops and fortifications; (4) to free the five barons; (5) to frame a liberal constitution.

The Bourbons did not yield without resistance; and the crisis was verging on civil war. Amid the confusion compounded by the disclosing of a filo-French conspiracy, Bentinck put 14,000 British soldiers on alert, threatened to deport the king and queen, and suspended all their subsidies. In effect, this was an ultimatum.

Bentinck, however, found a way out himself by meeting with Ferdinand's son, Francesco. Apparently the latter was the only person who understood the needs of the moment and Bentinck's message. Francesco was convinced that London did not want to dethrone the Bourbons or take possession of Sicily but merely to protect English interests in the Mediterranean. By January 16, 1812, Ferdinand had also listened to reason, making his son Francesco the Vicar of the King with "ample powers as his *alter ego*." Furthermore, before he withdrew to his Ficuzza palace, the monarch named Bentinck Captain General of the Army and Fleet of Sicily. The queen, stung to the quick, retired to the Marquis of Santa Croce's villa in Mezzomonreale.

### 3. The Constitution of 1812

Thus 1812 found Ferdinand at Ficuzza, hunting rabbits and pheasants from dawn to dusk with Marquis Agostino Cardillo; Maria Carolina far from her capital in the Santa Croce family's villa; and Francesco in Palermo, acting as the king's Vicar General and *alter ego*. Suddenly, calm seemed to reign at the Court. Taking advantage of this "truce," Francesco took two quick steps: he abolished the one percent tax on payments and had the five barons released from their island internments.

Returning to Palermo on January 20, 1812, the barons were publically acclaimed. Shortly thereafter, all five were chosen for the new liberal government demanded by Lord Bentinck. Prince Belmonte served as Minister of Foreign Affairs, Prince Castelnuovo as Minister of Finance, Prince Aci as War Secretary, and Prince Carini as Minister of Justice. These four ministers, along with Prince Cassaro, formed the Council of State where Lord Bentinck, as Captain General of the Army and Fleet, also sat. Every one of the queen's ministers was relieved of his duties and invited to leave Sicily.

1. The abbot Paolo
Balsamo.
Engraving.

The above arrangements were more than agreeable to the majority of Sicilians. Unfortunately, though, this new government was too soon put to the test of a food shortage that weighed equally upon the citizenry and the State Treasury. But an *ad hoc* commission managed to acquire grain from abroad, and Lord Bentinck met the emergency by having wheat stored in Messina's fortress distributed to the populace. While Bentinck made this distribution in the form of a loan, the gesture was deeply appreciated by the people.

The next urgent matter was the reform of the Kingdom's Constitution. Determined yet capable of listening, Lord Bentinck advised the vicar general not to drag his feet and to give Sicilians a more liberal body of laws and rights. Simultaneously, the Englishman, not wanting to impose a model from without, goaded the new government to propose its own constitutional reforms. Entrusted with this delicate task, Princes Belmonte and Castelnuovo turned for guidance to the illustrious Abbot Paolo Balsamo, Professor of Political Economy and Agriculture at Palermo University. Born in Termini Imerese in 1764, Balsamo, at 48, was a man of experience who had traveled widely and written numerous treatises. At the peak of his maturity, the professor drew up the proposal for a new constitution on the basis of his in-depth studies of the Kingdom's ancient charters and the existing constitutions of Spain, France and, naturally, England.

Paolo Balsamo composed his elaborate document consulting periodically with "the Constitutional Barons" Castelnuovo and Belmonte. The body of laws and rights that was ultimately approved by the Parliament and

Lord Bentinck was the result of countless hours of meditation on the inspiring significance of the English Constitution. Balsamo, however, failed to take into account the barons' interests. Deprived of their feudal privileges by the new document, the barons would soon stake their claims for damages and obtain compensation for their losses.

The Parliament met to vote on the Constitution on the momentous date of July 18, 1812. The fifteen articles of this historically vital document were approved the night of July 19 after more than 20 hours of debate. The representatives also decided to merge their Ecclesiastical and Baronial Branches.

That same night, it was solemnly proclaimed that Sicily's feudal system had been abolished forever. Few, if any, of those present could foresee that this constitution, approved so resoundingly, would be contested not only from without but also precisely within the chambers where it had been elaborated and ratified.

### 4. The Split in the New Parliament

The fifteen articles approved by the Sicilian Parliament in its historic session of 1812 provided the foundation of the new kingdom. Strangely enough, however, conservatives considered the Constitution reactionary. According to a British newspaper article published by a Palermitan Court denizen, "the government of Sicily, as presently defined in its parliamentary charter, is purely republican. And the king is, in effect, dethroned, as was Louis XVI by the Constitution of 1791."

It is true that King Ferdinand, after heated discussions with his personal advisors and considerable resistance, sanctioned the articles limiting the monarch's prerogatives and reducing the estates of the crown. Although these articles were modified to defer to a perplexed king, the fact remained that Ferdinand was obligated, in the event that he reconquered the Kingdom of Naples or acquired new territories, to step down from the independent throne of Sicily in favor of his son.

Notwithstanding such issues of *lése majestè*, a new, innovative spirit informed this constitution that, shaped primarily in the British mold, evinced the utmost respect for humanity and the individual. To this purpose, the document abolished torture and the use of iron shackles and, in penal matters, asserted that sentences could be appealed and absolutions were irrevocable. Furthermore, the constitution established that arrests could not be made on the basis of circumstantial or prejudicial evidence and that all citizens had the rights to express any political views and to protest against any injustices. Outlawing the censorship of printed matter, the document guaranteed the inalienable freedom of expression of personal ideas.

The new constitution would strike the bbarons as truly revolutionary, especially for its abolition of privileges and exclusive hunting reserves, its provisions against illiteracy, its elimination of private courts with the exception of the ecclesiastical, its institution of a Supreme Court of Appeals and five district tribunals for the same purpose. Paradoxically, the barons themselves, caught up in the tides of change, had approved these anti-feudal reforms and thus consented to making considerable sacrifices.

But, after voting for the Constitution, many barons continued to demand their feudal rights. They mounted opposition, above all, to the abolition of an heir's prerogative to transfer all or a part of his inheritance to another person. Most noteworthy among the opponents of the elimination of this ancient "right" were the conservative Princes of Belmonte and Cassaro.

The liberal Prince of Castelnuovo and other nobles who advocated democracy backed what they saw as a necessary reform in this area of inheritance. Thus, among the barons, a major split occurred that was to deepen *in re* another article of the Constitution designed to transfer properties of the aristocracy and the crown directly to the liberal State. Further lines of division were also established by the constitution itself, which split the Parliament into two houses, that of Lords (clergymen and hereditary nobles) and that of Commons (deputies elected by cities, rural districts and guilds).

Meanwhile, Maria Carolina, intriguing and fostering dissension within the realm, had spurred Ferdinand to attempt a return to power. Making his way in secret from Ficuzza back to Palermo on March 9, 1813, the king surfaced at the cathedral to the acclaim of those nobles still loyal to him. Two days later, he was proceeding to the Church of Saint Francis to be reinstated openly when Lord Bentinck had him detained "to prevent public disturbances."

Bentinck was already prepared to impose order with an iron fist after learning of the arrest of a German emissary of the queen who had made contact with the commander of the French troops in Calabria. Contradicting Ferdinand's wishes, the English lord mobilized all his forces in Sicily against a possible French invasion and, in a stormy session with the king, convinced him to yield his power—according to the agreement of January 16, 1812—to his son Francesco. Bentinck also exacted from Ferdinand the promise not to intervene in affairs of State without consulting the English and the consent to the queen's departure from the Kingdom of Sicily.

On June 14, 1813, Maria Carolina, now 61, left from Mazara. Destined for Austria via Constantinople, she journeyed for almost eight months. Finally reaching Vienna on February 2, 1814, the queen fell ill soon thereafter. By September 7, she had retired to her death bed in the Castle of Hetzendorf. That same evening, she expired.

Ferdinand did not remain a widower for long. Less than two months after Maria Carolina's death (November 27), he was secretly wed in Palermo to Donna Lucia Migliaccio, Duchess of Floridia and Princess of Partanna. This widow and mother of nine children was 44, and Ferdinand was 63.

## 5. In a Climate of Restoration

In the spring of 1813, the Constitution elaborated by the barons under the auspices of Lord Bentinck received provisional endorsement from the Parliament. Moreover, the elections taking place shortly thereafter gave another boost to the reforms written into the document by changing the cast of characters governing Sicily. For instance, Minister of Justice Prince Cassaro, considered too dependent upon the Court, was defeated—as was Secretary of War Prince Aci, who had had a falling-out with Bentinck. The new ministers in question were, respectively, the liberal Prince Carini and Ruggero Settimo, the future head of the revolutionary government of 1848, who was, at the time, a brilliant superior naval officer well regarded by the British.

When the Parliament met again on July 8, 1813, the prince vicar stressed the urgency of approving the State's financial plan for the following year. But his proposal for immediate approval was tabled after the most prominent advocate of democracy, the Catanese lawyer Emanuele Rossi, known for his Jacobin sympathies, declared that to discuss taxation before the official publication of the Constitution would "jeopardize the liberty and independence of the Chamber." Therefore, the Parliament deliberated on other issues, especially the prices of staple foods and vital consumer goods.

The Parliament's fixing of prices, however, put an end to the festive mood permeating Palermo. When riots broke out in the city to protest "democratic decisions," two of the instigators were condemned to death.

Parliament reconvened on July 25, but social tension could not be alleviated. Compounding this crisis was the struggle between the followers of Prince Belmonte and those of Prince Castelnuovo/ Villaermosa. Belmonte proposed that King Ferdinand be reinstated to restore order. In fact, that same month, after fishing tuna at Solanto, the deposed king had returned to his beloved Chinese Palace.

In the meantime, Lord Bentinck, who had been on a mission to Spain as part of his French-containment policy, came back to Palermo, setting the stage for a dramatic meeting with Ferdinand. The latter, loving power more than life itself, let himself be courted. Then he confessed that he would never seize the reins of the kingdom again without British consent and begged Lord Bentinck to exonerate him from this heavy commitment in such an emergency. It seems that the Englishman, in the face of this charade, suffered a moment of indecision, or even weakness. Surreptitiously, Ferdinand stepped in to announce his return to the throne "with all the authority and prerogatives attributed to the crown by the existing Constitution."

Bentinck, at this point, was tempted to rebel and, as he had done in the past, mobilize his troops. But, instead, he was content with suspending the payments of British subsidies.

In Europe at this juncture, times were changing rapidly. Napoleon was on the decline, the Bourbons were re-emerging in France, and alliances were shifting. In July of 1814, Lord Bentinck himself was relieved of his duties in Sicily and replaced by William A'Court, a modest functionary chosen by the conservatives to get back to "business as usual." Thus, on the international scene, Sicily lost its role as anti-French bastion; and once Murat had fallen into disgrace, the Kingdom of Naples could be reclaimed by the aging Ferdinand.

On May 15, 1815, in this climate of restoration, Ferdinand dissolved the Sicilian Parliament. He then flaunted his disrespect for what was left of Sicily's Constitution by going off to Naples without further consultation. Moreover, to avoid reminders of unhappy times for him, Ferdinand nominated his son as lieutenant general of the island, rather than as vicar.

In response, Sicilians, deluding themselves once again, urged that their land become an autonomous realm ruled by Francesco of Bourbon at the head of a constitutional government. The next year, however, Sicilians' hopes were dashed when, on December 8, 1816, Ferdinand abolished their constitution and, superseding his status as Ferdinand III of Sicily and IV of Naples, declared himself King Ferdinand I of the Kingdom of the Two Sicilies.

In short, the island was thus put in Neapolitan chains. But Sicilians never forgot the affront that this gesture of an absolutist monarch entailed. Their desire for revindication of the prerogatives lost with the abolition of the Constitution of 1812 would subsequently be the driving force of the revolts occurring on the island between 1820 and 1848 and of the ferment finally exploding in 1860.

### 6. The Heavy Hand of Naples

The aging sovereign regarded the title of King Ferdinand I of the Two Sicilies as his new skin. He, therefore, looked upon his obligations as Ferdinand III of Sicily and IV of Naples as null and void. Howsoever ludicrous his reasoning might have seemed at this juncture, he carried out his charade. Once in Naples, he assigned to oblivion the subjects of the island that had hosted him for so long. Furthermore, he surrounded himself with people who had suffered most from the British occupation of Sicily and who were apparently bent on exacting revenge from Sicilians.

As a consequence of Ferdinand's associations with the enemies of Sicily, the Neapolitan ministers, in 1816, imposed heavy taxes on the islanders. The Neapolitans' apparent purpose was to compensate Ferdinand I for the enormous expenses he had incurred to reconquer the Kingdom of Naples.

**45. 18th century map showing the three valleys of Sicily.**

In the following year, in accordance with Murat's administrative model adopted in Naples, the Bourbon government undertook profound political transformations "to frame a unified monarchy where all state functions would merge in one organism to produce the mutual happiness of each and every part." The result for Sicily was that such unifying tendencies not only "neapolitanized" the island but also deprived the region of those prerogatives its inhabitants had jealously guarded for centuries. The long and short of the whole matter was that Sicily was totally dependent on Naples socially, politically and economically.

The chief architects of this Bourbon domination of the island were the Ministers Luigi Medici and the Marquis of Tommasi. Their first step was to give the police extraordinary powers to prevent crimes against state security and to forbid "sectarian and factional associations." At the same time, the Neapolitan government in Sicily introduced a stamp tax on all court proceedings and abolished Palermo's lottery via a decree that enraged and mortified the city's inhabitants. To divide and conquer, Sicily's new rulers, in January of 1818, declared the old division of the island according to the valleys of Mazara, Noto and Demone invalid. From then on, Sicily was administered via the establishment of seven intendancies (or provinces): Palermo, Messina, Catania, Trapani, Syracuse, Agrigento, and Caltanissetta.

These provinces, in turn, oversaw the governance of subintendancies, which administered the various communes. A law of the Kingdom of Naples stipulated that every intendancy had specific "privileges to be respected" by the communes, especially a one percent duty to be paid on all their revenues. Needless to say, this new tax weighed heavily on cities like Palermo.

Soon after Naples took control of Sicily, other causes of discontent emerged on the island. For instance, a mandatory draft for young men from twenty to twenty-six was instituted—with exemptions only for those who had married before the age of twenty and for those who had degrees in jurisprudence and medicine.

This conscription law in a land which had never known compulsory military service engendered profound social disturbances. Marriages of convenience escalated—as did matriculations at Sicilian universities. To avoid the draft, many young men mutilated themselves or became fugitives from justice.

In this same period, a new concordat was signed between the Holy See and the Kingdom of the Two Sicilies. According to this pact, Catholicism was officially declared the sole religion of the realm. Simultaneously, the ecclesiastical properties confiscated in the past and not yet repossessed were restored to their original owners. This restoration was viewed in Palermo with great apprehension since Naples intervened in the retransferral of estates in favor of Messina, the city so dear to the Bourbons for having called, in 1815, for the abolishment of the constitution of Sicily.

But the royal decree that weighed most onerously on Sicilians was that of putting Neapolitans in charge of the legal and court system. The ancient laws of Sicily were thereby substituted by the Napoleonic codes that, a few years before, Ferdinand had ordered to be burned. Now he was adopting their ashes in the Kingdom of the Two Sicilies.

To add insult to injury, in August of 1819, the Supreme Police Council of Sicily was eliminated, and the exercise of all functions of Law and Order was entrusted to Marquis Ugo of Favare. At this point, Sicilians' righteous indignation against "an evil seigniory" reached its peak. Revolution was in the Sicilian air. From Spain, where the "Carbonari" had already made converts, the currents of discontent would flood Sicily as well.

# Chapter XV: 1820: The Beginning of the End

## 1. The Winds of Revolution

The year 1820 brought storms of revolution over Europe. Military leaders and liberal politicians, united in discontent, called for the re-establishment in Spain of the Constitution of 1812, and Ferdinand VII was forced to accept it with all its attendant prerogatives, including the right of new elections, amnesty for political prisoners and freedom of the press. The aftermath of these concessions in Spain were similar reforms enacted from Portugal to Germany, Poland and Greece.

**46. The revolt in Messina in 1848. Lithograph.**

Meanwhile, in the Kingdom of Naples, where underground Carbonari organizations were deeply rooted, revolution found fertile terrain. The imminent threat of such rooting induced Ferdinand I to recall his son Francesco from Sicily and to send a replacement in the person of General Diego Naselli, a weak and inept man who was hostile to Sicilians. And while the sovereign was on his very own ship the Galatea out in the Bay of Naples, where he was to celebrate his son's return from Palermo, the revolt of the Carboneria within the capital of the kingdom—an insurgency backed by the clergy and the military—would turn the tide against the aging Ferdinand. In effect, this uprising would force him to recognize the Spanish Constitution of 1812 that Francesco, now Vicar General with all the prerogatives of his father's *alter ego*, had endorsed.

In Sicily, Messina was first to heed the call for revolution. To this city, where most of the island's "Carbonari" were concentrated, Colonel Gaetano Costa directed his Princess Regiment after sweeping from Torre Annunziata through Campania, Basilicata and Calabria to incite these regions to revolt. The Messinese welcomed the colonel jubilantly; and the mayor of the city had gigantic barrels of wine brought to Cathedral Square to contribute to the festivities.

In Palermo, however, events in Naples and Messina went unnoticed until July 8, when the crew of an English ship reached the Sicilian capital bearing news of trouble in the whole kingdom. Still celebrating their sovereign's promulgation of the Constitution of 1812, the Palermitans were in the process of organizing their Patron Saint Rosalie's Feast. But this joy was quickly transformed into disappointment when Palermo's citizens learned that, from Naples, Ferdinand I had actually sanctioned the Spanish constitution for the Kingdom of the Two Sicilies instead of their own document and, under the aegis of the British, had abolished all feudal rights, not to speak of the freedoms of speech and the press. Subsequently, even those Sicilian nobles—the Princes of Villafranca and Cassaro and General Fardella—who had assumed high positions in the government of Naples

**47. A print depicting the 1848 revolt in Palermo.**

refused to swear allegiance to the king. Categorically stating their opposition to "the humiliating dependency of Sicily on the Kingdom of Naples" that their monarch was proposing, the nobles unfurled their yellow banner, symbol of Sicilian independence, to billow in the same winds of revolution as the red, black and turquoise pennant of the Carbonari. Thus the revolutionaries found a new and unforeseen inlet: Palermo.

On July 16 and 17, violence erupted in the city. Public offices were looted and destroyed, and a statue of Ferdinand was toppled and smashed. An angry mob invaded Castellammare Fort, taking possession of 14,000 guns and tons of ammunition. All men conscripted in the compulsory draft were liberated. Guerrilla warfare in the streets took its toll: 300 dead and 400 wounded. Given this crisis, General Naselli could think of nothing but flight under the protection of two wings of his army. Embarking on a sloop that was to escort him to the ship Tartaro, however, he was wounded in one knee by an insurgent. Before setting out to sea, Naselli rapidly penned a letter to the Council of State, affirming that he "had not disobeyed the king's commands" and entrusting the maintenance of law and order to that royal body.

## 2. New Hopes Dashed to the Ground

The Palermitan revolt was now in full swing. After Naselli had fled, the violence escalated when the military, flirting with the popular forces, suddenly regrouped and turned against them. Aiming its cannons on the people, the army drove them up the Cassaro. Scattering in back alleys, the rebels engaged the soldiers in hand-to-hand combat. At this point, prisoners liberated from the Vicaria came to the people's aid. In the outlying countryside, peasants mobilized with their pitchforks and other improvised weapons. All in all, 4,500 armed men rose up in and around Palermo, and many units of the army surrendered to the insurgents.

Excesses were not uncommon. Scores of houses were looted, and there were cases of gratuitous violence. Many criminals, released from the Vicaria, took revenge on their old enemies. In this state of anarchy, the consuls of the 72 worker and artisan organizations of the city requested that the mayor, Prince Torrebruna, set up an emergency council for the maintenance of the public peace.

The mayor acted quickly, instituting a board of eighteen aristocrats and bourgeoises. Cardinal Gravina accepted the duty of heading this emergency council. But its task was an arduous one. Excesses continued. For instance, the Princes Aci and Cattolica were killed when a mob vented all its hatred of authority by literally tearing them to pieces. Finally, on July 24, Prince Giuseppe Alliata of Villafranca, dispatched by Naples, reached

Palermo. This Neapolitan originally of a noble Palermitan family was noted for his non-partisan approach and considered the right man to act with decision and firmness in the interests of law and order.

Prince Villafranca was Naples's man-of-the-moment, chosen after a Sicilian delegation sent to Naples had made two seemingly contradictory requests: that Sicily form a government able to guarantee national independence and that the Spanish constitution be adopted on the island. Arriving at the port of Palermo, Villafranca was escorted triumphantly to his palace. Shortly after Cardinal Gravina resigned, the prince was elected President of the Council.

Nevertheless, Villafranca failed to restore tranquility. On the contrary, Palermitans became even more tense and exasperated when the vicar prince issued a proclamation deploring the state of affairs and urging all citizens "to respect law and order and to obey the king once again." The emergency city council itself responded by choosing the noted polemicist and patriot Giovanni Aceto to write a rejoinder. In this document, he went so far as to assert that the Palermitan Revolution was an appropriate and legitimate answer to Bourbon misrule. Naturally, this firm stand angered the king and his court; and, after a final appeal made by Villafranca that Palermitans return to business as usual under the aegis of the new lieutenant general, the Prince of Scaletta, Naples and Palermo broke irrevocably.

The Prince of Villafranca deluded himself into thinking the formation of "a guerrilla army" would be the solution to Palermo's problems. Believing in the myth of "the people's war," he enlisted volunteers from city and country and armed these popular forces. While this may have been a laudable, albeit dubious, experiment in democracy, these "guerrillas," nonetheless, could not stop the subsequent invasion of an army of 6,000 men commanded by General Florestano Pepe. Nor could the popular forces impede the surrender of Palermo which was formalized by the October 5 treaty signed on board the English cutter "The Racer."

In spite of all the difficulties that Pepe encountered in working out a compromise arrangement with the new president of the Sicilian Council, Prince Luigi Moncada of Paternò, Naples was neither sympathetic with the general nor satisfied with the treaty. Thus, in November of 1820, the Bourbons replaced Pepe with Pietro Colletta, the future historian of the Kingdom of Naples. Still not content with his commander in Sicily, Ferdinand sent a new one (Lieutenant General Vito Nunziante) to Palermo in January of 1821.

The situation on the island was still in flux and confusion. Misunderstandings, conflicts and uncertainties reigned. In this climate most unfavorable to Sicilian liberals, who were branded hot-headed separatists by Naples, lightning struck on February 9, 1821, in the form of the news that the king had abolished the Constitution in accordance with decisions taken in Ljubljana at a summit manipulated by Austria, "the epitome of reaction." Moreover, it was learned that, to enforce this landmark decision, an Austrian army of 50,000 men under the command of General Fremont had already crossed the Po River and was headed for the Kingdom of Naples to back Ferdinand.

Carrying out the king's wishes and commands, the Austrian troops occupied Palermo on May 1, 1821. Their arrival put a virtual end to Sicily's momentary hopes and grand illusions and signified the triumph of absolutism. This invasion, however, did not snuff out the patriots' fire nor stifle Sicilians' autonomist aspirations.

### 3. Moment of Challenges

As destiny would have it, more patriots paid with their lives for their noble efforts to change the order of things. From 1821 until the Sicilian Revolution of 1848, groups of courageous souls constantly challenged the vigilant Bourbon tyranny. With virtually no outside support, weapons, or military apparatus, these revolutionaries were strong only in spirit and daring. Moreover, so much worked against them to nullify all their efforts to mount an insurrection: betrayals from within their small cadres and co-conspirators' last minute "repentance" and—from without—the repressive machine of the Neapolitan State. With odds like these, many Sicilian liberals were marched to the gallows.

Nevertheless, the arrival of Austrian troops in Palermo, where they harassed and intimidated the populace, and the May 30, 1821 decree strictly prohibiting any kind of public meeting failed to lead to the disbanding of the Carbonari. In July of that year, Salvatore Meccio, legal counsel and official of the Internal Guard, organized a "Carbonari" sect with the participation of Ferdinando Amari (the historian Michele's father), several priests, and the Marquis of Favare's only son. But infighting within the cadre and fellow-conspirators turned informers caused Meccio's plot to backfire. Nine rebels, including two priests, were subsequently executed on January 31, 1822; and, on September 18, Meccio himself was guillotined after a mock-trial during which he denied his participation in any subversive group.

In the following years, capital punishment for sectarian crimes and minor conspiracies continued to be a matter of course. For instance, in 1824, Doctor Girolamo Torregrossa and the tailor Giuseppe Sessa were put to death for belonging to the French "Carboneria" for New Reforms; and in December of 1826, Gaetano Abela, a major leader of "Carbonari" activity in 1820, was shot by a firing squad. Apparently, a number of policemen tried to help Abela escape at the moment the carriage escorting him to his death left Castellammare Fort. But the prisoner failed to break free and was safely conducted to his fate. In September of 1829, five members of the secret Reform Carboneria—Isidoro Alessi from Palazzo Adriano, Giuseppe Ragusa from Sciacca, Cosimo Cambria from Palermo, and Michele Zurlo and Niccolò Saulle from Foggia—were pitchforked to death in the infamous Fort of Saint James on the island of Favignana.

The 20 year old Ferdinand II's ascension to the Neapolitan throne on November 8, 1830, struck many Sicilian liberals as a significant turn of events, especially since, simultaneously, Lieutenant Pietro Ugo, Marquis of Favare, head of the Bourbon police force, was replaced by King Leopold's brother, the Count of Syracuse. Such a choice appeased Sicilians in that they

48. Historian Michele Amari in a photo of 1865.

now had a prince of royal blood as ruler in Palermo. Therefore, when the count entered the city on March 10, 1831, he was regaled by the populace. Similar festivities took place in July of that same year on the occasion of Ferdinand II's visit to the island.

Continually naive, Sicilian liberals believed the time was ripe to ask for independence from Naples and for their own prince. As Valentino Labate, the perceptive author of a history of Sicilian Carboneria, wrote, "in the burning southern Italian imagination, such a design must have seemed easily realizable." With this aim in view, a Carbonari-style conspiracy of more than 2000 persons was organized in Palermo, designed to take shape in a July, 1831 revolt during Saint Rosalie's Feast, precisely when Ferdinand was visiting Palermo. But, as usual, certain co-conspirators informed the police of the plot, allowing the forces of repression to mobilize. Nevertheless, on the evening of September 1, 1831, Domenico Di Marco, ex-bell-foundryman and later royal tax guard, led a handful of insurgents in a revolt originating at Termini Gate. Shouting "Long Live the Constitution," Di Marco's band proceeded according to their pre-determined itinerary, trying to join forces with other conspirators. But the group found no supporters along the way; and, realizing that they had been betrayed, the rebels launched desperate cries of rage at frightened passers-by. Thus, their appeals faded into the dark—although the police tracked eleven of the conspirators down and, accusing them of robbery and murder, had them condemned to death. The sentence was executed in Consolation Square on October 26.

The following year, the first issue of Giuseppe Mazzini's *Young Italy*, published in Marseille on March 18, 1832, affirmed the justice of DiMarco's cause. As the author of the relevant article wrote, "Di Marco and his eleven friends (actually, the number was ten) were sacrificed for having tried to liberate their country from its abhorrent servitude."

### 4. The Pretext of Cholera

The presence in Palermo of King Leopold's brother, the Count of Syracuse, did not change the Neapolitan Court's authoritarian approach to Sicily. On the contrary, via the intervention of the lieutenant's advisors, Minister Antonino Mastropaolo and Prince Antonio Lucchesi Palli of Campofranco, Naples continued to apply its repressive measures in total indifference to the Sicilian people's discontent. Forewarned by the 1831 riots in Romagna and the disturbances in Modena, the Marches, and Umbria, the Neapolitan Court was wary of any liberal concessions.

Nevertheless, via mediation, the Count of Syracuse succeeded in easing tensions between Naples and Palermo. In January of 1833, for example, the count granted to Neapolitan and Sicilian ministers the right to choose their own bases of operation. In addition, he re-instituted the Secretary of State for Sicilian Affairs, an office set up after the 1820 Revolution, then subsequently abolished by the Bourbons.

Naples, however, remained on guard, never failing to doubt Sicilians' loyalty to its court. The Bourbons' suspicions were further aggravated by unconfirmed rumors of a planned invasion of Sicily by exiles now in France. While the time and the place of such a venture were never verified, the rumor was enough to worsen the general climate of mistrust and to lead to the Count of Syracuse's ousting in the winter of 1835.

The pretext for removing the count was, in truth, ludicrous. The king's brother was accustomed to participating during the Carnival season in a parade where, dressed in a costume like the most notable of Sicilian aristocrats, he would ride in an elaborately decorated cart. That year, the theme of the procession happened to be the triumphant entrance of King Roger into Palermo; and Leopold, decked out in the style of a Norman king, was acclaimed and applauded in the streets as he headed the traditional parade.

The report of this event that the police sent to Naples, however, did not please Ferdinand II. The suspicious monarch read between the lines, detecting in the masquerade a hidden significance: that Sicilians had symbolically chosen Leopold as the future King of Sicily. Therefore, Ferdinand ordered that a frigate set sail immediately for Palermo to collect Leopold and escort him back to Naples. In Leopold's stead, his advisor, the Prince of Campofranco, was made lieutenant.

During Campofranco's term of office, the dread Asiatic disease of cholera struck both Naples and Sicily in 1836. This calamity, creating an atmosphere of mourning all over the island and dealing death to many illustrious men and women, was one more cause for Sicilians to revolt, especially after a general quarantine throughout the island brought on an economic crisis. The situation was most grave in Messina, a city hit particularly hard by the suspension of its port activity and maritime commerce. In response, on June 23, 1837, riots broke out, and the authorities managed to quell them only in the middle of July.

At about the same time in Palermo, the cholera epidemic was raging. For Saint Rosalie's Feast alone (July 15), 1,000 deaths were reported. Among the victims were historians Domenico Scinà and Niccolò Palmeri, the philanthropist Pietro Pisani, and the painter Vincenzo Riolo.

In the grim context of a virtual witch-hunt, alleged "plague-spreaders" reputed to be the cause of contagion were persecuted. Syracuse witnessed how innocent citizens were accused of "importing cholera" and indiscriminately slaughtered. Catania saw armed mobs, organized to hunt down plague-spreaders, ignite an anti-Neapolitan riot. In the piazzas, it was announced that this so-called Asiatic disease was in fact Bourbonic. Such an outrageous statement sufficed to cause the disturbances to grow even more violent.

Hearing of this resurgence of disorder, Ferdinand did not hesitate to grant all his *alter ego* powers to Minister of Police, the Marquis Francesco Saverio Del Carretto. The Marquis, from 1820 on, had distinguished himself for his repressive ferocity. Now, as Francesco Guardione observed in his essay on the Bourbons in Sicily, "the minister used violence, injustice and tyranny to convince the king that his presence and decisive actions in Sicily had crushed the revolution previously so widespread throughout so many provinces." Equally widespread, and seemingly everlasting, was Sicilians' martyrdom.

## 5. Still, the Carrot and the Stick

The repression organized by Del Carretto as the head of the "commando forces" sent by Naples to Sicily became a veritable Bourbon vendetta. The king's *alter ego* landed at Catania in August of 1837 and, after setting up a military tribunal to try insurgents, rushed to Syracuse to meet the emergency there.

In the latter city, among those condemned to death was one Mario Adorno who had attempted to prove that the cholera epidemic was the work of "poisoners." Adorno was to face the firing squad along with his 18 year old son. Asking to witness the boy's execution, he was granted this strange privilege. Satisfied, he then fell under another hailstorm of lead.

As a corollary to Bourbon repression, Ferdinand II demonstrated that it was time for islanders to abandon all their precious illusions by eliminating the Ministry of Sicilian Affairs and by sending to Sicily a mere lieutenant, Duke Onorato Gaetani of Laurenzana, as Campofranco's replacement. Ferdinand was apparently convinced that his heavy-handed approach had finally subdued Sicilians. Therefore, in 1838, the king returned to the island and, the following year, granted amnesty to political prisoners and dissolved his military tribunals.

In the decade of 1830-40, a new interest was developed in Sicily: the taste for classical Italian literature. The numerous editions of the works of Alfieri, Foscolo and Leopardi are testimonies to this Sicilian passion. Manzoni, however, was not well-received on the island because, in this period of political tension, his form of Christianity seemed too resigned and fatalistic. Sicilians preferred to "Manzonian fatalism" the periodical literature, both scientific and humanistic, that was published and distributed all over their island.

A great contributor to both scientific and humanistic Sicilian culture during this period was Michele Amari, son of the anti-Bourbon conspirator. An advocate of Sicilian independence and the Constitution of 1812, Amari firmly believed that "the pen could circumvent the king's censorship and usher in the Revolution." Amari's *History of the War of the Sicilian Vespers* was deeply rooted in this conviction. With historical perspective, he argued that the lesson of the events of 1282 could be applied for a better understanding of the state of affairs in the Sicily of 1830-40 and that Palermo's anti-French revolt during the 1300s could be a model for instigating

Sicilians to vent their hatred of the Bourbons in the nineteenth century. The book he called *A Period of Sicilian History in the Thirteenth Century* to avoid censors' suspicions was designed for such revolutionary purposes. As Amari later revealed, this work was almost done by 1837, but a cholera epidemic detained him from completing the final version. This volume was eventually published in Palermo in 1842 with the Bourbon censors' approval. While Amari's real message eluded these steadfast bureaucrats, its tremendous success among Sicilian intellectuals for its historical associations and explosive tendencies did not escape Del Carretto. Consequently, the lieutenant warned the king of "this subversive book," Amari's work was withdrawn from circulation, and the censor who has consented to its publication was branded as the author's accomplice and summarily discharged. Amari himself was relieved of his post in the Secretaryship of State, transferred to Naples, and put under surveillance. Fearful of being arrested, he fled to France soon thereafter.

But the spirit of insurrection in the Kingdom of the Two Sicilies was all-pervasive by now. Revolution was no longer a matter of isolated initiatives, but a coherent movement spurred by Neapolitan and Sicilian patriots and spread like wild fire down the peninsula and across the island. While the Sicilian insurrections of 1843 and 1844 were thwarted, and while, in June of 1844, an ill-fated landing on the Calabria coast cost the brothers Attilio and Emilio Bandiera and seven fellow-conspirators their lives, uprisings did not cease. Witness those of 1847, in both Messina and Reggio Calabria.

Ferdinand returned to Palermo in July of 1847 for the customary celebrations. As he was riding in his carriage, an unidentified subject threw a pamphlet through the window. The king picked up this document and grew pale upon reading its title: *The Protest of the People of the Two Sicilies*. After thumbing through the text, Ferdinand flew into a rage. In the pamphlet, His Majesty was described as "a true Bourbon: foolish, presumptuous, avaricious, superstitious, insensibly cruel and overweaningly proud." Del Carretto, "the spy," was accused of "getting fat by filching 40,000 ducats per year." This harsh indictment, later identified as the work of Luigi Settembrini, amounted to the ultimate condemnation of Ferdinand's kingdom.

# Chapter XVI: The Ultimate Conspiracy

### 1. The Dawn of 1848

A key to the Sicilian Revolution of 1848 was the tightening of relations between Sicilian and Neapolitan conspirators. This association solidified an insurrectional movement originating in Italy and spreading throughout continental Europe. While in other parts of Europe prolonged struggles were aimed at eliminating the despotism of Metternich, Sicilians tried to launch their revolution—one that lasted little more than fifteen months and, ultimately, failed—against Bourbon absolutism. Whatever the outcome, Sicily's dreams, unlike its separatist and independentist designs of 1820, were informed this time by a nationalist spirit—i.e., the desire to unite the island with the League of Italian States.

**49.
Francesco
Crispi.
Engraving.**

The Palermitan conspirators, challenging the ever-vigilant Bourbon police, set a date for their revolt: January 12, when Ferdinand would turn 38. Things, in fact, happened according to the insurgents' plans. That day, in Palermo, crowds of people were anxiously awaiting the ritualistic cannon salute from Castellammare Fort that normally announced the king's birthday. After the cannons had been fired, many Palermitans remained in the streets or at their windows out of curiosity to see what would happen next. Suddenly an abbot was seen making his way up one of Palermo's main streets. As this clergyman brandished a cross and urged people to rise up and overthrow their oppressors, a certain Giuseppe La Masa appeared and, with indomitable revolutionary spirit, began to wave a canestalk at the tip of which were tied red and white handkerchiefs linked with a green ribbon. Although the revolt, at the start, did not have any organic unity, the conspirators' first skirmishes with Bourbon soldiers at Maqueda and Saint Antonino Gates and on Calderai Street—encounters in which several children were among the casualties—helped to fan the embers of anti-Bourbon hatred. At the sight of other Sicilians' blood, moreover, secret backers of the revolution mustered their courage and took to the streets.

On that first day of violent encounters between insurgents and Bourbon troops, attempts were made in a building on Piazza Fieravecchia to form a provisional committee to organize and carry out the revolution. But this democratic initiative fizzled in spite of the fact that it had been the most disinherited of the poor classes to lead the charge against the enemy. On the second day, however, popular participation in the insurrectional movement was more extensive and focused thanks to the arrival of peasants armed with knives, pitchforks and even pistols and rifles from the towns of Villabate, Bagheria and Misilmeri. These reinforcements were the key to the insurgents' initial victory against the royal troops on Via Toledo. The same popular army without a leader subsequently stormed the police barracks, tried and executed many of the "spies" there, occupied government offices and the military hospital, induced many Sicilian soldiers to back the "people's war," and seized weapons and currency to further the revolutionary cause.

This groundswell of popular activity finally materialized in a revolutionary committee of which La Masa was a key member. Patriotic nobles and other individuals whose allegiances had previously been declared "underground" finally took open stands. The only class to hesitate at this point was the bourgeoisie, inclined as it was to accept reforms within the Bourbon system. Such reformism had already led to progress and prosperity for entrepreneurs in industry, commerce, and maritime shipping. Yet even some Sicilian capitalists were opposed to these developments encouraged by the Bourbons. Damaged by Neapolitan protectionism, these dissenting entrepreneurs expressed their grievances by siding with the aristocracy. At the hour of the outbreak of the revolution, the common front that enlightened bourgeoises and nobles chose to defend was the reinstating of the Constitution of 1812 as modified to meet the changing needs of the times.

The revolt spread from Palermo to other major Sicilian cities. Catania rose on January 24, Messina on the 25th, and Trapani and Caltanissetta on the 29th. With the formation of a provisional government and a national guard, the revolution seemed to be consolidated. Such institutionalization also encouraged bourgeoises to participate in the hopes of curtailing possible excesses.

At this juncture, the events in Sicily brought the Neapolitan government's crisis to its peak. Consequently both the Bourbon Court and the Sicilian rebels requested the mediation of England, a nation considered the champion of people's constitutional rights. The English representative in Naples, Lord Minto, then took the initiative to propose to Ferdinand II the following reforms: the nomination of a lieutenant for Sicily who would be Sicilian by birth or by noble blood and the creation of a Sicilian Ministry that could convene its own parliament "yet still function under the aegis of the Bourbon monarchy." The sovereign wisely accepted this proposal and nominated the 70 year old Ruggero Settimo as his lieutenant and virtually all members of the provisional government as his ministers. This concession on the part of the king, dictated by fear, was, nonetheless, a compromise Palermitans refused to accept.

## 2. The Formal Break With Naples

In open defiance of the Neapolitan monarchy, the Provisional Sicilian Government made the unanimous decision to reject the king's proposal on the grounds of its violation of the Constitution of 1812. Accepting Lord Minto's advice, Sicilians also sent a counterproposal to the king via this same British mediator. This document made it clear that, while the principle of union of the Two Sicilies was still upheld, the monarch's representative on the island should exercise the prerogatives and functions befitting a real viceroy, the ministers should be directly responsible to this governor, and Sicily itself should control one-fourth of the fleet and army around and on its own territory.

Ferdinand II regarded these counterproposals from Palermo as an ultimatum to be scorned. Therefore, he registered his "protest," declaring his previous concessions null and void. The die was cast; and Naples and Sicily made a formal break. That noon of March 25, 1848, in the Church of Saint Dominic, when the reconstituted Sicilian Parliament recognized such a "divorce," was indeed a solemn moment for Sicilians. Ruggero Settimo himself, unanimously proclaimed as President of the Realm, was entrusted to form an autonomous government. Complying, he chose Mariano Stabile as Minister of Foreign Affairs and Commerce, Baron Riso as Minister of War and the Navy, the Marquis of Torrearsa as Minister of Finance, Pasquale Calvi as Minister of Internal Affairs and Police, the Prince of Butera as Minister of Education and Public Works, and Counsel Gaetano Pisanò as Minister of Justice and Religious Cults.

On April 13, after a preliminary discussion, the Parliament entertained the proposal that King Ferdinand's rule be forfeited. The atmosphere of this session was tense. After all, royal troops were still occupying Messina's citadel. Nevertheless, in the midst of a heated debate, Emerico Amari proposed that, every time the Parliament met, its delegates should rise and swear openly that "Ferdinand II's dynasty in Sicily has come to an end." At this highly-charged and solemn moment in Sicilian history, Amari's declaration was unanimously approved by both the House of Commons and the House of Lords. Later, referring to this milestone decision, Stabile would write: "Every Sicilian, in his heart, knew that the decline of the Bourbons was imminent. No emergency act of their government could have stopped or even delayed Ferdinand's fall." In effect, the throne of Sicily was proclaimed vacant, pending the choice of a new king from the House of the Bourbons.

This compromise was based on the conviction that the English, who had by then committed themselves to supporting the Sicilian Constitution, would stop Ferdinand from invading Sicily. The concession of choosing a new Bourbon monarch was made to avoid an open conflict with Naples. At the same time, the Parliament was trying to stem the republican tides upon which Sicilian democrats were aiming to sweep into power. But, for the nth time, Sicilians' aspirations were thwarted. Lord Palmerston, speaking for London on November 27, categorically stated that "the British government could not endorse the Constitution of 1812." This declaration, in effect, confirmed England's neutrality regarding the upheavals of 1848.

A new Sicilian statute, approved on July 9, endorsed the principle of popular sovereignty and limited the exercise of executive power. This legislative measure, so progressive in those times, was, however, resisted by Ferdinand via all the resources left in his repertoire. To mount his opposition, the king obtained a loan of eight million ducats from the banker Rothschild, who had been a long-time supporter of the Kingdom of Naples. Thus financed, Ferdinand sent an expedition against Sicily commanded by General Carlo Filangeri, an old officer of Murat's. Filangeri's fleet departed from Naples on August 30 and, by September 7, had occupied Messina. Three days later, Filangeri was in control of Milazzo. On the 13th of September, Sicily was forced to make a formal peace treaty with Naples.

All eyes in Europe were turned toward the dramatic events in Sicily. Under this pressure, Ferdinand, who still failed to comprehend the political import of these agons, decided to be generous. Issuing his own ultimatum, he offered Sicilians their own viceroy. He also granted amnesty to all islanders except the leaders of the insurgency.

As the revolt flared up again in several Sicilian towns and cities, both houses of the island's Parliament rejected Ferdinand's "offers." By now, in 1849, however, the revolutionary fervor of certain sectors of Sicilian society had waned, especially that of a bourgeoisie no longer sympathetic to popular uprisings. As Baron Riso stated opportunely: "The times have changed. It is not 1820, it is 1849." Riots occurred once more in Palermo toward the end of April and on May 3rd; but, when Filangeri's troops entered the city on May 15, they found ubiquitous manifestos signed by Riso urging Palermitans to regard the soldiers as brothers.

Ferdinand's amnesty, meanwhile, excluded only 43 persons, but his recourse to repression was, nonetheless, ruthless. The Neapolitan Court also retaliated by imposing new taxes on Sicily. Fortunately, many patriots had already left the island. For instance, Ruggero Settimo, the most prominent of revolutionaries, took refuge on Malta. Other insurgents managed to escape to Piedmont and Liguria.

### 3. The Last Decade

During the last decade of Bourbon domination in Sicily, the poor classes emerged once again as protagonists of revolution. In spite of their bloody suppression by an all-pervasive, ruthless police/spy network, common people driven by political passion organized a series of attempted *coups*. These uprisings, progressively vexing and enraging Naples, constituted the popular support of and foundations for the actions of the enlightened patriots working for change "at the top"—notably, Francesco Crispi, Emerico and Michele Amari, Giuseppe La Farina, Vito D'Ondes Reggio, and Filippo Cordova.

In the meantime, Giuseppe Mazzini, that great romantic spirit and political agitator, was acting as coordinator-in-absentia for the liberal Sicilian cadres struggling for the kind of Italian unity Mazzini himself envisioned. Many political leaders in Sicily, however, were qualifying these goals, convinced as they were of the absolute need for Sicilian autonomy. As Michele Amari summed up their point of view, "while Sicily's annexation to the emancipated provinces of Italy is necessary, the island's autonomy is indispensable."

In the aftermath of the events of 1848-49, Sicily was subjugated once again under the Bourbon yoke. But no one could put a stop to political agitation and riots. This time, in spite of brutal repression and numerous arrests, Catania took the initiative. Palermo followed suit at the end of January, 1850. Of course, the city paid the usual price: the heavy Bourbon hand and big stick. Moreover, six conspirators, including the twenty year old student Niccolò Garzilli, were condemned to death and shot post-haste.

As internal revolts flared, revolutionaries kept up the pressure outside

Sicily by constantly urging the natives of the island to organize an all-out effort to liberate themselves. Francesco Crispi, in exile in Turin, sent passionate appeals to his fellow islanders. Mazzini himself, from London, communicated with the central revolutionary cadre of Palermo, also contributing funds to the cause.

Mazzini, however, was agitating for a form of republican government undesirable for most Sicilians. In response to his missives, the Genoese leader received a letter from Palermo stating that "the prevailing public spirit of our agitation affirms our desire to be independent of Naples, but few of us envision the kind of republic you propose." In this epistle, the Palermitan patriots also stressed their need of weapons and their openness to a *condottiere* like Giuseppe Garibaldi as leader of their insurrectionary movement.

Mazzini continued to press for his objectives in Sicily, sending one of his emissaries to Palermo. Undaunted when his man and his Sicilian contacts were arrested, Mazzini organized a landing of political exiles on the coast of Messina Province. But these insurgents were apprehended by the Bourbon police.

In spite of the rebellious mood of the times, when Ferdinand II arrived in Messina in October of 1852, its citizens, who had suffered the dire consequences of the Revolution of 1848, gave him a triumphant welcome. While this reaction shocked Sicilian patriots, it confirmed Ferdinand's own intentions to lift the state of siege that had been declared on Messina in 1849 and to reduce royal taxes in the interests of developing commerce. Clearly, at this moment of tension and danger for the Neapolitan monarchy, the king's moves were conciliatory, if not propagandistic.

The Bourbons, however, did nothing to improve the kingdom's climate of suspicion, going so far as to ban the Neapolitan song "Palommella biuanca" (Little White Dove). Apparently the censors thought this air was the anthem of revolutionary Sicilians to be used as a rallying cry during insurrections.

But censorship and repression did not stop with music. Vincenzo Florio was severely reproved for having named his steamship the *Independant*. And in October of 1852, the commissioner of Catania Province informed the rector of the city's university that, "by a supreme decree," all beards sported by professors, students and staff "must be shorn in accordance with proper moral conduct."

Riots continued throughout Sicily—many of them organized with extraordinary dedication and improvisation. For example, in response to letters written by Rosolino Pilo, Francesco Bentivegna (a young Corleonese deputy in the Sicilian Parliament) was spurred to action. On the evening of

November 22, 1856, Bentivegna, a few comrades from Mezzojuso and Villafrati, and a number of prisoners they had freed from jail tried to incite Palermitans to riot on the pretext of an alleged English landing in the port. As Bentivegna and his men marched toward the city, joined by other dreamers from Lercara, Pizzi, Marineo and Ciminna, the Bourbons met them with an imposing army of foot soldiers and artillery and cavalrymen. Realizing that no support would come from Palermo, Bentivegna disbanded his forces and tried to flee. Tracked down, he was tried by a war council, condemned to death, and executed on December 20.

At the same time, news reached Sicily of the attempt on Ferdinand's life by the Cosentino Agesilao Milano, infantryman of the Third Cacciatori Battalion. While the actions of this soldier of republican sympathies and the deputy from Corleone had little, if anything, in common, many people construed these spontaneous expressions of rebelliousness as the beginnings of a widespread insurrection.

### 4. Torturers and Patriots

The period from 1857 to 1860 was distinguished for its virtually hysterical repression. The servile and sadistic Police Commissioner Salvatore Maniscalco, carrying on the work of Filangeri (1848-55) and his successor, Field Marshall and Aide-to-the-King Prince Paolo Ruffo of Castelcicala (1855-57), was charged to eliminate the slightest traces of resistance to the Bourbons. A study of the Ligurian and English press during this time gives one a good idea of all the methods of torture Maniscalco adopted in Bourbon police offices and jails to exact confessions from Sicilian patriots: the "shoe" applied with screws to the feet; the "glove," also called "the angelic tool," that crushed the thumbs; and that refined instrument, the "hood of silence," a device developed during the Middle Ages by the Inquisition.

As the climax of social upheavals and official intransigence approached, Sicily became an arena for the ideological confrontation between Mazzinians and Cavourians. The former, supported by illustrious exiles like Michele Amari (then in Paris) and Francesco Crispi, who was in constant contact with Mazzini himself, organized a series of specific actions to inspire Sicilians to take arms under the banner of a united Italy. The latter, led by Giuseppe La Farina, favored unity under the Piedmontese monarchy. Neither group was particularly comfortable with Mazzini's declared republican sympathies.

In the midst of this political ferment, in March of 1858, Mazzini's emissary from London, Maurizio Quadrio, arrived in Messina to distribute Mazzini's underground pamphlet on guerrilla warfare. About the same time, the patriot-in-exile, Rosolino Pilo, snuck into Genoa to meet with Crispi and inform him of his plot to return to Sicily and launch the decisive insurrection.

News in Palermo of French-Piedmontese victories on the battlefields of Lombardy filled the Liberals with hope. The evening of June 26, 1859, egged on by a few "hot heads," the Lodge of Good Friends on Via Toledo and the Circle of Nobles on Piazza Bologna both lit candles to celebrate, cautiously, the triumph of Solferino. This small gesture, in turn, infuriated Maniscalco, who, already exercising limitless power on the island, had his police close down these two social clubs and arrest the scions of many noble Palermitan families.

Among those detained was Brancaccio of Carpino, who narrated the events of the period in his autobiographical *Three Months in Palermo's Prison*. Carpino, in this volume, describes a feast held in the home of the Marchioness of Spedalotto that spring. Allegedly, the banquet ended with cries of "Long Live Verdi." Carpino adds, "the five letters of the name of the great Italian composer and maestro comprised an acronym for 'Vittorio Emanuele Re d'Italia' (i.e., Victor Emanuel, King of Italy). Such was the rallying cry heard throughout the kingdom at that point, repeated with great enthusiasm by lords and ladies toasting with their full cups raised on high."

In August of that year, Crispi entered Palermo under an alias with falsified documents: Emanuele Pareda, Argentine merchant. During his brief stay in the city, the Sicilian political leader taught co-conspirators how to fabricate "Orsini-style bombs." Demonstrating the technique himself, Crispi made terra cotta shapes, then covered them with fused iron. Filled with gunpowder and provided with a fuse to ignite them, these bombs were designed to explode into thousands of deadly pieces of shrapnel as soon as they hit the ground. Shortly thereafter, the Sicilian patriots received from England a clandestine shipment of enough lead and gunpowder to adapt the Orsini bomb by coating clay flasks of the liquor Curaçao with the metal.

From Bologna, September 29, Giuseppe Garibaldi sent a message to all Sicilian liberals which was a virtual manifesto announcing his up-coming expedition: "The cause championed by my comrades-in-arms and myself is not a provincial one. On the contrary, it is the aspiration of all Italians from the Isonzo River to Trapani, from Taranto to Nice. The redemption of Sicily is ours as well, and we urge you to unite as one under our banner: 'Italy and Victor Emanuel'. If you are ready now, rise up! If not, organize and grow strong in your union."

The Eve of the Revolution, the year of 1859, came to a close with an October insurrection, resulting in the usual repression, and a direct attempt on Maniscalco's life in November. While he received only minor back wounds, no one, not even he in his rage, could be blind to what was happening.

## 5. 1860: The Year

Preparations for the Sicilian Revolution were accelerated at the beginning of 1860 by the zeal of exiles who not only agitated for armed revolt against the Bourbon oppressor via their letters, proclamations and messages, but also accumulated and smuggled into Sicily guns and ammunition. By now, nobles, bourgeoises and poor all believed extreme social and political transformation was inevitable. As concrete proof of the broad-based, classless appeal of the revolutionary movement, a single committee was constituted in Palermo and composed of representatives from every level of the social hierarchy, not simply of a few enlightened patriots or liberals. In cities throughout Sicily, manifestos endorsing insurrection were printed and distributed via extensive networks.

For Sicilians, two essential tasks had to be carried out at this point: (1) Garibaldi had to be persuaded to lead the revolt on the island; (2) Cavour's intentions had to be better understood. Meanwhile, Mazzini continued to agitate and insist that "the health of Italy depends on action from the South."

In a state of constant alarm, Police Commissioner Maniscalco seemed finally to comprehend the full dimensions of the social and political upheaval around him. As he wrote in his April 1, 1860 report, "the voices of imminent tumult, aiding and abetting these immoral disturbances, echo everywhere from morning till night."

An actual revolt was set in Palermo for the 4th of April. Its prime mover was Francesco Riso, a waterworks employee's 34 year old son who had participated, at 22, in the riots of 1848. Riso's plan was to amass enough weapons in a warehouse next to the Monastery of Gancia and then call for the uprising. His men had also prepared two tricolored flags to wave at the right moment.

But the police were forewarned of the conspiracy at hand and stationed their forces throughout the whole area around the monastery. The conspirators, having already manned their stations, were thus trapped. Riso and his small cadre of trusted friends managed to slip into the monastery and barricade themselves there. Then, they had the church bells rung to call for help. In response, Bourbon troops opened fire on the monastery. At this point, a few of the most audacious conspirators burst out of their places of refuge and charged the soldiers with guns blazing. However, after throwing the enemy into some confusion and wounding a number of soldiers, the insurgents were surrounded. Six of them died in battle, and the rest, with wounded among them, were captured. The Bourbon troops were not satis-

**50. Giuseppe Garibaldi. An engraving from Jessie W. Mario's *Garibaldi e i suoi tempi*, Milan 1885.**

fied, though, and launched a bayonette charge on the monastery, looting the monks' cells and destroying their library. The monks themselves were reviled and beaten before being tied together with the cords of their habits and dragged through the city as a warning.

Pursuant to this uprising, 13 conspirators, including Riso's aged father, were summarily tried by a war council and shot on April 14. Francesco Riso himself, who had received four bullet wounds in battle and a bayonette lesion while he was being transported on a stretcher to the hospital, died 13 days later. Before Riso expired, nevertheless, Maniscalco tried to cajole him into talking. Going to Riso's bedside himself, Maniscalco later spread the rumor that the conspirator had named names.

Two of the April 4th conspirators, refusing to leave the Monastery of Gancia, hid in a tomb. But after three days, their own hunger drove them out to ask the monks for help. Fortunately, these clergymen did not betray the insurgents. In fact, the monks showed the conspirators a secret passageway called "the hole of salvation" through which they could go free. This passageway can still be found in one of the Gancia's walls, where a tablet commemorates the event and its protagonists, Gaspare Bivona and Filippo Patti.

The Gancia episode had tremendous resonance, and emulators, throughout many Sicilian cities and towns. Messina experienced agitation and arrests; and as the riots escalated for days, a state of siege was declared. Yet this repression failed to deter Catania, Caltanissetta, Syracuse, Agrigento and Noto from revolting. In the latter city, a small group of courageous rebels attacked Bourbon soldiers head on. This assault caused the authorities to put Noto under siege as well.

In Trapani, the insurrection was better organized and sustained. An enormous popular demonstration took place during which participants shouted "Long Live Victor Emanuel!" The rebels had to scrap their plan to liberate all political prisoners on the nearby island of Favignana; nonetheless, the revolutionary ferment of the city did not fizzle. Ultimately, it would help set the stage for Garibaldi's Sicilian Campaign.

### 6. The Hour Comes and a New Age Begins

Following the Gancia Monastery Incident, Maniscalco claimed to have "seized the Revolution by the hair." But, in reality, Sicily's revolutionary momentum was unstoppable. Not even the new Neapolitan King Francesco II, having succeeded Ferdinand II in 1859, could delude himself into thinking Sicilians would be satisfied with his assurances that they could have a viceroy of royal blood on the island or with the new monarch's promise to spend two months a year in Sicily to court the aristocracy and the populace alike.

The Neapolitan monarchy, especially for its repressive measures taken on the island, had lost all its credibility on local, provincial and international levels. As a case in point, apropos of the death of Ferdinand II, the *London Times* had coldly reported: "The king was called from his earthly realm to the ultimate Seat of Judgment where he will have to pay a severe penalty for his governance." The *Times* obituary concluded: "During his life, Ferdinand made many tears flow; yet few will be shed for his death."

The best touchstone whereby the people's feelings for the Bourbons could be gauged is in the nicknames pinned on the representatives of their dynasty. Ferdinand I was dubbed Big Nose, Ferdinand II the Bomb, and Francesco II Little Frankie.

With Sicily as the hot-bed of revolt, the Bourbons' last resort was to send fresh reinforcements to Palermo in an attempt to cool the insurgents down. About 40,000 men were driven on a forced march from their posts near Gaeta, which they left unguarded, all the way to the island. Simultaneously, the munitions factories of the kingdom were in operation day and night to produce enough fire power for these mobilized troops. And the naval bases of Naples and Castellammare were ordered to be on the alert and send out ships to guard the Sicilian coastline. In addition, a high-ranking officer in the Neapolitan navy was transferred to Palermo to bolster the city's defenses in cooperation with the lieutenant general.

These various precautionary measures of the Bourbons, whose nerves were understandably frayed, were reinforced by a more and more unbridled yet faltering repression. Sicilian towns and cities, no matter what their military resources, continued to rebel. In the long run it would not matter that scattered insurgents were menaced by thousands of armed men. In spite of the odds again them, the patriots of Carini, on April 18, defied the royal troops in a bloody pitched battle that left only 250 Sicilians dead as compared to 320 Bourbon soldiers. Not even when Carini was put to the sword and fire, with every possible form of violence wreaked upon it and its women slaughtered as they sought asylum in churches, nor when Trapani, revolting once again, was overwhelmed by massive Bourbon mobilizations, did the flames of revolution subside in Sicily. As witness to Sicilians' indomitable spirit, Messina, Catania and Termini Imerese continued to fight.

Taking immediate advantage of this situation, Rosolino Pilo, Giovanni Corrao and Agostino Castelli, all patriots of exceptional courage, ventured to land in Sicily near Messina and proceed with great effort and risk as far as Piana dei Greci. Maniscalco, as usual informed by his spies of the arrival of "subversives" in Sicily, ordered that these insurgents be hunted down. The squadrons he sent for this purpose actually reached Piana and were about to apprehend the patriots. But the mere presence in the town of Rosolino Pilo encouraged its citizens to resist the Bourbon advance and assure that Sicily could truly hope a new age had begun.

At this juncture Garibaldi was virtually forced to make a decision. Mazzini had already demonstrated a willingness to compromise with regard to his once rigidly anti-monarchical, intransigently republican stand. In March of 1860, he had categorically stated, "if Italians want to be united under the Savoy Dynasty, let them—as long as we have a unified Italy!" Moreover, the declaration of Garibaldi, the future leader of the Thousand Red Shirts' Invasion of Sicily, resonated in Sicilians' ears: "All of Italy in an indissoluble union with Victor Emanuel!" Cavour himself, convinced that there was no way the Bourbons could survive, after many hesitations and political compromises, had decided to back, albeit unofficially, Garibaldi's plan of action.

Garibaldi, until he made his ultimate commitment to invade Sicily, remained indecisive. He was spurred to act, however, after being shaken by

"La Trinacria caccia il Borbone"

**51. Trinacria kicks out the Bourbons. Popular print.**

the accounts of Raffaele Motto, the captain of the trawler that had brought Rosolino Pilo and Giovanni Corrao to the island, and by a letter written by Pilo in which the latter overly-dramatized the reign of terror in Messina. Pilo had affirmed, moreover, that 30,000 insurgents, armed in the vicinity of Palermo, were awaiting the Liberator (Garibaldi).

The Expedition of the Thousand was planned in less than a week in an atmosphere of uncertainty and enervating expectancy. Most impatient among the conspirators were La Masa, Bixio, La Farina, Carini, Orsini and Crispi, who were ready to launch the attack at any price. Finally, two ships, the Piedmont and the Lombard, were put at Garibaldi's disposal. His volunteer army of 500 guerrillas quickly grew to the famous Thousand when it became clear that a ship would really disembark from Quarto.

Naples, since it had already heard upon many occasions the news that an expedition commanded by Garibaldi would be launched, was not surprised when it received word, on May 6, of the Liberator's action. As Harold Acton wrote, "everything was in Garibaldi's favor, working to frustrate the designs of poor little Francesco." The Bourbons' time had come to bend under the weight and the pendulum stroke of history and leave space for new times to flourish.

Sicily, with the advent of Garibaldi's victorious campaigns, cut its ties with the past. In the name of that freedom dreamed and sought for centuries, the island became an integral part of United Italy. Ironically, this unification would assure that certain Sicilian realities would not change. Disillusionments, often of a dramatic nature, would weigh upon the island's future generations for many decades to come after its supposed liberation.